RETHINKING *the* AMERICAN UNION *for the* TWENTY-FIRST CENTURY

RETHINKING *the* AMERICAN UNION *for the* TWENTY-FIRST CENTURY

Edited and with an Introduction by
DONALD LIVINGSTON

PELICAN PUBLISHING COMPANY
Gretna 2012

*The word "Pelican" and the depiction of a pelican are
trademarks of Pelican Publishing Company, Inc., and are
registered in the U.S. Patent and Trademark Office.*

Library of Congress Cataloging-in-Publication Data

Rethinking the American union for the twenty-first century / edited
and with an introduction by Donald Livingston.
    p. cm.
Includes bibliographical references and index.
ISBN 978-1-58980-957-4 (hardcover : alk. paper) -- ISBN 978-1-
4556-1546-9 (e-book) 1. Federal government--United States. 2.
Nullification (States' rights) 3. States' rights (American politics)
4. Secession--United States. 5. Republicanism--United States. 6.
United States--Politics and government--Philosophy. I. Livingston,
Donald W.
JK311.R47 2011
320.473'049--dc23
            2011041868

Printed in the United States of America
Published by Pelican Publishing Company, Inc.
1000 Burmaster Street, Gretna, Louisiana 70053

For Harry Teasley, a friend of liberty

Contents

Preface

This book grew out of a conference sponsored by the Abbeville Institute on "State Nullification, Secession and the Human Scale of Political Order" held in Charleston, South Carolina on February 4-7, 2010. Scholars from across the ideological spectrum, from left to right, examined the modern paradigm of centralization that has led to the creation of vast-scale unitary states and to the consequent loss of a human scale in political association. In discussions after the conference, a number of us thought a book on the topic we had explored would be beneficial at a time when many of our political and cultural elites are shifting their allegiance to supranational and subnational entities and when the nineteenth-century nationalist language of large unitary states "one and indivisible" is losing its salience. To a perplexed public, these essays might provide fresh insights into our condition. The essays were commissioned especially for the volume.

We are grateful to acknowledge the Teasley Foundation, which from the beginning has generously supported the Abbeville Institute with scholarships for college and graduate students and which provided the financial support for the conference. We are grateful also to the Watson-Brown Foundation and to the Mary Elizabeth Sanders Foundation for funding student scholarships over the years. And the Institute is especially grateful for the friendship and support of the Rockford Institute.

Each contributor to this volume would have a number of scholars to recognize in gratitude, but space does not permit such a listing. As editor, however, I must acknowledge three Abbeville colleagues whose work on the neglected topic of the constitutionality of State nullification undergirds the spirit of this study: Thomas Woods, *Nullification: How to Resist Tyranny in the 21st Century;* Marco Bassani, *Liberty, State, and Union: The Political Thought of Thomas Jefferson;* and the magisterial two-volume study of W. Kirk Wood, *Nullification: A Constitutional History, 1776-1833.* To these we should add the work of our friend William Watkins, *Reclaiming the American Revolution: The Kentucky and Virginia Resolutions and Their Legacy.* These four works comprise the definitive study on the constitutionality of State nullification—a dormant part of the American political tradition that has once again become topical. Lastly, I would like to recognize the great Calhoun scholar, Clyde Wilson, Distinguished Emeritus of the University of South Carolina and M. E. Bradford Distinguished Fellow of the Abbeville Institute, who had been ploughing the ground long before many of us came to plant.

—Donald Livingston
Emeritus, Emory University

Contributors

Kent Masterson Brown is a practicing attorney who has prosecuted and argued constitutional-law cases from his offices in Lexington, Kentucky, where he lives, and as counsel to Webster, Chamberlain & Bean in Washington, D.C. He is the author of five books on Civil War history, including the critically acclaimed *Retreat from Gettysburg: Lee, Logistics and the Pennsylvania Campaign.* Brown has received numerous awards for his writing as well as his efforts at battlefield preservation.

Dr. Marshall DeRosa is professor of political science at Florida Atlantic University. His book publications include *The Confederate Constitution of 1861, The Politics of Creative Jurisprudence, Redeeming American Democracy: Lessons from the Confederate Constitution,* and *Robert E. Lee: Politics and War Through the Eyes of a Christian Realist.*

Dr. Thomas DiLorenzo is professor of economics at Loyola University Maryland and a senior faculty member of the Ludwig von Mises Institute. He is the author or coauthor of thirteen books, including *The Real Lincoln, How Capitalism Saved America, Lincoln Unmasked,* and *Hamilton's Curse: How Jefferson's Archenemy Betrayed the American Revolution— and What It Means for Americans Today.* He has published in academic journals such as the *American Economic Review, Economic Inquiry, Southern Economic Journal, Public Choice, International Review of Law and Economics, The Independent Review,* and the *Quarterly Review of Austrian Economics.* His articles have also appeared in the *Wall Street Journal, Barron's,* the *Washington Post,* and dozens of other newspapers and magazines. He is a regular columnist for LewRockwell.com.

Donald Livingston is professor emeritus of philosophy at Emory University, a National Endowment for the Humanities Fellow, and a Fellow of the Institute for Advanced Studies in the Humanities at the University of Edinburgh. He has published in the areas of American constitutionalism and the history of modern philosophy. His books include *Philosophical Melancholy and Delirium, Hume's Pathology of Philosophy,* and *Hume's Philosophy of Common Life.* He is president of the Abbeville Institute, an organization in higher education devoted to a study of what is true and valuable in the Southern tradition.

Yuri Maltsev is professor of economics at Carthage College. He received a doctorate from the Institute of Labor Research in Moscow, Russia and was a member of a senior team of Soviet economists that worked on President Gorbachev's program for economic reform. After coming to the U.S., he served as a consultant for different departments of the U.S. government and has testified before Congress. He has lectured at leading universities, colleges, corporations, banks, churches, schools, and community centers all over the U.S., Canada, and Europe. He has appeared on Cable Network News, Financial Network News, PBS News Hour, C-Span, CBN, CBC, and other American, Canadian, Spanish, and Finnish television and radio programs. He has authored five books and over a hundred articles published in *The Christian Science Monitor, Newsday, Washington Times, San Diego Union Tribune, Journal of Commerce, Milwaukee Journal Sentinel, Seattle Times,* and others.

Kirkpatrick Sale is the author of twelve books, including *Human Scale, The Conquest of Paradise: Christopher Columbus and the Columbian Legacy, Rebels Against the Future: The Luddites and Their War on the Industrial Revolution,* and *After Eden: The Evolution of Human Domination.* He is the director of the Middlebury Institute "for the study of separatism, secession, and self-determination."

Rob Williams is professor of media/communications at Champlain College as well as being a Vermont-based historian, public speaker, journalist, and editor/publisher of *Vermont Commons: Voices of Independence,* an independent multimedia news journal. He is also a yak farmer and co-owner of Vermont Yak Company in the Mad River Valley, a farm business raising grass-fed yaks for meat and agri-tourism. He moonlights as a musician, performing "pholkgospel grassicana music for happy brains" in an acoustic power "phoursome" called the Phineas Gage Project.

Introduction:
The Old Assumptions No Longer Apply

Donald Livingston

The conflicts that divide Americans today are as profound as in any period of our history. In addition to the usual policy conflicts—unprecedented debt placed upon future generations, inefficiency, waste, corruption, misguided and failed military adventures, runaway centralization—there are foundational moral and cultural divisions of an incommensurable kind that make rational discourse nearly impossible. Moreover, the nation-state itself and national identities created after the French Revolution no longer have the salience they once had and, in some cases, have disintegrated through secession. By 1991, fifteen states had peacefully seceded from the "indivisible" Soviet Union, and Soviet national identity vanished like smoke.

Just as nineteenth- and twentieth-century *nationalism* was a centripetal force that destroyed the independence of smaller states, provinces, and social authorities by consolidating them into large unitary states "one and indivisible," so is *globalism* challenging the independence of these very nation-states in favor of supranational organizations. Many political, business, and cultural elites are shifting their allegiance away from their nation-states to *supranational* entities. Others, such as the Basques in Spain, the Scots in Britain, Islamic immigrants in Europe, and self-sustaining Hispanic-speaking communities in America, are shifting their allegiance to *subnational* identities and away from the nation-states they inhabit. American national identity, for instance, has long been identified with the English language. Today, Spanish is becoming a second "American" language. Harvard's Samuel Huntington, in his book *Who Are We? Challenges to America's National Identity,* provides convincing evidence that the American national identity that emerged in the late nineteenth century is in a state of disintegration. The book is a plea to recover that identity, but even Huntington suggests that the prospects are not promising, short of a protracted war.

These challenges require some fundamental rethinking of the political and philosophical assumptions that have led to our current condition. But this is seldom done. Instead, public discourse is politics as usual: elect better leaders who will cut spending, slash the size of government, enforce our immigration laws, restore the Constitution, and the like.

How Big Is Too Big?

One topic is seldom mentioned, much less explored, and that is the question of *size and scale.* Leopold Kohr once observed that when things go wrong in the human world, it is often because something has grown too large. As Aristotle taught, everything in nature has a proper size, beyond or below which it becomes dysfunctional. A jury of 12 is well suited in size to determine the facts of a case. But a jury of 120 would be dysfunctional, even if everyone were virtuous and motivated to seek the truth. At that size, not everyone would be able to speak and answer challenging questions put to them by other jurors. Or if they did, the deliberations could last a year or more. And could one remember and process the reasoning of all? Some would not speak at all and suppress their views. Under these conditions, could one ever expect a unanimous verdict? A resort would have to be made to majority rule, in which case a *jury* would no longer exist. Size alone would have destroyed the jury system.

The same holds for the functioning of other social entities such as committees, lawmaking assemblies, and bureaucracies and the ratio of population to representative (e.g., one representative for every million persons is not representation at all). None of these can function well if they are too large or out of scale.

It should be surprising that the topic of size and scale has dropped out of political discourse, since Americans think of the United States as a republic, and the republican tradition for 2,000 years taught that a republic must be small. Having just broken with monarchy, which places no limit on size, the Founders were more attuned to this demand of the republican tradition than we are. Their solution was division of the territory into States, with a central government limited to foreign affairs, declaring war, and regulating commerce. All other matters were left to the States, where the government of everyday life would be closer to the people. In this view, the States were republics, but the central government was not. It was an artificial corporation created by the States for their mutual benefit. To think of the United States itself as a republic would mean consolidating the States into a single unitary state.

Thomas Jefferson viewed this prospect with horror. In a letter to Gideon Granger, August 13, 1800, he warned: "Our country is too large to have all its affairs conducted by a single government. Public servants at such a distance, & from under the eye of their constituents, must, from circumstances of distance, be unable to administer & overlook all details necessary for the good government of the citizens, and the same circumstances, by rendering detection impossible to their constituents, will invite the public agents to corruption, plunder & waste. And I do verily believe, that if the principle were to prevail, of a common law being in force in the U.S., (which principle possesses the general government at once of all the powers of the State governments, and reduces us to a single consolidated government) it would become the most corrupt government on the earth."

Have we not reached that condition today where the States are considered little more than administrative units of the central government? Nearly every aspect of life is under regulation of the central government. A lawmaking majority in Congress along with the president is only 269. That small number rules 305 million people and will spend an annual budget of $3.84 trillion. That along with a deficit of over $1 trillion is some $5 trillion. If $1 million a day were spent from the time of Christ until now, one would not have spent $1 trillion, much less $5 trillion. Never in human history has so much financial power been put in the hands of so few. It is simply not possible for that small number to manage such a vast sum for the public good. And what could the "public good" even mean at the scale of 305 million people? By virtue of size alone, Washington could not be anything other than a scene of frenzied pork-barrel spending, waste, inefficiency, corruption, and special-interest patronage for the politically well connected.

But there is more. Most of the laws we live under are not passed by Congress at all but flow from anonymous regulatory bureaucracies of continental scale that are under control of the imperial president: the EPA, EEOC, IRS, FCC, FDIC, FDA, etc., not to mention the presidential czars. But the presidency is not the only *extralegislative* body that makes laws. The Supreme Court has become the most important social-policymaking body in the Union, legislating policies regarding religion, education, morals, marriage, law enforcement, voting, welfare, and other things that the Constitution reserves to the States. It does this under the mask of "judicial review," a power nowhere authorized in the Constitution. So the consolidation of State powers into the central government that Jefferson feared has come to pass.

George Kennan Divides the Union

From the late nineteenth century on, ever-increasing

centralization and the hollowing out of State and local power were considered progressive, and not only in America but throughout the West. But after two world wars, the global Cold War, the dissolution of the Soviet Union (the most centralized regime in history), and the rise of globalist ideology, the merits of such centralization began to be challenged. One of these challenges came from George Kennan, architect of the United States' policy to contain the Soviet Union. Kennan is known for his realism and moderation in foreign policy and described by some as "the conscience of America." In a chapter titled "Dimensions" in his autobiography *Around the Cragged Hill,* Kennan argued that the United States has become simply too large for the purposes of self-government. The central government can rule 305 million people only by imposing one-size-fits-all rules that necessarily result in a "diminished sensitivity of its laws and regulations to the particular needs, traditional, ethnic, cultural, linguistic, and the like of individual localities and communities."[1] The sheer size of the United States has encouraged an abstract ideological style of politics that favors universalist, egalitarian solutions applying across the board to all elements of the population: "Particularly is this true of the United States, with its highly legalistic traditions, its dislike . . . of any sort of discriminating administration, its love for dividing people into categories, its fondness for regulating their lives in terms of these categories and treating them accordingly, rather than looking at the needs of individuals or of smaller groups and confronting these on the basis of common sense and reasonable discrimination."[2]

Congress is more interested in the struggle over how to spend $5 trillion in a single year than in tackling politically controversial issues and has turned these over to the federal courts. The Constitution reserves the regulation of abortion to the States, each of which could and did, for 177 years, adjust its regulations to suit the moral requirements of its political society. But through a fanciful reading of the Due Process clause of the Fourteenth Amendment, the Supreme Court in *Roe v. Wade* (1973) took on the task of making a single policy on abortion for the federation of States. In doing so, however, it transformed a question of *policy* into a question of *constitutional right*. Constitutional rights are and should be rigid things that cannot easily be adjusted to local traditions and circumstances. Policies, however, are contingent adventures in trying to establish what is thought to be good. Consequently, they are often in need of revision as new facts and unintended consequences arise. And this is best done by a legislature close to the people. But America today (in its social life, at least) is a country governed not by the people, whose representatives in legislative assemblies make the laws they live under, but largely by federal judges. This regime of "government by judiciary," as law professor Raoul Berger calls it, is unique in history.[3] And a similar rigidity is to be found in the regulatory agencies under the presidency. "Rarely, if ever," Kennan concludes, "can the workings of the federal laws be adjusted to meet unusual but reasonable requirements of the affected locality or individual."[4]

Another disease of large regimes is what Kennan calls "the hubris of inordinate size," the tendency to think that "the nation's role in the world must be equivalent to its physical size, with the consequent relative tendency to overweening pretensions and ambitions . . . to dreams of power and glory." The belief in American exceptionalism, the doctrine of Woodrow Wilson that America should fight global wars "to make the world safe for democracy," and George W. Bush's mission after 9/11 to lead a "global democratic revolution" are just such dreams and ones nourished by the sheer size of the regime. But even when well intentioned, "the belief that one country can do much good for another country by intervening forcefully in the latter's internal affairs is almost invariably an illusion."[5]

Finally, it is well known that bureaucracies, once established, tend to grow quite independent of the original reason for their existence. This is true of business corporations, churches, and governments. Churches are limited by revenue and more easily fall under the scrutiny of their members; businesses are restrained by cost. Small governments are restrained by the scrutiny of their members and by cost. For example, most American States have constitutional limits on spending. But in a vast centralized regime such as the United States, there is no constitutional limit on spending. The national government can borrow and even print money at will. Consequently, "the governmental apparatus of the great country grows around itself a thicker and more formidable bureaucratic coating than does the smaller [country]."[6] And "the problem grows and grows exponentially, with the size of the country and the government, so that the government and the people of the great power are more heavily burdened by this disease than are those of the smaller entity."[7]

The topic of size raised here is not to be confused with the way the term is used today in ordinary American political discourse. There one hears invective against "big government," of "reducing the size of government," or of "limiting government." These expressions usually mean limiting the *increase* in government spending; or, much less often, reducing the government's budget; or reducing its functions; or reducing the size of its bureaucracy. Kennan, however, means something quite different. He means a *territorial division* of the Union into a number of smaller political societies. If the regime has grown too large with respect to population and territory, it should be divided. But he is quick to add that this should not be done unless people see the advantages of it and really want it. To this end, he thinks we should begin a public debate on size and scale and how we might downsize a regime that has grown simply too large for the purposes of self-government. This book of essays is a contribution to that discussion.

To begin the debate, and without being dogmatic, Kennan

suggests the Union could be divided into "a dozen constituent republics." These might include: "New England; the Middle Atlantic states; the Middle West; the Northwest (from Wisconsin to the Northwest, and down the Pacific coast to central California); the Southwest (including southern California and Hawaii); Texas (by itself); the Old South; Florida (perhaps including Puerto Rico); and Alaska; plus three great self-governing urban regions, those of New York, Chicago, and Los Angeles—a total of twelve constituent entities. To these entities I would accord a larger part of the present federal powers than one might suspect—large enough in fact to make most people gasp."[8]

Such a reform would make evident the diverse character and special problems of these regions now able to govern themselves. Liberation from the older "national" norms would open room for local innovation and diversity. The goal of the reform is not to achieve racial or ethnic homogeneity for each region, as was often the case with the nineteenth-century nation-states (including the United States after the Civil War), nor to impose an inflexible ideology of "multiculturalism" on each region, as is the current policy of the United States. Rather the goal is merely to achieve "ease, flexibility, and intimacy of government."[9] Another achievement would be to reinvigorate and encourage the flourishing of regional cultures and character that have been increasingly hollowed out by the acid of "national" norms and regulations imposed from the center and to which a hapless mass of 305 million people must conform.

Rethinking the American Union

Kennan's suggestion is a thought experiment more than a policy proposal. It is an effort to open our eyes to the problems posed by *size alone* and an invitation to explore and confront them. The essays of this book can be viewed as a response to George Kennan's invitation. They do not offer policy solutions. They are rather efforts to *rethink* the philosophical, political, moral, and constitutional assumptions that have led us to think that size and scale do not matter in political things and that have produced a regime suffering from elephantiasis, with little understanding of its condition and even less inclination to seek such understanding.

If the United States has grown too large for the purposes of self-government, how could it be downsized within the framework of the Constitution? The answer depends on what we understand the Constitution to be. Two contrary theories of the Constitution have been offered by leading American statesmen: the compact theory (Thomas Jefferson, James Madison) and the nationalist theory (Justice Joseph Story, Daniel Webster, Abraham Lincoln). The former holds that the Constitution is a compact between sovereign States that created a central government and delegated to it only enumerated powers. If this were true, a State, being a sovereign political society and a party to the compact, could interpose its authority to nullify an unconstitutional act of the central government—that is, an act that intruded into powers it enjoyed before entering the Union and that it never delegated to the central government. And if necessary, a State could withdraw the powers it had delegated to the central government, secede from the Union, and resume its status as a sovereign State.

The nationalist theory flatly denies that the States are or ever were sovereign. Sovereignty is vested in the American people in the aggregate. If so, the States are administrative agencies of the general will of the American people. As such, they can neither nullify an act of the central government judged to be unconstitutional nor secede from the Union, any more than a county can lawfully nullify the acts of a State legislature nor lawfully secede from the State.

Kent Masterson Brown, in "Secession: A Constitutional Remedy that Protects Fundamental Liberties," argues that the text of the Constitution and the public acts that created it establish, to any honest mind, that the Constitution ratified by the States in 1789 was understood to be a *compact* between the States. The common law of contracts going back to the Magna Carta allows rescission or annulment of a contract as a remedy in law. Since the States are parties to the constitutional compact, they could employ this right of rescission to secede and re-federate, if they so desired, to form something like the commonwealth of twelve federative polities imagined by Kennan. Or a State could go it alone. This could not be done in the nationalist theory of the Constitution, which is "one and indivisible."

If, as Brown argues, the public acts creating the Constitution contain no textual or historical support for the nationalist theory, how are we to understand its emergence and dominance today? Thomas DiLorenzo, in "The Founding Fathers of Constitutional Subversion," argues that the nationalist theory was an imagined and wished-for constitution and not the one ratified by the States in 1789, which (as Brown has shown) was a compact between the States. From the first, there were those, such as Alexander Hamilton, who wanted a unitary state constitution modeled on Britain. Hamilton proposed a president for life with power to appoint State governors and veto State laws. Hamilton along with would-be nationalists such as Chief Justice John Marshall, Justice Joseph Story, and Daniel Webster, by isolating certain passages of the Constitution from the whole, systematically misdescribed a federative constitution between the States as being a unitary state constitution where the central government would be able to define the limits of its powers in relation to the States. In DiLorenzo's view, the rise of the nationalist theory is a story of incremental constitutional subversion.

Marshall DeRosa, in "The Tenth Amendment Awakening, the Supreme Court Be Damned," further documents this story of constitutional subversion put forth by DiLorenzo and observes that the Tenth Amendment movement, with its resolutions and amendments regarding State sovereignty and the right of States to nullify unauthorized acts of the central government, is making a big mistake in seeking a remedy in federal courts. The federal judiciary is after all a branch of the central government and is, consequently, a party to the dispute (between the central government and the States) and cannot act as an impartial umpire. In addition, DeRosa sketches out a melancholy history of how the Court has served, and is serving, the interests of the ruling political class, which, of course, has no interest in State sovereignty.

Donald Livingston, in "American Republicanism and the Forgotten Question of Size," observes that the republican tradition going back 2,000 years held that the virtues of republican life (self-government and the rule of law) were possible only in small polities. Historically these seldom went beyond a population of 200,000 and were often considerably smaller. The republican tradition also taught that the government of a large territory would necessarily end in a centralized monarchy. Upon seceding from Britain, Americans were determined to enjoy a republican style of politics, but they had acquired a territory so vast as to demand centralization. Livingston explores how Americans at first were acutely sensitive to the necessary connection between republicanism and size; how they tried to reconcile the two; and how they eventually abandoned the quest, allowing the emergence of the massively centralized regime we have today. He observes, however, that after World War II a great number of small states were created in the world by secession from larger states. Over half the states in the world today are under 5 million people; some are smaller than the land area of Washington, D.C., and the Vatican is smaller than the

Washington Mall. Today there is hardly any limit as to how small a state can be. And the peaceful secession of the Soviet republics has unmasked the pretensions of the modern nation-states created after the French Revolution to be "one and indivisible."

Kirkpatrick Sale, in "'To the Size of States There Is a Limit': Measurements for the Success of a State," revives the Aristotelian argument that everything in nature has a proper size, beyond or below which it tends to dysfunction. He assumes the existence of modern states (which are considerably larger than the classical republics) and asks whether there is an optimal size to such states. By using internationally recognized criteria of prosperity, human rights, rate of crime, healthcare, literacy, and sense of well-being, and by applying these criteria to the states recognized by the United Nations, he concludes that a state in the range of 3 to 5 million seems the optimal size. Looking at the United States, he finds a majority of States in this range and argues that they would be better off as independent countries.

Yuri Maltsev, in "Too Big to Fail? Lessons from the Demise of the Soviet Union," gives us a close-up look at how fifteen states were able to secede from the Soviet Union, the most centralized regime in history. The regime failed because, as Ludwig Von Mises and Nobel Laureate Friedrich Hayek taught, a centrally controlled economy is impossible and must eventually implode. This lesson, Maltsev thinks, is far from being understood by so-called "liberal" regimes in the West, including the United States. However, he observes that some of the former Soviet states have learned the lesson. Little Estonia, for example, is now one of the freest and most prosperous states in the world.

In the final essay, "Most Likely to Secede: U.S. Empire and the Emerging Vermont Independence Effort," Rob Williams examines the history and prospects of an actual secession movement, the Second Vermont Republic, so named because

Vermont was an independent State from 1777 until it joined the United States in 1791. The mission is to return Vermont to its original status as an independent republic. Williams is a cofounder of the Second Vermont Republic along with Thomas Naylor, a retired economics professor from Duke University and international businessman who was the original driving force behind the movement. Before retirement, he was a consultant on economic matters to various Soviet groups and very early predicted the collapse of the Soviet regime (an event that shocked Soviet "experts"). He sees the U.S. headed down a similar path and, like George Kennan (with whom he carried on an approving correspondence about Vermont secession), believes the remedy is and can only be division of the Union into States closer to the people.

Williams observes that although there are now many secession movements in the United States, the Vermont movement is different in having attracted national and international media attention and the support of distinguished thinkers such as George Kennan, Walter Williams, and John Kenneth Galbraith. Williams recounts the history and growth of the movement, which has its own Internet radio station featuring Vermont music and independence politics and a sub-stantial journal, *Vermont Commons: Voices of Independence,* with around ten thousand readers. In October 28, 2005, the Second Vermont Republic held a secession convention in the House Chamber of the State House. This was the first statewide convention called in the United States since North Carolina's secession convention on May 20, 1861. In the fall of 2010, the Second Vermont Republic fielded candidates for governor, lieutenant governor, and state legislative positions on a platform seeking independence from Washington. Whether or not the Second Vermont Republic will succeed, it is a telling instance of the fundamental rethinking of the Union that is needed and is actually going on.

Rethinking *the* American Union *for the* Twenty-First Century

Secession:
A Constitutional Remedy that Protects Fundamental Liberties

Kent Masterson Brown

We live in interesting times. Texas governor Rick Perry asserted in April 2009 that Texas always retains the right to secede from the Union. A Rasmussen poll indicated that nearly one in three Texas voters believes that the State has that right.[1] In a hotly contested race for the Republican nomination for governor of Tennessee, Rep. Zach Wamp of Chattanooga suggested in July 2010 that Tennessee and other States may have to consider seceding from the Union if the federal government does not change its ways regarding mandates.[2]

Indeed, States are confronting the federal government these days. Much of it has come about because of the enactment of a federal health-reform bill in excess of two thousand pages that, among other things, mandates the purchase of health insurance. Nearly 60 percent of the American public has consistently opposed the health-reform bill before and since its enactment in March 2010.[3] Nearly every State has introduced or enacted resolutions fundamentally "nullifying" the health-insurance mandate.[4] Missouri voters approved a constitutional referendum nullifying the mandate with a whopping 71 percent of the vote.[5]

The federal government is totally out of control. The nation is $13 trillion in debt, paying $600 billion in interest each year. The debt burdens every citizen and is a security threat to the nation.[6] It is a small wonder that efforts are under way to nullify federal enactments and that there are even discussions about secession.

The federal government appears absolutely unwilling to rein in its voracious appetite for power and control. Health-insurance mandates, controls over what we eat, and regulations about how much we weigh and how we live our

31

lives are now a reality, even in the face of overwhelming majorities who oppose it all. When asked about the power of the federal government in a town-hall meeting in August 2010, Rep. Pete Stark (D-CA) responded, "The federal government can do most anything in this country."[7] Unfortunately, he echoed the beliefs of most of the current members of Congress and the executive branch even though the federal government was created by a Constitution that gave to Congress "certain limited and enumerated powers."[8]

The remarks by Governor Perry and Congressman Wamp reminding people of the right of secession are in direct response to the federal government's relentless drive for power and control. Secession was—and is—a remedy that has evolved over the centuries and has been understood in the Constitution itself, to address just that problem.

Although many of the framers and ratifiers of the Constitution expressed distrust of the English common law, they, as lawyers, judges, and businessmen, were part of that ancient tradition. From the reign of Edward I in England (1272-1307), the phrase *jus commune* began being applied to the un-enacted, non-statutory law common to all Englishmen. The "common law" came to refer to the law as applied by the three then-developing courts in England: King's Bench, the Common Bench (or Court of Common Pleas), and the Exchequer.[9]

Within the Exchequer, the king's fiscal office, evolved the Chancery, the secretarial department. At its head was the chancellor, whose duty, among other things, was to issue writs over the great seal of the king to begin actions in the courts of law.[10] The department came to be known as the Court of Chancery. By the fourteenth century, the Court of Chancery developed two sides, a "common law" side and an "equity" side.[11] The common-law side evolved into a court system that heard cases involving all sorts of damage claims.[12]

Often, however, a petitioner would seek a remedy that, in the ordinary course of justice, could not be obtained. The king was literally asked by the petitioner to find a remedy. Many of the cases involved the poor or dispossessed, who petitioned the crown for help against those who were more wealthy and powerful and who were threatening harm or harming the petitioner. Petitioners in these cases went to the chancellor, not directly to the king. The chancellor, without the use of a jury, would order the defendant to appear before him and be examined to determine whether some extraordinary relief ought to be granted. By the sixteenth century, the chancellor's powers were defined by "the rules of equity and good conscience."[13] As the "law" courts entertained claims for money damages, the "equity" courts entertained claims for extraordinary relief.

The two great pillars of civil justice, law and equity, denote the bodies of law—and the specific courts that enforce same— that provide the means by which citizens may seek redress for the whole panoply of civil wrongs committed, or being committed, against them. They have evolved over 700 years and are applied in all American courts to this day. If a party is injured in property or person by another, and such injury can be quantified by an amount of money (damages), the action would be one "at law" and brought in a law court presided over by a judge, who would often empanel a jury to decide questions of disputed fact. If, on the other hand, a party is about to be injured, or is in the process of being injured by another—and no monetary relief would be adequate to redress the wrong, and the offending party can be restrained by some extraordinary action by a court—the action would be one "in equity" and brought in a court of equity. The judge would sit as a "chancellor," deciding all questions of law and fact.[14]

The law-equity division of the courts was planted in the American colonies upon settlement. English settlers established their English jurisprudential system. Courts of

Chancery existed in one form or another in every one of the thirteen colonies prior to the American Revolution. After the Revolution, most of the new States established Courts of Chancery, although there was little or no American equity jurisprudence. Nevertheless, the English tradition of the division of law and equity was well known and understood by the framers and ratifiers of the Constitution. No greater evidence of such knowledge may be found than the words the framers chose for Article III, Section 2, of the Constitution of the United States: "The judicial power [of United States courts] shall extend to all cases, in Law and Equity."[15]

How the two great pillars of civil justice are actually used is understood when one examines the law of contracts, a body of law as old as the Anglo-American division of law and equity. A contract is a promise, or set of promises, for the breach of which the law gives a remedy, or the performance of which the law in some way recognizes as a duty.[16] Synonyms for the term "contract" are "agreement" and "compact." When asked to define the term contract, courts have stressed the classic concept of an agreement resulting from mutuality of assent between two or more parties having capacity to contract, and an obligation based on consideration in the form of an agreement.[17]

If two parties enter into a contract whereby each promises to perform a particular task, and one of the parties fails to perform as promised—or breaches the contract—the other party may seek certain remedies that Anglo-American law has historically provided. A "breach" of a contract is simply a failure on the part of one or more of the contracting parties, without legal excuse, to perform any promise that forms the whole or part of the contract.[18]

Throughout Anglo-American judicial history, to remedy a breach of a contract, an aggrieved party was given certain choices by the law. First, he could choose to proceed to a law court and seek damages for the loss of money in reliance upon the contract being fulfilled. In the law court, he would seek from the party in breach such sums as would place him in as good a position as he would have been had the contract been fully performed.[19] Alternately, a court of equity could enforce the contract for an aggrieved party by making the defaulting party "specifically perform" his contractual obligations.[20] If the defaulting party failed to comply with the court order, the court would exercise its contempt powers against him.[21]

Finally, Anglo-American equity jurisprudence provided for another remedy for breach of contract—"rescission," or, the annulment of the contract.[22] Since the end of the eighteenth century in England, rescission has often been used as a remedy in conjunction with "restitution."[23] The aggrieved party would ask the court to annul the contract and, at the same time, ask that he be made whole for his own performance, thereby placing him in the same position he occupied before he entered into the contract.

For a State to secede from the Union, the Constitution must be construed to be an agreement created by the States as parties. There is simply no other legal construct known to the English-speaking people that would entitle a State to withdraw from the Union. If the Constitution is an agreement—a compact—and the States are parties to it, then the States have the equitable right of rescission in the event of a breach of the agreement. If the States are not parties to an agreement, they would be fundamentally powerless to do anything to protect themselves or their citizens; they would be considered nothing more than federal precincts. To establish the Constitution as an agreement—a compact, if you will—and the States as parties thereto, is essential to the protection of the States and of the liberties of the citizens of the States.

The evolution of remedies in equity and, particularly, the equitable remedy of rescission in the law of contracts was one of the most important concepts applied by the framers and ratifiers of the Constitution to their understanding of that document. To illustrate the application of that concept, one must delve into the history of the call of a Federal Convention and the drafting and ratification of the Constitution.

During the waning years of the Revolution, the thirteen sovereign States entered into a "firm league of friendship" by the Articles of Confederation.[24] The Articles, however, did not create a sovereign national government; rather, they created a government wholly dependent upon the several States. Nevertheless, the Articles were entitled "Articles of Confederation and Perpetual Union," and the framers inserted at the conclusion thereof that the Articles "shall be inviolably observed by the States we respectively represent, and that the union shall be perpetual."[25] Any alteration of the Articles required the agreement of Congress and confirmation by the legislatures of every State. With national postwar finances in crisis, however, most people lost faith in the Confederation government. Trade was chaotic and the "nation" was unable to pay its debts. Stability in foreign relations had never been achieved.[26]

The crisis created by the impotence of the Confederation government brought about a conference in March 1785 at Alexandria, Virginia and at Mount Vernon, George Washington's nearby estate. Representatives of the legislatures of Maryland and Virginia convened for the purpose of discussing mutual navigation problems along the lower Potomac River and the Chesapeake Bay. The conference ended without substantive resolution, but the germ of a broader conference among the States was planted.[27]

In January 1786 the Virginia legislature, acting on a resolution drafted by James Madison, invited all the States to another conference to deal with domestic and foreign trade and to make recommendations to the States and the Confederation government for the improvement thereof. Meeting at Annapolis, Maryland from September 11 to 14, 1786, were twelve representatives from five States: Delaware,

New Jersey, New York, Pennsylvania, and Virginia. Alexander Hamilton and James Madison convinced the commissioners that they should exceed their limited mandate and recommend a national meeting to consider the adequacy of the Articles of Confederation.[28]

After recounting the "defects in the system of the Federal Government," the report of the commissioners at Annapolis, Maryland, penned by Alexander Hamilton, recommended to the Confederation Congress that the States appoint commissioners to meet in Philadelphia in May 1787 for the purpose of "considering the situation of the United States [and] to devise such further provisions as shall appear to them necessary to render the constitution of the Federal Government adequate to the exigencies of the Union" and to report same to Congress.[29]

After receiving the report, Congress called upon the States to send delegates to a convention. Dated February 21, 1787, the call "recommended to the States composing the Union that a convention of representatives from the States respectively be held . . . for the purpose of revising the Articles of Confederation."[30] Clearly, if anything was to be accomplished to amend the Articles of Confederation, it had to be done by the States. The States agreed to formulate the Articles of Confederation, and the States had to be called upon to revise them. The Articles of Confederation formed a classic "compact," and the States were the parties to it.

All State legislatures, except that of Rhode Island, appointed delegates to attend the convention in Philadelphia. In every instance, the respective States paid the expenses of their delegates. Some States actually compensated their delegates. The States, not individual delegates, cast the votes in the convention, and the journal of the convention records only the votes of the States. Each State specified what portion of its delegation needed to be present to act and cast the State's vote.[31]

The Federal Convention

The convention began in Philadelphia on May 25, 1787. Fifty-five delegates attended some or all of the proceedings. By the end of the convention on September 17, 1787, only thirty-eight delegates would cast votes for their respective States on the proposed Constitution of the United States.[32]

After meeting, debating, drafting, and redrafting the document through an intensely hot Philadelphia summer, the convention agreed to a constitution that did, in fact, create a more powerful federal government than had the Articles of Confederation. Article I of the proposed Constitution created the Congress, with a Senate and House of Representatives. Each State would have two senators, and the makeup of the House would reflect the population of each of the States.[33] Article I, Section 8, set forth the powers of Congress. They were "enumerated" powers and included, among other things, the power to coin money, regulate interstate commerce, and declare war. The section even included a "necessary and proper" clause, giving Congress the power to do those things necessary and proper to carry out its enumerated powers.[34] The Constitution withheld from Congress the power to pass bills of attainder and ex post facto laws and further limited Congress's power to lay direct and indirect taxes or suspend the writ of habeas corpus.[35]

Article II created the offices of president and vice president of the United States and defined the limits of their authority.[36] Article III created the Supreme Court of the United States and defined the jurisdiction thereof.[37] Finally, subsequent Articles, among other things, provided that full faith and credit shall be given in each State to the public acts, records, and judicial proceedings of every other State, granted to all citizens of each State all privileges and immunities of citizens in the several States, and guaranteed a republican form of government to every State.[38] Importantly, Article VI provided that the laws and treaties of the United States would be the "supreme law of the land," a provision not without significant controversy.[39]

Finally, the Constitution made crystal clear the role of the States as the parties thereto by setting forth the terms whereby it could be amended and was to be ratified. Article V required all amendments to be "ratified by the legislatures of three-fourths of the states, or by conventions in three-fourths thereof."[40] And if there was any doubt about the fact that the Constitution was an agreement entered into by and between the States, Article VII proclaimed, "The ratification of the conventions of nine States shall be sufficient for the establishment of this Constitution *between the States so ratifying the same.*"[41] Plainly and simply, the Constitution agreed to by the delegates in Philadelphia and, ultimately, the ratifiers in each of the States, was a "constitution between the States so ratifying the same." It was not a constitution among the people.

During the session, the delegates considered, and favorably voted on, a preamble to the Constitution, which read, "We the people of the States of New Hampshire, Massachusetts, Rhode Island and Providence Plantations, Connecticut, New York, New Jersey, Pennsylvania, Delaware, Maryland, Virginia, North Carolina, South Carolina and Georgia do ordain, declare and establish the following Constitution for the Government of ourselves and our posterity." The preamble reflected the role of the States in the creation of the instrument; it was identical to the preamble found in the Articles of Confederation.[42]

In the end, the Committee of Style and Arrangement, not knowing if every one of the enumerated States would actually ratify the document, replaced the list of the States with the now-famous words "We the People of the United States." Much would be made of those words by ardent nationalists in the years ahead, but their insertion was never the result of any vote on the floor of the convention; rather, it was an effort by the Committee of Style and Arrangement to avoid embarrassment. No meaning was ascribed to the rewritten preamble by any of the framers that was different from the original preamble. The delegates finally signed the formally drafted document for and on behalf of their respective States on September 17, 1787, sending it to the Congress of the Confederation and, ultimately, the States for ratification.[43]

The ratification of the Constitution followed a somewhat difficult path. Although its proponents wanted it quickly ratified, that did not happen. Proponents, known as Federalists, received initial momentum in December 1787 and January 1788 when the conventions of five States promptly ratified the Constitution: Delaware (December 7, 1787), New Jersey (December 18, 1787), and Georgia (January 2, 1788)—all unanimous—and Pennsylvania (December 12, 1787) and Connecticut (January 9, 1788) by narrower margins.[44] Between February 6 and June 2, 1788, the conventions of four more States ratified the Constitution: Massachusetts (February 6, 1788) by a vote of 187 to 168 after recommending nine amendments, Maryland (April 28, 1788), South Carolina (May 23, 1788) after recommending multiple amendments, and finally New Hampshire (June 2, 1788).[45] Although New Hampshire's ratification gave the Federalists the nine States necessary to approve the Constitution, Virginia and New York had not ratified the document. They were the largest States, and without their support the new Federal Union would never be fully realized.

Virginia proved to be a battleground. At the Virginia convention in Richmond, such eminent statesmen as George Mason, Patrick Henry, and James Monroe argued *against* ratification, while James Madison, John Marshall, George Wythe, and Edmund Pendleton urged ratification. From June 2 to June 26, 1788, heated debates continued until a vote was taken and the Constitution was ratified by the narrow margin of eighty-nine to seventy-nine. Identifying multiple rights that should forthwith be added as amendments to the Constitution in the Virginia resolution made ratification more palatable to the delegates. But ratification was made possible only so long as the people of Virginia expressly retained the right of rescission. The Virginia resolution of ratification of June 26, 1788, read, in part, "We, the delegates of the people of Virginia . . . do, in the name and in behalf of the people of Virginia, declare and make known, *that the powers granted under the Constitution, being derived from the people of the United States, may be resumed by them, whensoever the same shall be perverted to their injury or oppression.*"[46] Virginia ratified the Constitution expressly subject to its people's right of rescission.

In New York the battle was as fierce as in Virginia. Held in Poughkeepsie, the New York convention was bitterly divided. New Yorkers Alexander Hamilton and John Jay and Virginian James Madison were compelled to publish arguments in the New York press reassuring the delegates about the proposed Constitution and advocating ratification. Those arguments became known collectively as *The Federalist Papers.* Finally, on July 26, 1788, New York narrowly ratified the Constitution by a vote of thirty to twenty-seven. In New York, like in Virginia, the resolution of ratification was made expressly subject to the State's people's right to rescind. It read, in pertinent part:

We, the delegates of the people of the State of New York . . . do declare and make known—

That the powers of government may be reassumed by the people whensoever it shall become necessary to their happiness.

The delegates then presented a veritable catalogue of rights that they believed should be added to the Constitution by way of amendment.[47]

Interestingly, North Carolina and Rhode Island did not ratify the Constitution until after George Washington was sworn in as president of the United States. North Carolina, on August 2, 1788, voted to defer any action on the Constitution until a second federal convention considered a declaration of rights and other amendments. Only on November 21, 1789, did North Carolina finally ratify the document.[48] Rhode Island, likewise, expressed deep misgivings. In fact, its legislature defeated resolutions calling for a convention to consider ratification seven times! Finally, on May 29, 1790, Rhode Island ratified the Constitution after the federal government threatened it with economic sanctions. Like Virginia and New York, Rhode Island ratified the Constitution, or, what it deemed to be a "social compact," subject to its people's right of rescission. The Rhode Island resolution of ratification—a virtual copy of New York's resolution—read, in pertinent part:

> We the delegates of the people of the state of Rhode Island and Providence Plantations, duly elected and met in Convention . . . do declare and make known—
> I. That there are certain natural rights of which men, when they form a *social compact,* cannot deprive or divest their posterity—among which are the enjoyment of life and liberty, with the means of acquiring, possessing, and protecting property, and pursuing and obtaining happiness and safety. . . .
> III. *That the powers of government may be reassumed by the people whensoever it shall become necessary to their happiness.*[49]

The Constitution is an agreement "between the States so ratifying the same." It has parties—the States. Each of those parties agreed to surrender some powers in exchange for receiving a "common defense" and some regulation of commerce between the States where it was necessary. The Constitution is an "at will" agreement; it has no definite term and is, by no means, perpetual. Each party retains the right to rescind its ratification of the Constitution if there is a material breach by other States or by the federal government created by the Constitution. That right to rescind is retained by the operation of law; the State need not have expressly reserved it in writing.

The Constitution clearly was created after the States agreed to send delegates to the Federal Convention to draft revisions to the Articles of Confederation. The States paid their own delegates, and the delegates voted on the final draft for and in the name of their respective States. Each of the twelve States that sent delegates to the convention were identified by the name of the State on the signatory page of the Constitution as agreeing to the terms thereof. To ratify the Constitution required the favorable vote of the conventions of nine States. To amend the Constitution required the ratification of three-fourths of the State legislatures. The document was sent to the Congress of the Confederation and, in turn, to the States for ratification. And although State legislatures did not vote to ratify the document but rather voted to turn over to their respective citizens the decision to elect delegates to State ratifying conventions, the States nevertheless provided the machinery and funding for the elections and conventions, and those conventions ratified the Constitution in the name of the people of their respective States.

Textually, the Constitution read that it was a "Constitution between the States so ratifying the same." No matter whether the States ratified the Constitution by conventions of delegates (as they, in fact, were called upon to do and did) or by the votes of the State legislatures, the Constitution they ratified was a "constitution between the States." Notably, at least three States, including the two largest States, Virginia and New York, ratified the Constitution expressly subject to their citizens' right to rescind or annul it if necessary.

The framers and ratifiers of the Constitution unquestionably understood it to be a "compact." Not only did the document, in form, contain all the elements of a contract, but the prevailing political thought of revolutionary America underscored the fact that written constitutions were "compacts."

Probably no political writer had more influence on American thought during and immediately after the Revolution than John Locke. In his *Second Treatise on Civil Government*, he developed a theory that government was the creature of a "social compact" between individuals in a state of nature to combine in society.[50] As the war progressed, Americans used Locke's theory to develop and understand the relationships established between themselves and their States. Wrote Prof. Gordon S. Wood, "Only a social agreement among the people, only such a Lockean contract, seemed to make sense of their rapidly developing idea of a constitution as a fundamental law designed by the people to be separate from and controlling of all institutions of government."[51] Wood echoes what Thomas Paine wrote in 1776 about the Pennsylvania Constitution: "That Charter should be the act of all and not of one man," Paine wrote. "[It should be] the charter or compact of the whole people, and the limitation of all legislative and executive powers."[52]

The Massachusetts Constitution of 1780 actually declared itself to be a "social compact by which the whole people covenants with each citizen and each citizen with the whole people, that all shall be governed by certain laws for the common good."[53] Massachusetts was not alone in the 1780s. "From South Carolina to New Jersey," Professor Wood has noted, "the constitution [the written, organic documents of the States] had become [known as] a social compact entered into by express consent of the people."[54] And there was historical precedent for such a conclusion. The first written constitution on the North American continent was called the "Mayflower Compact" for the very same reasons.

So embedded was the concept that a State constitution was a social compact that many of the framers and ratifiers of the Constitution used the term to describe the Articles of Confederation and the United States Constitution. The only difference was that the Articles of Confederation and the

Constitution were considered by them to be compacts among and between the States, as sovereigns, not among the people.

On the floor of the Federal Convention, James Madison eloquently argued that the document the delegates were drafting was a compact. On June 19, 1787, he argued the classic theory of contract law as applied to the possible rescission or annulment of the Constitution: "If we consider the federal union as analogous to the fundamental compact by which individuals compose our society, and which must in its theoretic origin at least, have been the unanimous act of the component members, it cannot be said that no dissolution of the compact can be affected without unanimous consent. A breach of the fundamental principles of the compact by a part of the Society would certainly absolve the other part from their obligations to it."[55]

Madison then argued that the Federal Union was not analogous to social compacts among individual men but "to the conventions among individual states." Then, again drawing upon the ancient law of contracts, he concluded, "Clearly, according to the Expositors of the law of Nations, that a breach of any one article, by any one party, leaves all other parties at liberty to consider the whole convention to be dissolved, unless they choose rather to compel the delinquent party to repair the breach."[56] Other delegates referred to the document they were creating as a "compact." For instance, Gouverneur Morris of New York, who would author the final preamble, was recorded to have argued on July 12, 1787:

> It has been said that it is a high crime to speak out. As one member, he [Morris] would candidly do so. He came here to form a compact for the good of America. He was ready to do so with all the states: He hoped and believed that all would enter into such a Compact. If they would not he was ready to join with any states that would. But as the Compact was to be voluntary, it is vain for the Eastern states to insist on what the Southern states will never agree to.[57]

Notably, both James Madison and Gouverneur Morris not only used the term "compact" to describe the Constitution, they also invoked the idea that the States were "parties" to the compact, as one would reference parties in the context of contract law.

The Constitution as a Compact

In the ratification conventions in the States, the Constitution was repeatedly referred to as a "compact." In those proceedings, unlike the proceedings in the Federal Convention, delegates freely resorted to the invocation of political theory. New Hampshire, when formally ratifying the new Constitution, considered itself and other States as "entering into an explicit and solemn compact with each other." Rhode Island referred to the Constitution as "a social compact" in its resolution of ratification.[58]

Although it is not good form to assert what the framers and ratifiers understood the Constitution to mean (because no one can assert that they all had one understanding), it is unquestionably correct to state that virtually all of them understood the Constitution to be a compact in some form and that they understood that one of the remedies for its breach was rescission. Manifestly, few, if any, of the framers or ratifiers would have understood the Constitution to be an instrument from which a State could not extricate itself if necessary. The idea that the Constitution that they had drafted and ratified was entered into "by the people," as opposed to the States, and was irrevocable once ratified was absolutely unknown to the framers and ratifiers. They left no record of such an idea in their voluminous debates in the Federal Convention or the State ratifying conventions.

The Constitution, as drafted and ratified, was a "Constitution between the States so ratifying the same" because it says so.

The only legal construction for the Constitution that any of the framers and ratifiers understood was that it was a compact between the States, and, like all compacts, it was subject to the equitable remedy of rescission or annulment upon a breach, whether that right was explicitly reserved in writing or not.

In the years after the ratification of the Constitution, the document was often referred to as a compact. Chief Justice John Jay referred to it as a compact in his opinion in the famous case of *Chisholm v. Georgia* in 1793.[59] Notably, the legislatures of both Kentucky and Virginia referred to the Constitution as a compact in their famous resolutions of 1798-99, adopted in response to the enactment by Congress, and the enforcement thereof by John Adams' administration, of the hated Alien and Sedition Acts.[60] Written largely by Thomas Jefferson and James Madison, the Virginia and Kentucky resolutions are virtual lessons in the compact theory. Reads the Kentucky Resolution of November 10, 1798, a document penned by Jefferson and refined by John Breckinridge of Kentucky, "Resolved, that the several States composing the United States of America are not united on the principles of unlimited submission to their General Government; but that by compact under the style and title of a Constitution for the United States . . . and that whensoever the General Government assumed un-delegated powers, its acts are un-authoritative, void, and of no force. That to this compact each State acceded as a State, and is an integral party, its co-States forming as to itself, the other party."[61]

Kentucky did not seek secession but, rather, the "nullification" of the despised federal laws. Through the pen of James Madison, Virginia sought to "interpose" itself between the challenged laws and those against whom they were enacted to operate, Virginia's citizens. States, claimed the Virginia Resolution, were "duty-bound to interpose for purposes of arresting the evil."[62] The issue resolved itself short of actual nullification, but the compact theory and the related doctrines of "nullification" and "interposition" were firmly enunciated in a crisis only eleven years after the ratification of the Constitution by two of the nation's foremost "founding fathers."

James Madison declared long after the ratification of the Constitution, "Our governmental system is established by a *compact*, not between the Government of the United States and the State governments, but *between the States as sovereign communities, stipulating each with the other a surrender of certain portions of their respective authorities to be exercised by a common government,* and a reservation, for their own exercise, of all their other authorities."[63]

Then in 1814, the shipping embargo imposed by the James Madison administration during the War of 1812 led the New England States to openly speak of secession. Relying upon the compact theory, and speaking of the Constitution as an association of States, one Boston newspaper, the *Columbian Centinel,* wrote, "Whenever [the Constitution's] principles are violated, or its original principles departed from by a majority of the States or of their people, it is no longer an effective instrument, but that any state is at liberty by the spirit of that contract to withdraw itself from the union."[64] Again, the issue passed without a confrontation, although the 1814 Hartford Convention came close to actually embracing secession as a remedy.

These arguments would be repeated over and over in the first half of the nineteenth century. In the 1830s, John C. Calhoun would echo the compact theory and the Virginia and Kentucky "Resolutions of '98" in the great "nullification" crisis over the 1828 Tariff of Abominations. And in the end, the compact theory would form the basis for the secession of South Carolina and her ten sister Southern States in 1860 and 1861.[65]

The theory was absolutely sound. Unquestionably, the Constitution was a compact. It had all the requisites of a contract. There were parties: thirteen States, to which were added those that similarly ratified the document in the years after 1789. There was mutuality: each State promised to give up some of its sovereignty in exchange for what the Union promised to deliver. The Constitution was created by the States and ratified by the States. It could only be amended by the States. And the Constitution reads that it is a "Constitution between the States so ratifying the same." If, then, the Constitution is a compact, what is the remedy for a State or a group of States harmed by a breach of the Constitution by the federal government or other States? The only remedy, short of persuading the party or parties in breach to conform, is the equitable remedy of rescission.

If the Constitution is a compact, and it could be rescinded or annulled upon a breach, what would be sufficient to constitute a breach? Whatever would constitute a breach is left wholly to the State seeking the extraordinary remedy of rescission. Obviously, in the words of the 1800 Report on the Virginia Resolution of 1798, the offensive act would have to be "a deliberate, palpable and dangerous exercise of power not granted by the compact."[66]

It has been argued that the Constitution was meant to be perpetual, and, because of same, States cannot withdraw from it. Importantly, the Constitution does not include the word "perpetual" in any of its provisions. The Articles of Confederation, on the other hand, were entitled "Articles of Confederation and Perpetual Union," and the Articles were textually meant to be perpetual. That did not occur. Instead, the Articles of Confederation were completely replaced without one mention of them in the text of the Constitution that replaced them. The Articles were replaced without the States even conforming to the requirement in the Articles that its amendment be unanimous.

The English-speaking people have never, at any time in their long and storied history, subscribed to a rule of law that recognized any agreement as being perpetual. Parties to an agreement were always protected in their right to rescind the agreement, even an agreement for a specific term of years. That rule of law was true whether the right to rescind was explicitly provided in writing or not. That rule of law was true even if the contract was, by its terms, "perpetual." No matter what a contract provided, parties were always provided with a right to rescind if another party or other parties breached the contract. If that was not the case, a party could be kept in a contract to his economic destruction while the other party or parties willfully and wantonly breached the terms thereof. Reads the ancient rule of law: *Perpetua Lex Est Nullam Legem Humanom Ac Positivam Perpetuam Esse, Et Clausula Quae Abrogationem Excludit Ab Initio Non Valet* ("It is perpetual law that no human and positive law can be perpetual, and a clause in law which precludes the power of abrogation is void *ab initio*").[67] No party can be forced to remain in an agreement while other parties are in breach of its terms.

The framers and ratifiers understood the Constitution not to be perpetual because they ascribed to it no such term. They understood it could never be perpetual even if they incorporated that very term in the text of the Constitution. Like the Articles of Confederation, it would remain in effect so long as all of the parties to it prospered and no party or parties breached its terms and, importantly, the federal government created thereby did not breach its terms.[68]

That the Constitution is a compact subject to the equitable remedy of rescission has been refuted by many notable individuals. Ardent nationalists objected to the compact theory because it diminished federal power and it provided the single most critical mechanism allowing the States to control the growth and actions of the federal government by exercising that right to rescind. Nationalists argued that the people ratified the Constitution, not the States. Not being parties to the Constitution, they claimed, the ancient remedies in contract law such as rescission were not available to the States.

The most famous early refutation of the theory that the Constitution is a compact may be found in the opinion of Chief Justice John Marshall in *McCulloch v. Maryland*.[69] That case was brought by the cashier of the Baltimore branch of the Bank of the United States, a corporation created by Congress, challenging the constitutionality of a tax imposed upon it by the State of Maryland.

Apart from arguing the power of Congress to create a bank through its power to "coin money" and "regulate the value thereof," "regulate commerce between the States," and do all of those things "necessary and proper for carrying into execution such power," as well as the "supremacy clause," Marshall embarked on a line of reasoning triggered by the argument of counsel for the State of Maryland. According to the latter, it was important to construe the Constitution as an "instrument not emanating from the people, but as the act of sovereign and independent States" in order to advance his argument. The counsel's argument was absolutely correct textually and historically. To Marshall, an ardent nationalist, such a construction could not stand no matter what the text or history of the Constitution indicated.[70]

Wrote Marshall in response:

> It would be difficult to sustain this proposition. The convention which framed the constitution was indeed elected by the state legislatures. But the instrument, when it came from their hands, was a mere proposal, without obligation, or pretensions to it. It was reported to the then existing Congress of the United States, with a request that it might "be submitted to a convention of delegates, chosen in each state by the people thereof, under the recommendation of its legislature, for their assent and ratification." This mode of proceeding was adopted; and by the convention, by Congress, and by the state legislatures, the instrument

was submitted to the people. They acted upon it in the only manner in which they can act safely, effectively, and wisely, on such a subject, by assembling in convention. It is true they assembled in their several states and where else should they have assembled? No political dreamer was ever wild enough to think of breaking down the lines which separate the states, and of compounding the American people into one common mass. Of consequence, when they act, they act in their states. But the measures they adopt do not, on that account, cease to be the measures of the people themselves, or become the measures of the state governments.

From these conventions the Constitution derives its whole authority. The Government proceeds directly from the people; is "ordained and established" in the name of the people; and is declared to be ordained, "in order to form a more perfect union, establish justice, insure domestic tranquility, and secure the blessings of liberty, to themselves and our posterity." The assent of the states, in their sovereign capacity, is implied in calling a convention, and thus submitting that instrument to the people. But the people were at perfect liberty to accept or reject it; and their act was final. It required not the affirmance, and could not be negatived, by the state governments. The Constitution, when thus adopted, was of complete obligation, and bound the state sovereignties. . . .

The Government of the Union, then, (whatever may be the influence of this fact on the case), is emphatically, and truly, a government of the people. In form and in substance it emanates from them. Its powers are granted by them, and are to be exercised directly on them, and for their benefit.[71]

For all the invented history and tortured logic of Marshall, the Constitution resolves the question textually. Article VII reads that it is a "Constitution between the States so ratifying the same." It is not a Constitution among the people, as Marshall proclaims. No matter what the preamble might proclaim, the text of the Constitution makes it absolutely clear that it is a "Constitution between the States" regardless of the ratification process. Marshall totally ignored the text of the Constitution and invented his own history. It would not be the last time the Supreme Court would do that.

The Webster Argument

Probably no single exponent of an "indissoluble Union" was greater than Daniel Webster, the senator from Massachusetts. He was an imposing figure, indeed. Tall and powerfully built, he had a barrel chest. His head was large, and his "deep-socketed, black eyes peered out from a 'precipice of brows' and glowed like coals in a furnace" when he spoke.[72] If anyone could articulate how the Constitution makes the Union indissoluble, it was Webster.

On February 16, 1833, Webster rose in the Senate to argue against three resolutions introduced by John C. Calhoun of South Carolina in opposition to a bill extending the hated Tariff of 1828. Calhoun's resolutions read, in part, "Resolved, that the people of the several states composing these United States are united as parties to a constitutional compact, to which the people of each state acceded as a separate sovereign community, each binding itself by its own particular ratification; and that the union, of which the said compact is the bond, is a union between the States ratifying the same."[73] Note that Calhoun's resolution actually quoted Article VII of the Constitution.

Webster took the floor and began by fundamentally arguing against himself: "I do not agree, that, in strictness of language, [the Constitution] is a compact at all. But I do agree that it is founded on consent or agreement, or on compact, if the gentleman [John C. Calhoun] prefers that word, and means no more by it than voluntary consent or agreement." He then argued against himself again:

> The Constitution, Sir, is not a contract, but the result of a contract; meaning by contract no more than assent. Founded upon consent, it is a government proper. Adopted by the agreement of the people of the United States, when adopted, it has become a constitution. The people have agreed to make a Constitution; but when made, that Constitution becomes what its name imports. It is no longer a mere agreement.[74]

What on earth was Webster arguing? He paraphrased Chief Justice John Marshall's words in *McCulloch v. Maryland*. The Constitution, Webster argued, is the "result of an agreement between the people," not the States. But according to Webster, the Constitution somehow ceased to be an agreement at all when it was ratified; with ratification it became a constitution.

Article VII of the Constitution answers Webster's tortured logic. It is a "Constitution between the States so ratifying the same." That parties can enter into a contract and then, somehow, the contract can change its form after it is signed is utterly nonsensical. Under Webster's understanding of history, the framers and ratifiers were duped. Without knowing it, they entered into an agreement that was designed to cease being what they thought it was when they signed it; it became something else after ratification.

Webster's argument, like Marshall's, cannot stand the tests of logic or history, although it has been the accepted line of reasoning by the courts—and by most Americans—ever since. It is contrary to the very text of the Constitution, and it is hardly supported by the history of its drafting and ratification. The Constitution was never, at any time during the Federal Convention, or during the ratifying conventions in any of the States, represented to be irrevocable. If the Constitution was designed to create a government from which the States could never escape, no matter how that government abused its power and authority, it would have never been reported out of the Federal Convention. It certainly would have never been ratified by the States, particularly given the tenor and language of the Virginia, New York, and Rhode Island resolutions of ratifications reserving their right to rescind their ratifications.

Abraham Lincoln provided no clearer guidance as to whether the Constitution created an indissoluble Union. On March 4, 1861, he delivered his first inaugural address. By that time, six States had already seceded from the Union.[75] Lincoln chose to direct his address at that matter, saying:

> I hold, that in contemplation of universal law, and of the Constitution, the union of these states is perpetual. Perpetuity is implied, if not expressed, in the fundamental law of all national governments. It is safe to assert that no government proper, ever had a provision in its organic law for its own termination. Continue to execute all the express provisions of our national Constitution, and the union will endure forever—it being impossible to destroy it, except by some action not provided for in the instrument itself.
>
> Again, if the United States be not a government proper, but an association of states in the nature of contract merely, can it, as a contract, be peaceably unmade, by less than all the parties who made it? One party to a contract may violate it—break it, so to speak; but does it not require all to rescind it?
>
> Descending from these general principles, we find the proposition that, in legal contemplation, the union is perpetual, confirmed by the history of the union itself. The union is much older than the Constitution. It was formed, in fact, by the articles of association in 1774. It was matured and continued by the declaration of independence in 1776. It was further matured and expressly declared and pledged, to be perpetual, by the Articles of Confederation in 1778. And finally, in 1787, one of the declared objects for ordaining and establishing the Constitution, was "to form a more perfect union."
>
> But if destruction of the union, by one, or by a part only, of the states, be lawfully possible, the union is less perfect than before, which contradicts the Constitution, and therefore is absurd.

It follows from these views that no state, upon its own mere motion, can lawfully get out of the union—that resolves and ordinances to that effect are legally nothing; and that the acts of violence, within any state or states, are insurrectionary or treasonable, according to circumstances.

I therefore consider that the union is unbroken; and, to the extent of my ability, I shall take care that the laws of the union be faithfully executed in all the states. Doing this I deem to be only a simple duty on my part; and I shall perform it, unless my rightful masters, the American people, shall withhold the requisite means, or, in some tangible way, direct the contrary.[76]

Lincoln rests his argument that the Union is perpetual upon the "contemplation of universal law" and the "law of all national governments." He could point to nothing in the Constitution that provided that it was perpetual. He could point to no utterances on the floor of the Federal Convention or any of the ratifying conventions. The "universal law" of which he spoke was a law that governments are not created by instruments that provide a mechanism for their own dissolution. That may be true for the governments of monarchs and dictators that ravaged Europe for centuries, but it was not true for the government created by the Constitution. The Constitution is a revolutionary instrument created by a revolutionary people at the end of a successful revolution fought to end the rule of a monarch and to guarantee fundamental liberty to all citizens. The government created by the Constitution was worth keeping only so long as it served that end. That fundamental understanding of the formation of the Union was utterly lost on Lincoln. It is sheer folly to argue that the Constitution is perpetual because other governments claim their constitutions are perpetual. Monarchs always claim the monarchy is perpetual. On the basis of this argument, nevertheless, Lincoln led the Union to war in 1861.

As the Constitution established "a more perfect Union," as set forth in the preamble, and the Articles of Confederation established a "perpetual Union," it followed to Lincoln that the Constitution must have established a Union more "perfectly perpetual" than the Articles of Confederation. The fact is the Constitution, unlike the Articles of Confederation, does not incorporate the term "perpetual" anywhere. In fact, no term is expressed at all. Likewise, the Constitution does not explicitly or implicitly incorporate any of the terms of the Articles of Confederation in its text. The Constitution does not use the term "perpetual" because the framers and ratifiers knew that no compact could ever be perpetual; all compacts are subject to the equitable remedy of rescission.

Finally, the Supreme Court considered the legality of secession in *Texas v. White* in 1869.[77] The case was brought by the Reconstruction State government of Texas to recover payment in United States currency on bonds that a military board of Texas had, during the Civil War, ordered delivered to agents for purposes of sale in order to raise money for the war effort.[78]

Chief Justice Salmon P. Chase wrote the opinion for the Court. That opinion was little more than the plagiarizing of Lincoln's first inaugural address. Wrote Chief Justice Chase:

> The Union of the States never was a purely artificial and arbitrary relation. It began among the colonies, and grew out of common origin, mutual sympathies, kindred. . . . When, therefore, Texas became one of the United States, she entered into an indissoluble relation. All the obligations of perpetual union, and all the guaranties of republican government in the union, attached at once to the state. The act which consummated her admission into the Union was something more than a compact; it was the incorporation of a new member into the political body. And it was final. The Union between Texas and the other states was as complete as perpetual, and as indissoluble as the Union between the

original states. There was no place for reconsideration, or revocation, except through revolution, or through consent of the States.

It began among the Colonies, and grew out of common origins, mutual sympathies, kindred principles, similar interests and geographical relations. It was confirmed and strengthened by the necessities of war, and received definite form, and character, and sanction from the Articles of Confederation. By these the Union was solemnly declared to "be perpetual." And when these articles were found to be inadequate to the exigencies of the country, the constitution was ordained "to form a more perfect union." It is difficult to convey the idea of indissoluble unity more clearly than by these words. What can be indissoluble if a perpetual Union, made more perfect, is not?[79]

Chase admits that the States formed the Union. Without them, there would be no "United States." Once the States formed the Union, however, that was it! Like Webster, Chase argued that the compact became something else upon ratification. When a State was admitted to the Union, Chase claimed, it was the "incorporation of a new member into the political body," and "it was final." It goes without saying that not one member of the Federal Convention nor one member of any of the ratification conventions ever argued that once the Constitution was ratified by a State, that ratification was irrevocable. Virginia, New York, and Rhode Island *explicitly* reserved the right to rescind their ratification if they were not "happy." Either Chase was ignorant of that fact or he chose to ignore it. It would not be the last time the Supreme Court followed such a course.[80]

To argue whether a breach occurred in 1860 and 1861 is, of course, beyond the scope of this discussion. Volumes have been written about it. A few words about the issue are appropriate, however. The threat of the abolition or limitation of slavery, in the eyes of the citizens of slaveholding States, was viewed as an act constituting a breach. There is no question that slavery is absolutely antithetical to the principles of liberty upon which the Constitution was based. Many Southerners abhorred slavery; most wished it had never been introduced into the region. But whether slavery was good or evil was not the question that haunted Southerners. The question they asked was who should initiate and oversee slavery's eradication?

To understand why the abolition of slavery, as advocated for many years by many representatives from the Northern States, was viewed as a constitutional breach by Southerners, one must place oneself in the position of those living in the slave States in 1860 and 1861. Although no major political party actually advocated abolition as part of its platform, the agitation for abolition had grown to such an extent that large voting blocs in Congress were able to limit slavery's extension into the territories. Southerners feared that federal policy would embrace abolition and that it was only a matter of time before that would become a reality. With nearly four million African-American slaves in the Southern States by 1860, the sudden release of them was unthinkable.[81] As a practical matter, there was no place for the freed slaves to go; they had no means by which they could provide for themselves and live. There was no public housing or public assistance then. If the slaves were suddenly freed, the region would be torn apart. There also had been threats of slave uprisings, and John Brown's Harpers Ferry raid in 1859 added fuel to the fear of the abolition movement. Southerners believed then that if slavery was to be abolished, only the States where slavery existed should be responsible for the method and timing. The States had to find mechanisms to address the myriad issues created by the abolition of slavery.

The abolition or limitation of slavery, short of a constitutional amendment, was unconstitutional. Slavery was actually recognized then by the Constitution.[82] That was never questioned. The abolition or limitation of slavery was unquestionably contrary to the Constitution. After years of intense argument and bitterness over the issue of slavery and its extension into the new territories, the election to the presidency of Abraham Lincoln, a candidate who did not even run in the Southern States and who was openly supported by abolitionists in the Northern States, was, to many Southerners then, sufficient cause for secession. Secession may well have been the result of a "crisis of fear," but the fear of those living in the South then was very real nevertheless.[83]

South Carolina rescinded its ratification of the Constitution on December 20, 1860.[84] Ten of her sister Southern States followed.

Few figures on the national scene were more erudite than Judah P. Benjamin, then a United States senator from Louisiana. A lawyer of significant distinction, Benjamin delivered a speech on the right of secession before the Senate on December 31, 1860. Relying upon the ancient law of contracts, Benjamin said, "I say, therefore, that I distinguish the rights of the States under the Constitution into two classes; one resulting from the nature of their bargain; if the bargain is broken by the sister states, to consider themselves freed from it on the ground of breach of compact; if the bargain be not broken, but the powers be perverted to their wrong and their oppression, then, whenever that wrong and oppression shall become sufficiently aggravated, the revolutionary right—the last inherent right of man to preserve freedom, property, and safety—arises, and must be exercised, for none other will meet the cause."[85]

Only a Civil War—the use of brute force—crushed the attempt by slave States to secede. The Constitution has been understood by many people since the Civil War as an instrument that was created by the "People of the United States" in order to form an "indissoluble Union" and that granted to the federal government plenary powers over virtually all aspects of the lives of its citizens. That meaning is not one understood by any of the framers or ratifiers. Rather, it is the result of the use of force against the States by the very government the States agreed to create in 1789. Justice Oliver Wendell Holmes, a thrice-wounded Union veteran of the Civil War, may have said it best when, in the landmark case of *Missouri v. Holland,* he wrote that the Constitution he was interpreting was one that "has taken a century and has cost [the] successors [of the framers and ratifiers] much sweat and blood to prove that they created a nation."[86]

Although Holmes' *dicta* may have the ring of truth, the Constitution's text and history before the Civil War did not change as a result of Appomattox. Contracts do not textually change by the use of brute force; contracts change only by the agreement of the parties. The Constitution was still a "constitution between the States" after the war as it was before. It remains so now.

That it is considered to be a "constitution between the States" is absolutely necessary to preserve the liberties of the people of the several States. Without the States being able to exercise their powers as parties to the Constitution, the people are totally subject to the dictates of the federal government. They have no power save through their respective States. In fact, the Supreme Court has consistently denied citizens standing, as citizens and taxpayers, to even challenge the constitutionality of revenue-spending acts of Congress.[87]

Secession is not only constitutional, it was understood by all the States to be available when they ratified the Constitution; three States explicitly reserved the right to rescind when they ratified the Constitution. Manifestly, the Constitution would not have been ratified if it had been understood to be otherwise. More than that, however, the Constitution is a revolutionary document created by a people who had prevailed in a revolution against the most powerful monarch on earth. The revolution had been fought to guarantee liberty. If what the framers and ratifiers created failed to protect the liberty of the people, the States were free to rescind their ratification of it.

If the government created by the Constitution ceases to guarantee liberty, there must be a remedy available to those oppressed by it. It is not the courts; the citizens may not even have standing to challenge the actions of the federal government, and, moreover, the courts are creatures of the very government that would be the oppressor. To be sure, courts are really not competent to even address constitutional challenges to acts of Congress that allege that those acts undermine the liberties of citizens and invade the powers reserved to the States.[88] Resorting to the ballot may be ineffectual; the votes of a few metropolitan areas may negate the votes of all other regions. More than that, fundamental liberties should never be subject to a majority vote.

What remains to protect individual liberties are the States as parties to the Constitution. As parties, they must exercise their "duty" to protect their citizens from a federal government that has grown too powerful, too intrusive, too dictatorial. They do that by exercising the right that parties to agreements have exercised for literally hundreds of years: to stand up to actions that invade the liberties of citizens and the reserved powers of the States by, first, nullifying the unconstitutional acts and then, if the federal government persists, seceding. The framers and ratifiers would not have thought any differently. After all, although they were revolutionaries who created a revolutionary form of government, they were also the inheritors of an Anglo-American legal tradition that had been developed over hundreds of years, which defined contracts and the remedies available to those injured by the breach thereof.

The Founding Fathers of
Constitutional Subversion

Thomas DiLorenzo

After spending his adult lifetime in politics, John C. Calhoun (U.S. senator, vice president of the United States, secretary of war) wrote his brilliant treatise, *A Disquisition on Government,* which was published shortly after his death in 1850. In it, he warned that it is an error to believe that a written constitution alone is "sufficient, of itself, without the aid of any organism— except such as is necessary to separate its several departments, and render them independent of each other—to counteract the tendency of the numerical majority to oppression and abuse of power."[1] The separation of powers is fine as far as it goes, in other words, but it would never be a sufficient defense against governmental tyranny, said Calhoun.

Moreover, it is a "great mistake," Calhoun wrote, to suppose that "the mere insertion of provisions to restrict and limit the powers of the government, *without investing those for whose protection they are inserted, with the means of enforcing their observance,* will be sufficient to prevent the major and dominant party from abusing its powers" (emphasis added).[2] The party "in possession of the government" will always be opposed to any and all restrictions on its powers. They "will have no need of these restrictions" and "would come, in time, to regard these limitations as unnecessary and improper restraints—and endeavor to elude them."[3]

The "part in favor of the restrictions" (i.e., strict construc-tionists) would inevitably be overpowered. It is sheer folly, Calhoun argued, to suppose that "the party in possession of the ballot box *and the physical force of the country,* could be successfully resisted by an appeal to reason, truth, justice, or

63

the obligations imposed by the constitution" (emphasis added). He predicted that "the restrictions [of government power in the Constitution] would ultimately be annulled, and the government be converted into one of unlimited powers."[4] He was right, of course.

This is a classic statement of the Jeffersonian states' rights position. The people of the free, independent, and sovereign states must be empowered with the rights of nullification and secession, and a concurrent majority with veto power over unconstitutional federal laws, if their constitutional liberties are to have any chance of protection. The federal government itself can never, ever be trusted to limit its own powers.

How did Calhoun come to such conclusions? One answer to this question is that he was a serious student of politics, history, and political philosophy for his entire life and understood the nature of government as much as anyone else alive during his time. He also witnessed firsthand (or quickly learned about) the machinations of the sworn enemies of limited constitutional government in America—men such as Alexander Hamilton, John Adams, John Marshall, Joseph Story, and Daniel Webster.

The Founding Enemies of Limited Government

America's first constitution—the Articles of Confederation and Perpetual Union—did a much better job of limiting the tyrannical proclivities of government than the U.S. Constitution did. It did so, moreover, while permitting enough governmental power to field an army that defeated the British Empire. The limits on government that the Articles contained were opposed by the advocates of unlimited governmental powers, such as Alexander Hamilton. Hamilton was the main instigator of the idea of "revising" the Articles at a constitutional convention. Rather than merely revising them, however, they were scrapped completely and the "Perpetual Union" that they created was abolished. All the states peacefully seceded from that particular union. The new Constitution did not commit the folly of calling the union "perpetual."

The constitutional convention was Hamilton's idea as much as anyone's. Upon arriving at the convention, Hamilton laid out the plan of his fellow nationalists: a permanent president or king, who would appoint all governors, who would have veto power over all state legislation. This monopoly government would then impose on the entire nation a British-style mercantilist empire without Great Britain, complete with corporate-welfare subsidies for "internal improvements," a large public debt, protectionist tariffs, and a central bank modeled after the Bank of England that would inflate the currency to finance the empire. John Taylor of Caroline exposed Hamilton's agenda when he explained that what was being proposed was "a national government, nearly conforming to that of England. . . . By Colonel Hamilton's project, the states were fairly and openly to be restored to the rank of provinces and to be made as dependent upon a supreme national government, as they had been upon a supreme British government."[5]

Hamilton did not get his way, of course, thanks to the Jeffersonians or Anti-Federalists. John Taylor relied on the notes taken by Robert Yates, the chief justice of New York who attended the constitutional convention and whose book, *Secret Proceedings and Debates of the Constitutional Convention,* was published posthumously. Quoting Yates, Taylor noted that the convention attendees viewed the Constitution as a compact among the free and independent states and not the creation of a "national" government. "It was proposed and seconded," Taylor wrote, "to erase the word *national,* and substitute the words United States [in the plural] in the fourth resolution, which passed in the affirmative. Thus, we see an opinion expressed at the convention, that the phrase 'United

States' did not mean a consolidated American people or nation, and all the inferences in favour of a national government are overthrown."[6]

What Hamilton and his fellow nationalists were up to, wrote Taylor, was essentially a scheme to create "Monarchy, and its hand-maiden consolidation, and its other hand-maiden, ambition, and a national government dressed up in popular guises" such as "national splendor" and "national strength."[7] It was all "only a pretext of ambition and monopoly . . . intended to feed avarice, gratify ambition, and make one portion of the nation [the South] tributary to another," Taylor wrote in 1823.[8]

Taylor also wrote of how "paradoxical" so many of Hamilton's economic and political views were. Hamilton and his party contended that: "the greater the [government] revenue, the richer are the people; that frugality in the government is an evil; in the people, a good; that monopolies and exclusive privileges are general welfare; that a division of sovereignty will raise up a class of wicked, intriguing, self-interested politicians in the states; and that human nature will be cleansed of these propensities by a sovereignty consolidated in one government."[9]

When the Constitution was finally ratified, creating a federal instead of a national or monopolistic, monarchical government, Hamilton denounced the document as "a frail and worthless fabric." He and his Federalist/nationalist colleagues immediately went to work destroying the limits on government contained in the Constitution. He invented the notion of "implied powers" of the Constitution, which allowed him and his political heirs to argue that the Constitution is not a set of limitations on governmental powers, as Jefferson believed it was, but rather a potential stamp of approval on anything the government ever wanted to do—as long as it is "properly" interpreted by clever, statist lawyers like Alexander Hamilton or John Marshall. "It seems certain," wrote Hamilton biographer Clinton Rossiter, "that Hamilton would have affixed a certain certificate of constitutionality to every last tax. . . . Hamilton took a large view of the power of Congress to tax because he took a large view of the power to spend."[10] Moreover, "having failed to persuade his colleagues at Philadelphia of the beauties of a truly national plan of government, and having thereafter recognized the futility of persuading the legislatures of three-fourths of the states to surrender even a jot of their privileges, he [Hamilton] set out to remold the Constitution into an instrument of national supremacy."[11]

One of the first subversive things Hamilton did was to rewrite the history of the American founding by saying in a public speech before the New York State Assembly on June 29, 1787, that the states were merely "artificial beings" and were never sovereign. The "nation," not the states, was sovereign, he said. And he said this while the constitutional convention was busy crafting Article VII of the Constitution, which holds that the Constitution would become the law of the land only when nine of the thirteen free and independent *states* ratified it. The states were to ratify the Constitution because, as everyone knew, *they* were sovereign and were delegating a few express powers to the central government *for their mutual benefit.*

Hamilton's superstition that the "nation," and not the states, was sovereign is the biggest political lie ever told in America. It would be repeated endlessly for decades by such Hamiltonian political heirs as John Marshall, Daniel Webster, Joseph Story, and Abraham Lincoln.

Hamilton invented the myth of "implied powers" of the Constitution during his debate with Jefferson over the constitutionality of a national bank managed by politicians out of the nation's capital (the "Bank of the United States"). "There are implied, as well as express powers [in the Constitution], and the former are as effectually delegated as the latter," he wrote in his *Opinion on the Constitutionality of the Bank of the United States.*[12]

Statist historians have long heaped praise on Hamilton's subversion of the Constitution with slippery, lawyerly rhetoric. "With the aid of the doctrine of implied powers," Clinton Rossiter wrote in a celebratory tone, Hamilton "converted the . . . powers enumerated in Article 1, Section 8 into firm foundations for whatever prodigious feats of legislation any future Congress might contemplate."[13]

This, of course, was exactly the kind of political poison that George Washington warned about in his Farewell Address when he said: "If in the opinion of the People, the distribution of modification of the Constitutional powers be in any particular wrong, let it be corrected by an amendment in the way the Constitution designates. But let there be no change by usurpation . . . the customary weapon by which free governments are destroyed."[14]

It was Hamilton who invented the expansive interpretations of the General Welfare and Commerce clauses of the Constitution, which have been used for generations to grant unlimited powers to the central state. "The terms general Welfare [in the Constitution] were doubtless intended to signify more than was expressed," he wrote, so that "it is therefore of necessity left to the discretion of the National Legislature, to pronounce upon the objects, which concern the general Welfare, and for which . . . an appropriation of money is requisite and proper."[15] Of course, leaving such decisions up to "the National Legislature" would inevitably result in that legislature declaring that *any and all appropriations* are "requisite and proper." In other words, there would be no limits at all on government spending, as doubtless intended by the framers of the Constitution.

Hamilton was the first to twist the meaning of the Commerce Clause ("the Congress shall have Power . . . to regulate Commerce with foreign Nations, and among the several States") as well. This clause was intended to give Congress the ability to regulate interstate commerce in defense of free trade.

But Hamilton asserted that since intrastate commerce ultimately affected interstate commerce when goods crossed state lines, the Commerce Clause contains the "implied power" of regulating *all* commerce.

In contrast to the constitutional views of Jefferson, Madison, and Washington, which held that the Constitution was necessary to limit "the violence of faction," as Madison put it, Hamilton "chose to interpret the Constitution as a reservoir of national energy," wrote Clinton Rossiter.[16] He "taught his friends how to read the Constitution."

Hamilton's Supreme Disciple

Hamilton's devoted disciple, John Marshall, was appointed chief justice of the United States in 1801 and served in that post for more than three decades. His career was a crusade to rewrite the Constitution so that it would become a nationalist document that destroyed states' rights and most other limitations on the powers of the centralized state. He essentially declared in *Marbury v. Madison* that he, John Marshall, would be the arbiter of constitutionality via "judicial review." These words are not in the Constitution; they are a complete fabrication at the hands of John Marshall. The Jeffersonians, meanwhile, had always warned that if the day ever came when the federal government became the sole arbiter of the limits of its own powers, it would soon declare that there were, in fact, *no* limits on its powers. This, of course, is what the nationalists wanted—and what has happened.

Jefferson himself explained in a September 6, 1819, letter to Judge Spencer Roane, "My construction of the Constitution is . . . that each department [i.e., branch of government] is truly independent of the others, and has an equal right to decide for itself what is the meaning of the Constitution in the cases submitted to its action."[17]

In the case of *Martin v. Hunter's Lessee,* Marshall invented out of thin air the notion that the federal government had the "right" to veto state court decisions. Marshall also made up the theory that the so-called Supremacy Clause of the Constitution makes the federal government "supreme" in all matters. This is false. The federal government is only "supreme" with regard to those powers that were expressly delegated to it by the free and independent states, in Article I, Section 8. As John Taylor wrote, "The expression in the constitution, 'shall be the supreme law of the land,' is restricted by its limitations and reservation, and did not convey any species of supremacy to the governments, going beyond the powers delegated or those reserved."[18]

Marshall also repeated Hamilton's bogus theory of the American founding, claiming that the "nation" somehow created the states. He amazingly argued that the federal government was somehow created by "the whole people" and not the citizens of the states through state political conventions, as was actually the case. In the name of "the people," Marshall said, the federal government claimed the right to "legitimately control all individuals or governments within the American territory."[19] In other words, John Marshall took it upon himself to personally repeal the Tenth Amendment, and most of the rest of the Constitution, in the name of "national supremacy" and totalitarian "control" of all people and governments.

The Subversion Continues

All of the Hamilton/Marshall superstitions about the founders having created a monopolistic, monarchical government and having abolished states' rights or federalism was repeated for decades by the likes of Supreme Court Justice Joseph Story and Daniel Webster. Story was "the most Hamiltonian of judges," wrote Clinton Rossiter. Story's famous book, *Commentaries on the Constitution*, published in 1833, could have been entitled "Commentaries on Alexander Hamilton's Commentaries on the Constitution," says Rossiter.[20] He "construed the powers of Congress liberally," i.e., there were virtually no limits to such powers; and "upheld the supremacy of the nation," i.e., of monopolistic, monarchical, and *unconstitutional* government. Story's *Commentaries* provided a political roadmap for "the legal profession's elite— or at least among the part of it educated in the North—during the middle years of the nineteenth century."[21]

Story's "famous" *Commentaries* are filled with false history and illogic. On the Articles of Confederation, he wrote, "It is heresy to maintain, that a party to a compact has a right to revoke that compact."[22] But the Articles of Confederation *were* revoked by the majority of the participants in the constitutional convention despite the fact that not all participants were in favor of doing so. Joseph Story's nationalist predecessors wanted to do it, and they succeeded despite strong opposition by the Anti-Federalists.

It is interesting that Story admitted that the Constitution was a compact among the states (the Jeffersonian theory) but then implied that the full force of the central government, presumably including the death and devastation of war, should be used to prevent "a party" from entertaining the belief that the constitutional compact was voluntary, as it undeniably was. Story was essentially laying the ideological groundwork for the destruction of federalism and the centralization of all political power that some future presidential despot would impose.

Secession of a single state would mean "dissolution of the government," Story wrote. It would mean the end of "the operation of the laws of the union." This is nonsense. After eleven Southern states seceded in 1860-61, the U.S. government proceeded to field the largest and best-equipped army in the history of the world up to that point. The government was hardly "dissolved." Indeed, war is the *health of the state*, as Randolph Bourne famously intoned.[23] A supposedly learned man like Story should have understood this from even a cursory study of world history. Furthermore, the whole point of secession or the threat of secession was to pressure the central government to *enforce* "the laws of the union" as written into the Constitution. That is why, as a condition of ratifying the Constitution, several states (New York, Rhode Island, and Virginia) explicitly reserved the right to withdraw from the union at a future time if at that time the union and its constitution failed to protect the rights of their citizens in the manners prescribed in the document. If the Constitution was to be enforced, it would have to be done by the citizens of the sovereign states, organized in local political communities and armed with such tools as nullification and secession. Otherwise, the government is merely another tyranny.

In a classic case of doubletalk, Story admitted, "The original compact of society . . . in no instance . . . has ever been formally expressed at the first institution of a state." That is, there was never any agreement by the citizens of any state to always and forever be obedient to those who would enforce what they proclaim to be "the general will." Nevertheless, said Story, "every part should pay obedience to the will of the whole." And *who is to define "the will of the whole"*? Why, nationalist Supreme Court justices like Joseph Story and John Marshall, of course.

This is essentially the Jacobin philosophy that was expressed over and over again by Alexander Hamilton, whom political scientist Cecelia Kenyon once described as "The Rousseau of the Right."[24] Rousseau was the intellectual father of the *French* Revolution, and a hallmark of his political philosophy was the notion of the existence of "a general will" that was somehow known by the ruling elite. As Felix Morley explained it, "No aspect of life is excluded from the control of the general will," and "whosoever refuses to obey the general will must in that instance be restrained by the body politic, which actually means that he is forced to be free."[25]

This collectivist philosophy was diametrically opposed to the individual-rights philosophy of the *American* Revolution, which is why Rousseau is also sometimes referred to as the intellectual inspiration for communism. As philosopher Claes Ryn has pointed out, Rousseau's philosophy, as articulated by Joseph Story in the above quotation, "collides head on with the advocates of [American] constitutionalism" and "could not be in sharper contrast to American traditions of constitutionalism, federalism, localism, and representation."[26] Of course, these were the American traditions that the nationalists hoped (and hope) to destroy.

Felix Morley wrote that the Jeffersonians "hated and feared" this philosophy, for if "the general will" were to become a political reality with regard to the operations of government, then all voluntary associations would be subjected to totalitarian control in the name of "the whole people" and their "will" (as defined by the ruling class alone).

Story admitted that social-contract theories of "voluntary" state formation were mere fantasies. He also held the rather totalitarian-minded view that "the majority must have a right to accomplish that object by the means, which they deem adequate for the end. . . . The will of the majority of the people is absolute and sovereign, *limited only by its means and power to make its will effectual.*"[27]

Story is *not* saying here that there should be a national vote on all policy issues that could somehow reveal the "will of the majority." As with Hamilton, he adopted the French Jacobin philosophy that such a "will" was possessed in the minds of the ruling class and that that class (the Storys, Hamiltons, Marshalls, etc.) somehow possessed "absolute" power as long as it had the *military* means to "make its will effectual." Here we have the theoretical basis for Abraham Lincoln's waging of total war on his own citizens. Dictatorship by ruling-class elite is only limited, in Story's worldview, by the will of the elite to brutalize and wage war against dissenters. That is what is meant by his phrase, the "power to make its will effectual."

Contrary to the political truths expressed by Calhoun— which have all borne out, by the way—Story articulated the childish view that the appropriate response to governmental tyranny should be only via "the proper tribunals constituted by the government," which would supposedly "appeal to the good sense, and integrity, and justice of the majority of the people." Trust the politicians and lifetime-appointed federal judges to enforce *their* view of "justice," in other words. If there is ever a problem with the government becoming tyrannical, citizens should just trust the "tribunals" operated by *that same tyrannical government* to restore "freedom." This sounds more like the system of "kangaroo courts" established by the Soviet Union than the system of government created by the original American union.

Story also repeated John Marshall's fable that the Supremacy Clause of the Constitution created a monopolistic government in Washington, D.C. with "supreme" powers over everyone and everything, and effectively abolished states' rights. He repeated the equally ridiculous myth that the Constitution was magically ratified by "the whole people" (presumably not counting women, who could not vote, or slaves and free blacks) despite the fact that no one had ever claimed that any such vote was ever taken. Not only that, but no mechanism existed that could have recorded such a vote. If there was, one can rest assured that Story, Marshall, Hamilton, and all other nationalists, to this day, would have been making endless references to it.

Story was as responsible as anyone for spreading the myth that the American union was not a constitutional compact among the states but was somehow established by "the whole people," by citing the preamble of the Constitution, which begins, "We, the people of the United States, do ordain and establish this constitution . . . " It was established by "the people of the United States, not the distinct people of a particular state with the people of the other states," wrote Story.[28] This, too, is unequivocally wrong. Quoting James Madison's *Notes on the Debates in the Federal Convention*, historian William J. Watkins explained that the first draft of the preamble stated, "We the People of the States of New Hampshire, Massachusetts, Rhode Island and Providence Plantations, Connecticut," etc., eventually naming all the states. Once it dawned on the founders that some of the states might not ratify the Constitution, they changed the language to "We the People . . . "

Madison himself explained this in Federalist No. 39, when he wrote that the Constitution was to be ratified by Americans "not as individuals composing one entire nation, but as composing the distinct and independent States to which they respectively belong," as signified in Article VII of the Constitution. Each state, wrote Madison, was "considered as a sovereign body, independent of all others, and only to be bound by its own voluntary act." Madison did *not* say that any state refusing to ratify the Constitution, or leaving the union after ratifying, would (and should) be forced back into the union by the "power" of the majority, as Story contended. In fact, all of the founders would have thought of such a thing as sinful and barbaric.

Daniel Webster's "Eloquent" Subversion of the Constitution

Another influential subverter of the Constitution was Daniel Webster, who invoked many of these same nationalist fables during his famous U.S. Senate debate with South Carolina's Robert Hayne in January of 1830. This is a debate that Hayne clearly won according to their congressional colleagues, and the media of the day, although nationalist historians have long claimed otherwise, making it an essential feature of nationalist propaganda.

The first Big Lie that Webster told during the debate was that "the Constitution of the United States confers on the government itself . . . the power of deciding ultimately and conclusively upon the extent of its own authority."[29] No, it does not. John Marshall may have *wished* that it did when he invented judicial review, but the document itself says no such thing. As Sen. John Taylor once said, "The Constitution never could have designed to destroy [liberty], by investing five or six men, installed for life, with a power of regulating the constitutional rights of all political departments."[30]

Webster then presented a totally false scenario: "One of two things is true: either the laws of the Union are beyond the discretion and beyond the control of the States; or else we have no constitution of general government."[31] *All* the laws? Are the people to have no say whatsoever about laws they believe are clearly unconstitutional? Apparently so, said Daniel Webster. His words are clearly contradicted by the *actions* of myriad American statesmen, most importantly Thomas Jefferson and James Madison, authors of the Kentucky and Virginia resolutions of 1798, which *nullified* the Sedition Act as unconstitutional. Before 1861, the New England states, including Webster's home state of Massachusetts, nullified the federal Embargo Law, and they essentially seceded from the union during the War of 1812 by not participating.

Webster's fellow New Englanders, who held a secession convention in Hartford, Connecticut in 1814, obviously did not agree with his admonition that all federal laws must be obeyed at all times, no matter how unconstitutional or tyrannical they seemed.

Pres. Andrew Jackson ignored the Supreme Court's ruling that the Bank of the United States was constitutional and defunded it; South Carolinians nullified the 1828 Tariff of Abominations; and during Webster's time (he died in 1852), some Northern states effectively nullified the Fugitive Slave Act by not enforcing it. All of this was done in the name of *maintaining* constitutional government, not destroying it as Webster argued.

The myth about the Constitution being somehow ratified by "the whole people" was repeated over and over by Webster. "It is, Sir, the people's Constitution, the people's government, made for the people, made by the people, and answerable to the people. The people of the United States have declared that this Constitution shall be the supreme law."[32]

Webster's strategy was apparently to convince his audience not by historical facts but by repetition and bluster. "The Constitution creates a popular government, erected by the people . . . it is not a creature of the state governments,"[33] he bellowed. Anyone who has ever read Article VII of the United States Constitution knows that this is utterly false.

In fine French Jacobin fashion, Webster asked, "Who shall interpret their [the people's] will?" Why, "the government itself," he said, and not through popular votes but through the government's dictates.[34] The people themselves were to have nothing to do with "interpreting" their own "will."

Article III, Section 3 of the United States Constitution clearly defines treason under the Constitution: "Treason against the United States shall consist in levying war against *them*, or in adhering to *their* enemies, giving *them* Aid and Comfort" (emphasis added). Thus, treason means levying war against "them," the sovereign states. This is why Lincoln's invasion of the Southern states was the very definition of treasonous behavior under the Constitution.

Webster attempted to *redefine* treason under the Constitution by claiming, "To resist by force the execution of a [federal] law, generally, is treason."[35] Thus, if the federal government were to invade a sovereign state to enforce one of its laws, a clearly treasonous act under the plain language of the Constitution, *resistance* to the invasion is what constitutes treason, according to Webster. He defined treason, in other words, to mean *exactly the opposite* of what it actually means in the plain language of the Constitution. Lincoln would redefine "treason" in the exact same way some thirty years later.

As Joseph Story would later do, Webster expressed a childish faith in "democracy" as the only necessary defense against governmental tyranny: "Trust in the efficacy of frequent elections," "trust in the judicial power."[36] With regard to the latter proclamation, Webster was essentially saying: "Trust in federal bureaucrats with lifetime tenure to diminish the power, perks, and budgets of their employer and to diminish their own prospects to attain wealth and power." The Anti-Federalists pointed out the folly of such thinking decades before Webster's time, and history has proven that they were right and he was wrong.

Conclusions

All of these false histories and logical fallacies were repeated by other nationalist politicians for decades. This includes Abraham Lincoln, who probably lifted his famous line in the Gettysburg Address from this statement by Webster during his debate with Hayne: "It is, Sir, the people's Constitution, the people's government, made for the people, made by the people, and answerable to the people. The people of the United States have declared that this Constitution shall be the supreme law."

As Lord Peter Bauer once said in commenting on the rhetoric of communism, whenever one hears of "the people's republic" the "people's government," etc., it is a sure bet that the people have very little, if not nothing whatsoever, to do with controlling that government.

Hamilton, Marshall, Webster, Story, and other nationalists kept up their rhetorical fog horning for decades, trying to convince Americans that the founding fathers did, after all, adopt Hamilton's plan of a dictatorial executive that abolished states' rights and was devoted to building a mercantilist empire in America that would rival the British Empire. But their rhetoric had little or no success during their lifetimes.

New Englanders plotted to secede for more than a decade after Thomas Jefferson was elected president in 1800 and even held a secession convention in Hartford, Connecticut in 1814;[37] all states, North and South, made use of the Jeffersonian, states' rights doctrine of nullification to oppose the Fugitive Slave Act, protectionist tariffs, the Bank of the United States, and other issues up until the 1860s. There was a secession movement in the Mid-Atlantic states in the 1850s,[38] and in 1861 the *majority* of *Northern* newspaper editorialists were in support of peaceful secession.[39]

The false, nationalist theory of the American founding was repeated by Abraham Lincoln in his first inaugural address—and praised decades later by Adolf Hitler in *Mein Kampf,* wherein Hitler made *his* case for abolishing states' rights and centralizing all political power in Germany.[40] "The individual states of the American union could not have possessed any state sovereignty of their own," Hitler wrote, referencing the argument of Lincoln's first inaugural address, "for it was not these states that formed the Union, on the contrary it was the Union which formed a great part of the so-called states."[41] "The National Socialists [Nazis] . . . would totally eliminate states' rights altogether," Hitler promised in *Mein Kampf,*[42] for "the National Socialist doctrine is not the servant of individual federated states, but shall some day become the master of the German nation."[43] All the worst tyrants in world history have been enemies of federalism and states' rights and champions of consolidated or centralized state power.

The only Americans to ever seriously challenge this false nationalist theory—Southern secessionists—were mass murdered by the hundreds of thousands (about 300,000 soldiers and some 50,000 civilians, according to historian Jeffrey Rogers Hummel);[44] entire cities and towns were bombed and burned to the ground; the entire Shenandoah Valley was set ablaze and turned into a burned-out ruin; 90 percent of the buildings in Atlanta were destroyed by General Sherman and the remaining 2,000 or so residents forced from their homes in November of 1864; tens of millions of dollars of private property was plundered by the U.S. Army, in addition to $100 million in private property that General Sherman claims to have destroyed during his "march to the sea"; Southern women, white and black, were raped; the region was left with over 200,000 homeless refugees;[45] and total war was waged on the civilian population. Standardizing for today's population, which is more than ten times what it was in 1860, the number of Southerners murdered by the U.S. government in the 1860s would be the equivalent of more than three and a half million today. Had the South won the war, this would now be considered one of the greatest war crimes in world history. Instead, it has been all but whitewashed from the history books.

Fully two-thirds of Southern wealth was either destroyed or stolen by the U.S. Army.[46] Because normal economic relationships between North and South were destroyed for four long years, it has been estimated that the war erased at least five years of wealth accumulation *nationwide.*[47] The direct financial cost of the war, financed by taxes, borrowing, and the printing of currency, would have been more than enough to have purchased the freedom of every last slave, which is how the British government ended slavery just twenty years earlier. It is doubtful that any nation on earth, up to that time, suffered such total destruction in any war. Total war, not the bloviations of Marshall, Story, Webster, and Lincoln, is what finally cemented into place the false, Hamiltonian/nationalist theory of the American founding.

This false theory of the American founding became the ideological cornerstone of the American empire with the help of generations of power-hungry, imperious, centralizing nationalists, as described by Michael Lind in his book, *Hamilton's Republic: Readings in the American Democratic Nationalist Tradition.*[48] First and foremost among this group is Abraham Lincoln, along with his self-professed political inspiration, Henry Clay. Moving into the twentieth century, the nationalist tradition (which at times became a national/ socialist tradition) was assisted by the most prominent writer/ editor of the "Progressive" movement, the Irish immigrant Herbert Croly, founder of *The New Republic* magazine. Croly supported fellow nationalist Teddy Roosevelt. Also included on Michael Lind's list of nationalist propagandists is the Harvard professor Samuel Beer; German immigrant Francis Lieber, who wrote Lincoln's military code; Henry Cabot Lodge; Walter Lippman, the cofounder of *The New Republic*; Dean Acheson; Franklin D. Roosevelt; and Lyndon Johnson, among many others.

Government of the people, by the people, for the people, is today "limited only" by the state's "power to make its will effectual," as Joseph Story proclaimed. The technology of mass murder in the hands of the state finally made this will "effectual" in the first half of the 1860s. With the rights of nullification and secession destroyed, Americans became the servants rather than the masters of their government and have been miseducated about their own political history ever since by the state's many court historians. It is this miseducation, this false theory of history, that serves to prop up the centralized, neo-mercantilist empire that Americans now slave under. Adorned with the pleasant-sounding rhetoric of "democracy," and the televised spectacle of frequent elections in which over 90 percent of all congressional incumbents are routinely reelected, it is a system of "participatory fascism," as economic historian Robert Higgs has aptly described it.

The Tenth Amendment Awakening, the Supreme Court Be Damned

Marshall DeRosa

> The accumulation of all powers, legislative, executive, and judiciary, in the same hands, whether of one, a few, or many, and whether hereditary, self-appointed, or elective, may justly be pronounced the very definition of tyranny.
>
> —*The Federalist Papers,* No. 47

> To consider the judges as the ultimate arbiters of all constitutional questions [is] a very dangerous doctrine indeed, and one which would place us under the despotism of an oligarchy.
>
> —Thomas Jefferson to William C. Jarvis, 1820

Over the past several years, growing numbers of States have been dusting off the Tenth Amendment in attempts to thwart ever-increasing intrusions of the U.S. government into their respective internal affairs.[1] Education mandates, universal healthcare, gun control, environmental policies, immigration rules, and other national impositions on State affairs have rankled some States to the point where the once-forbidden words of nullification and secession are in the political air.[2] Keeping the U.S. government within its constitutional limits is what the Tenth Amendment was intended to facilitate. But like birds long thought to be extinct, sightings here and there are not sufficient evidence that they will survive in the hyper-centralized twenty-first-century political environment.

That environment is evidenced by the Tenth Amendment movement. On the one hand, its advocates insist upon a recovery of the States' reserved powers and a curtailment of national powers. But on the other hand, it relies upon the U.S. government, and particularly the U.S. Supreme Court, to grant its request. The explanation for this servile posture towards the U.S. government is to be found in the broadly accepted belief that the States are inherently inferior to the U.S. government in regards to sovereignty. In other words, supreme political authority ultimately rests with the U.S. government. This inferiority complex on the part of the States is historically and constitutionally wrong. The States collectively created the national government; the States are the principals and the national government its agent. There is neither divided sovereignty, an oxymoron if there ever was one, nor an *imperium in imperio*. Each of the several States is sovereign, and as sovereigns they have the prerogative to inform the national government that it has exceeded the grants of its authority. Whether that is by nullification (or interposition) via blocking national policies or a complete withdrawal from the onetime voluntary union of States via secession is for each sovereign State to decide.

Of course, the controversy that such old-fashioned ideas provoke manifests the uphill battle that Tenth Amendment movements face, due to decades of political indoctrination that the national government created the States and has sovereignty over them. To put to rest this ignoble lie goes way beyond the scope of this chapter. Nevertheless, it should be axiomatic among Tenth Amendment political activists that the United States Supreme Court is a weak reed upon which to rest the long-term survival of Tenth Amendment states' rights. It cannot and was never intended by the framers to be relied upon as an honest broker in protecting the States against a usurping national government. Unless this political reality is accepted, current Tenth Amendment movements are headed for failure. In order to place these Tenth Amendment movements on track for ultimate success, three essential steps need to be taken.

First, Tenth Amendment advocates must recognize the U.S. Supreme Court as complicit in fraudulently stripping the States of their Tenth Amendment prerogatives. Second, Tenth Amendment advocates must be prepared to bypass the U.S. Supreme Court and look to their respective States as the guarantors of the States' reserved powers. And third, Tenth Amendment supporters need to be liberated from the constitutional apostasy propagated by Mr. Lincoln. This third step, in turn, necessitates facing the reality that the motive for stripping the Tenth Amendment of its original meaning was not the altruistic promotion of government "of, by, and for the people" but rather legitimizing imperialistic public-policy interests of a nationally based ruling class.

As a facilitator of the national ruling class's hegemony over the constitutional rights of the States, the Supreme Court will continue to have a prejudiced posture towards states' rights and its progeny, the Tenth Amendment. The purpose of this chapter is to make evident that recent Tenth Amendment movements will inevitably end in failure, sooner rather than later, if they continue to defer to the U.S. Supreme Court's judgment regarding Tenth Amendment controversies.

Stated another way, this chapter intends to take a hard, objective look at political realities. It is imperative that Americans rethink the nature of the Union by coming to grips with how and why the Union evolved from a voluntary association of sovereign States into an involuntary association of States under the dominance of the United States government with the blessings of the U.S. Supreme Court; the fact that the forces that subordinated the States to the Union are still in force today; and the fact that there is little chance that the current Tenth Amendment movement will have substantive long-term success in restoring to the States their reserved powers. Consequently, the Tenth Amendment movements must reject President Lincoln's *idée fixe*[3] that the U.S. government is legitimately omnipotent and the States constitutionally impotent to confront it. Tenth Amendment movements must be prepared to confront head on the consolidation of political power in an omnipotent national government, a power stemming from the implementation of the interests of a political class consisting of elites from the managerial, academic, military, political, and economic sectors that have converted the national government into an instrument of self-aggrandizement. This political class will not relinquish their power without a fight, a fight in which the U.S. Supreme Court will play a prominent role by attempting to beguile the American people into believing that Tenth Amendment advocates are either misguided or treasonous. Only by rejecting U.S. Supreme Court judicial review as the court of last resort over states' rights will the recovery of genuine Tenth Amendment states' rights be secured. The fact that this is a difficult task does not make it any less essential.

Judicial Awakening

Since the first quarter of the twentieth century, Supreme Court jurisprudence has been overwhelmingly partial to national interests at the expense of the States' Tenth Amendment reserved powers, i.e., regional and local interests. As national power expanded early in the century, the U.S. Supreme Court ratcheted up its assault against the States. It was a period of rapid economic, cultural, and political change, one in which the United States was transitioning from an agrarian- to an industrial-based economy. The ruling class had little tolerance for a political system of states' rights and decentralized political power. The national political class wanted power and they were determined to have it. In order to circumvent the constitutional rule of law that denied them the centralized power they craved, they focused on manipulating the U.S. Supreme Court to lead their coup against states' rights.

A case in point is Louis D. Brandeis, a leading light in transforming the Supreme Court into a Progressive legal vanguard sanctioning the new economic realities. Prior to his elevation to the Supreme Court, he called for a "judicial awakening to the facts of life":

> Courts continued to ignore newly arisen social needs. They applied complacently 18th century conceptions of the liberty of the individual and of the sacredness of private property. . . . The law had everywhere a tendency to lag behind the facts of life. But in America the strain became dangerous; because constitutional limitations were invoked to stop the natural vent of legislation. . . . Statutes to adjust legal rights to the demands of social justice were nullified by the courts, on the grounds that the statutes violated the constitutional guaranties of liberty or property.[4]

The intelligentsia was calling for a *creative jurisprudence* through which judges, and ultimately Supreme Court justices, would covertly supplant the 1789 Constitution of states'-rights federalism with a progressive unitary one. Under the guise of the "least dangerous branch" of government, academic elites constructed what was in reality a Trojan horse used to open the gates of constitutional constraints to willful elitist politics.[5] They deemed it their duty to dispense with Jeffersonian principles of government based upon the informed consent of the governed and replace it with social engineers who would direct the course of political, economic, and cultural developments. Their success is evidenced in a landmark 1920 Supreme Court case, in which one of their acolytes, Associate Justice Oliver Wendell Holmes, had this to say about a federal statute that was repugnant to the Tenth Amendment under an originalist's perspective: "The only question is whether it is forbidden by some invisible radiation from the general terms of the Tenth Amendment. *We must consider what this country has become in deciding what that Amendment has reserved.*"[6]

According to Justice Holmes, the clearest constitutional statement of the states' rights must be relegated to a meaningless verbiage, in order to accommodate the maturation of so-called national interests. The Supreme Court has not been shy about its intention. In several important decisions, the Court has been forthright about relegating the Tenth Amendment to impotence. So by deferring to Supreme Court case law precedent such as *Missouri v. Holland,* the States continued their slow and willful march from states'-rights federalism into the centralizing vortex of nationalism. Deferring to the U.S. Supreme Court was and continues to be a critical error on the part of the States. Why should an aggrieved sovereign State ultimately defer to its agent, the national government, in fairly resolving a constitutional conflict in which the latter has a substantial stake in the outcome? It should not and must not if it is to maintain its Tenth Amendment prerogatives.

The dilemma for and subservient pathology of the States is manifested in the complaint by States' attorneys general in challenging the constitutionality of the recently enacted universal healthcare regime, titled the Patient Protection and Affordable Care Act (ACA). On the one hand, the attorneys general acknowledge that "the Act also represents an unprecedented encroachment on the sovereignty of the states" and that each plaintiff "is a sovereign state in the United States of America." But then again, the attorneys general filed their lawsuit in the U.S. district courts, one of which is the Northern District Court, Florida, Pensacola Division, anticipating that the case will be appealed all the way to the U.S. Supreme Court.[7] Realizing that the end result will ultimately be against the States, why should, or more precisely would, a sovereign State defer to the judgment of a partner of the defendant? Such deference is illogical if not political madness. A sovereign State, in the final analysis, has no judicial, legislative, and/or executive superiors to which it does not consent. So why do the States submit?

In the Florida lawsuit challenging the constitutionality of the ACA, U.S. District Court Judge Roger Vinson explains why and how. Under the rubric of cooperative federalism, the States willfully submit to national mandates by accepting federal funds. Under an expanded interpretation of congressional commerce powers, the national government funds programs, such as the ACA. By accepting national funds attendant to Medicaid, the States waive their Tenth Amendment prerogatives. Citing case-law precedent, Judge Vinson concludes that when the States accept Medicaid funds, "federal legislation [e.g., the ACA] displaces laws enacted under the States' police powers."

According to Judge Vinson, the States maintain that this presents them with a Hobson's choice. They must either accept the ACA as an extension of Medicaid, with all its new obligations and costs, or exit both Medicaid and the ACA. This would require the States to forego all "federal matching funds that are necessary and essential for them to provide healthcare to their neediest citizens." Judge Vinson leaves a door open to the States: exit the Medicaid/Medicare programs altogether and challenge the ACA on Tenth Amendment grounds, or waive that option by staying in those federally funded programs.[8]

Of course, the States in all probability lack the political fortitude to reject billions of federal dollars in order to assert their Tenth Amendment prerogatives. So the key to the answer as to why the States willingly submit to national hegemony over their police powers, in this instance to healthcare, is wrapped around their dependence on federal dollars. But even if a State were to forego the federal funding and completely opt out of federal health programs, it is highly probable that the Supreme Court would condone national legislation coercing individuals into the program. In 1942, the Supreme Court concluded that anything that the U.S. Congress deems having a "substantial effect" on interstate commerce can be regulated with criminal and civil sanctions.[9] In other words, the primary if not only meaningful check on congressional commerce powers is political, not constitutional. The Supreme Court has essentially abdicated to the U.S. Congress the role of determining the limits of its powers.

The Tenth Amendment has for all intents and purposes been swallowed by congressional commerce powers. And with the impending fiscal crises facing national and state governments, the rules of political engagement may soon change. The success of the centralization is in large measure attributable to the almost unlimited funds the U.S. government has thrown at state governments. As those funds become scarcer, some States may begin to reconsider the benefits of centralization and begin to seriously assert some independence. Nevertheless, it should be expected that the U.S. government will put up a fight to keep the States under its imperial control. In essence, the Tenth Amendment movement is up against an illegitimate imperial, i.e., centralizing, power with much to lose if the movement succeeds. This tendency towards and resistance against imperialism is the core of American constitutionalism, with the U.S. Supreme Court functioning mainly as the agent of the imperialists.

Insidious Ideology

The Supreme Court's sanctioning of the national government's dominance over the states' rights can best be described as national imperialism over states' rights.[10]

Imperialism is woven into the American experience. The United States was founded with aspirations of becoming a "flourishing empire destined to expand its sphere of influence, or more benignly the blessings of commerce and liberty, far beyond the geographical limits of the thirteen original States."[11] This flourishing was to be fueled by free people pursuing their perceived interests, with local, State, and/or national governmental support not far behind if circumstances permitted. According to Hamilton, unlike the nations of Europe, the "industrious habits of the [American] people . . . absorbed in the pursuits of gain . . . and commerce" will not be inclined towards military adventures. By ratifying the Constitution and thereby conceding more powers to the national government, military conflict between the States would be neutralized. If the Articles of Confederation were not replaced, imperialistic wars between the States would commence in earnest as, according to Hamilton, European wars make manifest. It was the U.S. Constitution and its isolation that protected the Union from the war between and against the States.[12]

Hamilton was overly optimistic. Imperialistic impulses among the States post-1789 were essentially rechanneled from State capitols to the national Congress; moreover, the Union was not geographically isolated. Regarding the latter, Native Americans and European powers had claims and interests that in many ways necessarily provoked an imperialistic/expansionistic posture on the part of the States. Colonial charters and the national and State constitutions reflected this reality by establishing militias. Conflicts involving the French, Native Americans, and British kept the newly established nation on somewhat of a constant war footing. To varying degrees, State governments responded with violence, sometimes defensively and other times offensively. Early in the national experience, militarism was present, as the fate of hapless Native

Americans, the Barbary pirates, the War of 1812, and the Mexican War attest.

Nevertheless, it is significant that the War Between the States, the Spanish-American War, and World War I were on a scale substantially at odds with the previous conflicts. Lincoln had his Fort Sumter provocation, McKinley his *Maine,* and Wilson his *Lusitania,* but these "provocations" triggered shooting wars that were already de facto declared. All three were offensive wars that involved the subjugation of foreign countries, not ostensibly for commercial and national defense purposes but for militarized economic imperialism masquerading under the *idée fixe* flag of some vague pitch for democracy. In other words, the official pronouncements rationalizing U.S. policy towards the Confederacy, Cuba, and the Central Powers[13] were utilized to conceal from the public the predetermined resort to military imperialism. And not necessarily coincidentally, these imperialistic policies, especially those stemming from the War Between the States, had profound socializing effects in enhancing nationalism while diminishing states' rights.

If the pulsating quest for economic opportunities stoked American foreign imperialism, e.g., the Spanish-American War and World War I, one should not be surprised to learn that it would initially have the same posture towards domestic economic opportunities, the so-called American Civil War. Within the United States, there were and are regional tensions organized along economic and cultural fault lines. Augmenting national powers in 1789 facilitated the development of a type of internecine imperialism that the Articles of Confederation made difficult to realize. Under the U.S. Constitution, regional imperialism took root and flourished. Nineteenth-century regionalism took many shapes: Northern, Southern, deep South, upper South, New England, Western States, South-Atlantic seaboard, lower Mississippi Valley, Texas, etc. Regional imperialism is "the appropriation of Federal authority by the region which has had the means to lay hold upon it, and has reduced the regions (and within them the States) to the position of complaisant accomplices and servile dependants."[14]

Obviously, regional imperialism is facilitated and constrained by the rules of the game, including constitutional constraints and political parties that are national in scope. But what happens when these constraints break down? How does the American rule of law cope with an imperialism willing, able, and determined to maintain its policy hegemony at all costs, including the costs of war? How, in a manner of speaking, does an imperialist square the unconstitutional imperialism with the constitutional circle? If he fails to do so, he would presumably be characterized as a dictator and usurper. However, if he should succeed, he becomes deified and his policies the rule-of-law norm.

For this type of imperialism to reap the financial benefits its strategists anticipated, the suspension of basic rights, e.g., consent of the governed, is paramount. In some fashion, the vanquished must be subjugated so that they are more exploitable. Postbellum reconstruction policies in the South, the former Spanish colonies, and World War I Europe bear remarkable similarities in this regard. The U.S. Supreme Court specifically sanctioned U.S. jurisdiction over territories where the people were denied the fundamental right to have government based upon their consent. But how can this be, when U.S. presidents rationalized U.S. imperial policy on democratic grounds?

Considering the watershed presidencies of Lincoln, McKinley, and Wilson, political rhetoric was instrumental in selling imperialistic adventures to their supporters. Mr. Lincoln, however, was the master rhetorician to whose logic McKinley and Wilson hitched their imperialistic policies. It was Lincoln who subverted the voluntary Union of States in order to have the centralized national power to pursue his party's policy objectives.

To appreciate Lincoln's success as rhetorician *qua* politician, one must consider the salience of his rhetoric. "Rhetoric moves the soul with a movement which cannot be justified logically. It can only be valued analogically with some reference to some supreme image."[15] That "supreme image" is the *idée fixe*. Consider this example. In his Gettysburg Address, Lincoln stated that the carnage of the war is justified so that the nation will have a "new birth of freedom," so "that government of the people, by the people, for the people shall not perish from the earth." Implicit in Lincoln imagery is that, from the beginning, the Southern States befouled America. If the Confederate States of America (C.S.A.) were permitted to survive and eventually consume the Northern States, the America the founders envisioned would perish from the earth.

Lincoln rhetorically explained that he launched the U.S. into a war of aggression against the C.S.A. in order to re-found America without the Southern defilement; this is what he meant by a "new birth of freedom." The physical and political evidence lay all around him in Gettysburg that Southerners were not to have a government of, by, and for the Southern people but a coercive government based in Washington, D.C. Lacking empirical and theoretical evidence that his war was either constitutional or moral, his rhetoric moved the souls of his supporters then and continues to do so.[16] As a successful rhetorician, Lincoln instilled in a portion of Americans the *idée fixe* of a utopian government "of, by, and for the people." In the 1860s, the *idée fixe* emotionally moved them to action against the C.S.A., while currently it moves them to "make the world safe for democracy" by foreign interventionist excursions.

Lincoln's *idée fixe* is an insidious political ideology that incapacitates clear thinking about the war between the U.S. and C.S.A. and thereby the constitutional application of the

Tenth Amendment to an overbearing national government. "Political ideology purports to be an abstract principle, or set of related abstract principles, which has been independently premeditated," according to Michael Oakeshott. "It supplies in advance of the activity of attending to the arrangements of society a formulated end to be pursued, and in so doing it provides a means of distinguishing between those desires which ought to be encouraged and those which ought to be suppressed or redirected."[17] Under Lincoln's ideological *idée fixe,* the activity to be pursued is hyper-nationalism while suppressing states' rights. This has and continues to be the story of American federalism since 1861.

The success of Lincoln's rhetoric was not constrained to rationalizing military pursuits in places like Gettysburg, where Americans slaughtered each other presumably to protect the core founding principles. In reality, his rhetoric was an attack against the constitutional firewalls securing decentralization. By strengthening centralization, Lincoln secured national-government subsidies for what at the time was the largest corporate interest in America, the railroads. Historically, government subsidies for internal improvements were funded by high tariffs. The high tariffs not only raised revenue primarily from the importing Southern States but expended those revenues mostly north of the Mason-Dixon Line. Acknowledging the imperialistic motive and effect behind the tariff, one notable antebellum academic described it as "a system, whose effect will be to sacrifice the south to the north, by converting us into colonies and tributaries . . . in short to impoverish the planter, and to stretch the purse of the manufacturer."[18] Sen. John C. Calhoun articulated the political reality of the Northern States' posture towards the South in his March 4, 1850, speech:

> The next is the system of revenue and disbursements which has been adopted by the government. It is well known that

the government has derived its revenue mainly from duties on imports. I shall not undertake to show that such duties must necessarily fall mainly on the exporting States, and that the South, as the great exporting portion of the Union, has in reality paid vastly more than her due proportion of the revenue; because I deem it unnecessary, as the subject has on so many occasions been fully discussed. Nor shall I, for the same reason, undertake to show that a far greater portion of the revenue has been disbursed in the North, than its due share; and that the joint effect of these causes has been to transfer a vast amount from South to North, which, under an equal system of revenue and disbursements, would not have been lost to her. If to this be added that many of the duties were imposed, not for revenue but for protection—that is, intended to put money, not in the Treasury, but directly into the pocket of the manufacturers—some conception may be formed of the immense amount which in the long course of sixty years has been transferred from South to North.[19]

The same imperialistic predisposition permeated the postbellum conduct of the Republican Party. The U.S. Supreme Court, the national institution responsible for thwarting the consolidation of power that regional imperialism required, failed miserably. With the States of the former C.S.A. in utter ruins, rather than upholding the constitutional rule of law, the U.S. Supreme Court used it to sanction the political, cultural, and economic plundering of the South. This becomes evident by even a cursory review of the Court's postbellum Reconstruction case law, which served as its imprimatur of the U.S. government's imperialism over the Southern States.

Imperialistic Impulses

Reconstruction initially was a series of five congressional acts extending from March 2, 1867, to June 25, 1868, pushed through by the Radical Republicans. The acts placed the former Confederate States under the control of the U.S. Army. This placed Southerners in the awkward position of being American citizens but stripped of the fundamental rights of due process and self-government. The *post hoc, ergo propter hoc* claim that they forfeited those rights as a consequence of their being labeled insurrectionists is unsustainable. One would be hard-pressed to find anyone in the ruling political class who genuinely believed that Reconstruction could withstand legitimate constitutional scrutiny. A survey of what at the time were considered to be critical Supreme Court cases makes clear that what Mr. Lincoln's rhetoric set into motion made a mockery of Supreme Court judicial review.[20] The lynchpin of the Republican Party's policies was (and is) Lincoln's propaganda that the Union is supreme over the States. For example, in the landmark case determining the constitutionality of secession, Chief Justice Salmon P. Chase asserted:

> When, therefore, Texas became one of the United States, she entered into an indissoluble relation. . . . The ordinance of secession, adopted by the convention and ratified by a majority of the citizens of Texas, and all the acts of her legislature intended to give effect to that ordinance, were absolutely null. They were utterly without operation in law. The obligations of the State, as a member of the Union, and of every citizen of the State, as a citizen of the United States, remained perfect and unimpaired. It certainly follows that the State did not cease to be a State, nor her citizens to be citizens of the Union. If this were otherwise, the State must have become foreign, and her citizens foreigners. The war must have ceased to be a war for the suppression of rebellion, and must have become a war for conquest and subjugation.[21]

In his dissenting opinion, Justice Robert Cooper Grier stated the obvious:

The ordinance of secession was adopted by the convention on the 18th of February, 1861, submitted to a vote of the people, and ratified by an overwhelming majority. I admit that this was a very ill-advised measure. Still, it was the sovereign act of a sovereign State, and the verdict on the trial of this question, 'by battle,' as to her right to secede, has been against her.[22]

Chief Justice Chase had to falsify the constitutionality of secession; otherwise the war would be exposed for what it was, "a war for conquest and subjugation," according to Justice Grier. Thus, the C.S.A. was illegitimate and the secessionists insurrectionists/rebels. Thus, the refusal to recognize the constitutionality of secession sanctioned President Lincoln's designation of Confederates as insurrectionists and his calling forth the militia to subdue them because it maintained the U.S. jurisdiction over the C.S.A.[23]

Nevertheless, finding legal authority for Lincoln's invasion of the C.S.A. did not sanction the postbellum punitive policies against the former Confederates. If Southerners were U.S. citizens, the constitutional protections in Article I, section 9, clauses 2 and 3, which prohibit the suspension of habeas corpus, bills of attainder, and ex post facto laws, could be invoked on their behalf.[24] The congressional legislative designation of Southerners as insurrectionists was a bill of attainder, because it punished them without due process.

Lincoln's pocket veto of the Wade-Davis Reconstruction Bill, which declared "that every person who shall hereafter hold or exercise any office, civil or military, except offices merely ministerial, and military offices below the grade of colonel, in the rebel service, state or confederate, is hereby declared not to be a citizen of the United States," supported stripping citizenship from ex-Confederates: "I (President Abraham Lincoln) am fully satisfied with the system for restoration . . . as one very proper plan for the loyal people of any state choosing to adopt it, and that I am, and at all times shall be, prepared to give the executive aid and assistance to any such people."[25] This is a significant development, for the most part overlooked due to the misplaced focus on the peculiar institution. One needs to step back and consider the magnitude of Lincoln's stance. To arbitrarily strip Southern Americans of their citizenship is to place them in a stateless no man's land. It was nothing short of revolutionary in the truest sense of the word. The traditional rule of law ceased to apply; Republican Party membership and its policy objectives trumped the rights of citizenship. The primacy of party over citizenship is embodied in section 3 of the Fourteenth Amendment, which required a two-thirds vote of party partisans for the prerogatives of citizenship to be restored to former Confederates. If former Confederates failed to reject the old Jeffersonian states'-rights order and accept the new Lincolnian national order, they were denied citizenship.

If imperialistic impulses led to the U.S. war against the C.S.A., its military victory over the C.S.A. resulted in the Reconstruction policies that can be best described as a sort of political-party totalitarianism. Reconstruction's disregard for Southern political institutions and citizenship cut at the heart of the Declaration of Independence's core principle of government being based upon the consent of the governed.

Consider the Missouri Radical Republicans' 1865 amendment to the Missouri constitution: "SEC. 3: . . . No person shall be deemed a qualified voter, *who has ever been in armed hostility to the United States, or to the lawful authorities thereof,* or to the government of this State; or has ever given aid, comfort, countenance, or support to persons engaged in any such hostility; or has ever, in any manner, adhered to the enemies, foreign or domestic, of the United States, either by contributing to them, or by unlawfully sending within their lines, money, goods, letters, or information; or has ever disloyally held communication with such enemies; or has ever advised or aided any person to enter the service of such enemies; *or has ever, by act or word, manifested his adherence to the cause* of such enemies, or his *desire for their triumph* over the arms of the United States, or *his sympathy* with those engaged in exciting or carrying on rebellion against the United States . . . [or] *has ever knowingly and willingly harbored, aided, or countenanced any person* so engaged; or *has ever come into or left this State, for the purpose of avoiding enrollment for or draft into the military service of the United States.*"[26]

This amendment essentially subjected the overwhelming majority of Missourians to the de facto status of noncitizens, subject to the arbitrary rule of the Republican Party. Any word, mention, and/or thought of resistance to the U.S. government stripped the person of citizenship. To regain citizenship they had to submit to an "Oath of Loyalty", i.e., unqualified State submission to the U.S. government: "SEC. 6. The oath to be taken as aforesaid shall be known as the Oath of Loyalty, and shall be in the following terms: I, A. B., do solemnly swear that I am well acquainted with the terms of the third section of the second article of the Constitution of the State of Missouri, adopted in the year eighteen hundred and sixty-five, and have carefully considered the same; that I have never, directly or indirectly, done any of the acts in said section specified; that I have always been truly and loyally on the side of the United States against all enemies thereof, foreign and domestic; that I will bear true faith and allegiance to the United States, and will support the Constitution and laws thereof as the supreme law of the land, any law or ordinance of any State to the contrary notwithstanding; that I will, to the best of my ability, protect and defend the Union of the United States, and not allow the same to be broken up and dissolved, or the government thereof to be destroyed or overthrown, under any circumstances, if in my power to prevent it; that I will support the Constitution of the State of Missouri; and that I make this oath without any mental reservation or evasion, and hold it to be binding on me."[27] The oath stipulated that all Missourians and the once sovereign State of Missouri are hereafter in perpetual submission to the U.S. government. The Tenth Amendment for all intents and purposes was abrogated.

The stripping of citizenship and loyalty oaths were approvingly considered by the U.S. Supreme Court in several cases. In one involving a former Confederate lawyer's right to practice law, Justice Samuel Freeman Miller deferred to Missouri on the grounds that its Reconstruction constitution is "the fundamental law of the people of that State, adopted by their popular vote" and that it did not run afoul of ex post facto laws or bill of attainder prohibitions in Article I, section 10.[28]

In 1867, the Court considered a case in which a Roman Catholic priest was fined and jailed for not taking the oath. Justice Stephen Johnson Field reversed the Missouri Supreme Court's opinion, which upheld the conviction, imprisonment, and fine of Father Cummings for performing his priestly functions without taking the oath of allegiance. Justice Field maintained that Missouri was in violation of Article I, section 10, prohibitions against ex post facto laws and bills of attainder.[29]

The rule of law still presented an obstacle to the Radical Republicans' political and economic hegemony over the South. In a flurry of political maneuvers[30] to protect Reconstruction from a potential judicial setback, the Republicans withdrew from the Supreme Court jurisdiction over habeas corpus challenges in the conquered South. The Court could have and should have disregarded this maneuver, because it had already heard arguments and was about to issue its decision in a pending case. But it capitulated to the political pressures applied by the Republicans and left Southerners' habeas corpus rights twisting in the wind.[31] The constitutional rule of law in the conquered Confederacy was for all intents and purposes dead.

"Unchecked Power"

The political circumstances surrounding Supreme Court case law in the postbellum South manifest the destructive political forces Lincoln's *idée fixe* unleashed against the constitutional rule of law. The political abrogation of the Tenth Amendment was not questioned by the Court. The Court's few slings against Reconstruction were based upon important but circumspect constitutional protection against ex post facto laws. The question is why? Was there a fundamental flaw in the constitutional design that makes the Tenth Amendment "parchment barrier" futile when confronted with the sort of power Lincoln was willing and able to wield, a power that was not only political in the Machiavellian sense but also beguiling? Consider Lincoln's path to consolidated power. It is a path that even had the Supreme Court the fortitude to block it, its attempts would probably have been futile. And what is true for the Supreme Court in the 1860s is applicable today.

When Lincoln issued the call for 75,000 militiamen on April 15, 1861, he based his authority to do so on being the commander in chief (Article II, section 2) and on the 1792 Militia Act, amended in 1795.[32] Both the constitutional and statutory authority to call up the militia was predicated on the unconstitutionality of secession. If secession was unconstitutional, then the States were part of the Union and under the jurisdiction of the federal government. If not, the seceded States were outside that jurisdiction and under the jurisdiction of the newly formed C.S.A.). The relations between U.S. and C.S.A. governments would fall under international law, not the U.S. Constitution.

Although Lincoln's April 15 call for 75,000 militiamen was based upon the unconstitutionality of secession, his April 19 proclamation to blockade the Confederacy was implicit recognition of the constitutionality of secession and the C.S.A.'s independence. Under international maritime law, a nation can close but not blockade its own ports. The April 15 proclamation declared the Confederates to be de facto insurrectionists and the Southern States under U.S. jurisdiction, whereas the April 19 proclamation made them *de jure* belligerents and C.S.A. independence from the U.S. a *fait accompli.*

In order to suppress the Democratic opposition, on April 26, 1861, Lincoln issued the following order to Gen. Winfield Scott, suspending habeas corpus, including for Supreme Court justices:

My dear Sir: The Maryland Legislature assembles tomorrow at Anapolis [*sic*]; and, not improbably, will take action to arm the people of that State against the United States. The question has been submitted to, and considered by me, whether it would not be justifiable, upon the ground of necessary defence, for you, as commander in Chief of the United States Army, to arrest, or disperse the members of that body. I think it would *not* be justifiable; nor, efficient for the desired object.

First, they have a clearly legal right to assemble; and, we cannot know in advance, that their action will not be lawful, and peaceful. And if we wait until they shall *have* acted, their arrest, or dispersion, will not lessen the effect of their action.

Secondly, we *can*not permanently prevent their action. If we arrest them, we cannot long hold them as prisoners; and when liberated, they will immediately re-assemble, and take their action. And, precisely the same if we simply disperse them. They will immediately reassemble in some other place.

I therefore conclude that it is only left to the commanding general to watch, and await their action, which, if it shall be to arm their people against the United States, he is to adopt the most prompt, and efficient means to counteract, even, if necessary, to the bombardment of their cities and in the extremest [sic] necessity, the suspension of the writ of habeas corpus.[33]

Calling for 75,000 militiamen, the blockade, and the suspension of habeas corpus, all within the span of two weeks, signifies the unchecked power wielded by Mr. Lincoln. Where were the congressional hearings about the constitutionality of secession, the mobilization of the military, the blockade, and the suspension of the writ? Such opposition was met with a military response. The source of Lincoln's power was his willingness to exercise power not grounded in the original Constitution but in his creative abilities to undermine the Constitution while rhetorically defending it.

The political blanket thrown over the constitutional mechanisms to deal with the seceding States, including the Tenth Amendment, was Lincoln's *idée fixe*. Lincoln initially displaced the Union of 1789 with an abstract Union based upon his *idée fixe*. In time his abstract Union took concrete form, clearing the way for the exercise of arbitrary political power. The source of Lincoln's political power was his innate ability to rhetorically recruit and shape the political will of substantial numbers of Americans to his own. In short, his rhetorical skills, not the U.S. Constitution, were the font of his political powers. His rhetorical skills, not constitutional limitations, set the boundaries of his political action and his current political disciples of centralization. In order to restore the Tenth Amendment to its proper place, it is necessary to consider Lincoln's political *modus operandi* against it.

Conquest and Subjugation

Lincoln's unique rhetorical skills led Richard Weaver to conclude that Lincoln is "a father of the nation more convincingly than Washington." Citing Lincoln's law partner, Weaver provides insight into Lincoln's rhetorical ability: "Not only had he accurate and exact perceptions, but he was causative; his mind apparently with an automatic movement, ran back behind facts, principles, and all things to their origin and first cause—to the point where forces act at once as effect and cause. . . . All opponents dreaded his originality, condensation, definition, and force of expression."[34]

Opponents of centralization, including Chief Justice Roger Brooke Taney, had good reason to dread Lincoln. By reopening the debates of the 1787 constitutional convention and unilaterally resolving the issues to his own liking, Lincoln went on the political offensive against the Supreme Court and made it known that the justices risked their own arrests if they resisted. Early in his administration, "Lincoln issued an arrest warrant for Chief Justice Roger Taney after the eighty-four year old jurist issued an opinion that only the Congress, and not the president, can legally suspend the writ of *habeas corpus.*"[35] Lincoln's practice was to intimidate federal judges who took seriously their constitutional duties to enforce the constitutional rule of law. Imagine the chilling effect of placing some officers of the court under house arrest and incarceration in order to keep them from issuing habeas corpus. One federal judge wrote:

> After dinner I visited my brother judges in Georgetown, and returning home between half past seven and eight o'clock found an armed sentinel stationed at my door by order of the Provost-Marshal. . . . Armed sentries from that time continuously until now have been stationed in front of my house. Thus it appears that a military officer against whom a writ in the appointed form of law has first threatened with and afterwards arrested and imprisoned the attorney who rightfully served the writ upon him. He continued, and still continues, in contempt and disregard of the mandate of the law, and has ignominiously placed an armed guard to insult

and intimidate by its presence the judge who ordered the writ to issue, and still keeps up this armed array at his door, in defiance and contempt of the justice of the land.[36]

Contrast this with Pres. Jefferson Davis's directive for C.S.A. military and civilian officials to comply with habeas corpus issued by State judges, and the difference between the U.S. and C.S.A. political cultures becomes evident.[37]

A major chink in the Constitution's armor against Lincoln's rhetorical attack against the rule of law, i.e., his imperial power grab, was slavery. Arguing from first principles, it is unjust to enslave men; the Constitution sanctions slavery; consequently, the Constitution is unjust. Lincoln was not making an argument for equality *per se* but for higher-law justice.[38] Justice, according to Lincoln, trumps the Constitution, and a just man would not adhere to an unjust constitution. The pillars propping up the old Constitution must be torn down and "supply their places with other pillars, hewn from the solid quarry of sober reason."[39] By trumping the old Constitution with his version of higher law, Lincoln rhetorically dispensed with any political opposition grounded in the constitutional rule of law. This political trick facilitated the conversion of a decentralized federal republic into a centralized unitary national system.

This strategy marks Lincoln's successful path to power. In his 1838 Lyceum Address, he acknowledged that ambitious men would not be content with maintaining the status quo, by which other men, in this case the founders, reap the honor and glory of a grateful, but misguided, populace:

> Towering genius disdains a beaten path. It seeks regions hitherto unexplored.—It sees no distinction in adding story to story, upon the monuments of fame, erected to the memory of others. It denies that it is glory enough to serve under any chief. It scorns to tread in the footsteps of any predecessor, however illustrious. It thirsts and burns for distinction; and, if possible, it will have it, whether at the

expense of emancipating slaves, or enslaving freemen. . . . Distinction will be his paramount object, and although he would as willingly, perhaps more so, acquire it by doing good as harm; yet, that opportunity being past, and nothing left to be done in the way of building up, he would set boldly to the task of pulling down.[40]

Arguing from first principles, i.e., the nature of man, pulling down the pillars of the Constitution, using rationalism rather than circumstance as the foundation of a new political order, is characteristic of so-called Progressives. According to Weaver, "whereas for [Edmund] Burke circumstance was often a deciding factor, for Lincoln it was never more than a retarding factor."[41] In other words, facts need not get in the way of the *idée fixe*. One such fact is that the vast majority of Southerners never denied the slaves' humanity. The slaveowner did not own the slave *per se* but the slave's labor. Furthermore, the slave States placed legal restrictions on slaveowners' treatment of slaves, from maximum hours of work per week to abandonment of old and sick slaves. Lincoln must have known this but, in Jacobin fashion, was determined to ignore actual circumstances, radicalize the issue, inflame the passions of the electorate, and capture the reins of political power. In other words, his high-toned theoretical rhetoric was a means to undisclosed political ends, one being personal ambition.[42]

Lincoln's break with the constitutional rule of law and reliance on the *idée fixe* was immediate upon his taking the oath of office. This becomes evident by contrasting his inaugural address with Pres. James Buchanan's December 3, 1860, State of the Union Address. Buchanan asked:

Has the Constitution delegated to Congress the power to coerce a State into submission which is attempting to withdraw or has actually withdrawn from the Confederacy? If answered in the affirmative, then it must be upon the principle that power has been conferred upon Congress to declare and to make war against a State. After much serious reflection I have arrived at the conclusion that no such power has been delegated to Congress or to any other department of the Federal Government. . . . Without descending to particulars, it may be safely asserted that the power to make war against a State is at variance with the whole spirit and intent of the Constitution. Suppose such a war should result in the conquest of a State; how are we to govern it afterwards? Shall we hold it as a province and govern it by despotic power?

President Buchanan realized, as did his contemporaries, that declaring war against a seceded State would not preserve the Union but remake it, displacing consent of the States with national coercion:

But if we possessed this power, would it be wise to exercise it under existing circumstances? The object would doubtless be to preserve the Union. War would not only present the most effectual means of destroying it, but would banish all hope of its peaceable reconstruction. Besides, in the fraternal conflict a vast amount of blood and treasure would be expended, rendering future reconciliation between the States impossible. In the meantime, who can foretell what would be the sufferings and privations of the people during its existence?[43]

Buchanan's address is grounded in circumstances, such as the constitutional rule of law, State sovereignty, factual secession, limitations of national power to coerce sovereign States back into the Union, and the horrors of internecine war.

Lincoln's first inaugural address is essentially an ipso facto declaration of war against any and all seceding States. His *idée fixe* is that "the Union will endure forever." But his Union is not a compact of the several sovereign States but an aggregate of the American people, and one in which the numerical majority can bind the minority. The decision to secede is the prerogative of the States. Whether the decision was the correct one from a public-policy perspective, e.g., the pending fiscal policies of the Republican Party, enforcement of the fugitive-slave laws, the territorial questions, etc., is beside the point. A sovereign State is not accountable to external political units and/or public opinion. But according to Lincoln, the Union preceded the States and the latter never had the sovereignty requisite to unilaterally withdraw from the Union. He made it known "that the laws of the Union [must] be faithfully executed in all the States" and that "in doing this there needs to be no bloodshed or violence and there shall be none unless it be forced upon the national authority."[44] Lincoln was fully aware that if he attempted to enforce U.S. laws in what was by March 4, 1861, a foreign country, such attempts constituted casus belli. He also must have known that his argument denying the sovereignty of the States was a ruse concocted to rationalize a militaristic imperialism over the Confederacy.

In his first inaugural address, Lincoln laid out his authority under the rule of law to use coercion against the Confederacy. First, he claimed that the Union is perpetual:

> I hold that in contemplation of universal law and of the Constitution the Union of these States is perpetual. Perpetuity is implied, if not expressed, in the fundamental law of all national governments. It is safe to assert that no government proper ever had a provision in its organic law for its own termination. Continue to execute all the express provisions of our National Constitution, and the Union will endure forever, it being impossible to destroy it except by some action not provided for in the instrument itself.[45]

Lincoln continually stressed that "Articles of Confederation and Perpetual Union" were replaced by the "more Perfect

Union" of the U.S. Constitution, and if something "perpetual" is made "more perfect," then its perpetuity is not open to question.

This, of course, is nonsense. Theoretically, a perpetual union could be made more perfect by making it more consensual. "A perpetual union is not necessarily perfect and a perfect union is not necessarily perpetual."[46] More importantly, as a lawyer Lincoln had to know that the word "perpetual" in the eighteenth century was used as a diplomatic term, which signified that the document lacked a "built-in sunset provision." This is not to say that the Articles were binding forever but that their duration was unknown.[47]

Second, Lincoln asked: "If the United States be not a government proper, but an association of States in the nature of contract merely, can it, as a contract, be peaceably unmade by less than all the parties who made it? One party to a contract may violate it—break it, so to speak—but does it not require all to lawfully rescind it?" Obviously the Constitution is not "in the nature of a contract merely." It is a compact among sovereign States among whom there is not a neutral judge, including the U.S. Supreme Court, which is a branch of the national government. Where a neutral judge is lacking, a principal to the compact may terminate the agreement upon a breach by the agent, as may the agent upon a breach by a principal.

Third, to validate his "contract theory," Lincoln denied the sovereignty of the States and the compact theory[48] of the U.S. Constitution.

> Descending from these general principles, we find the proposition that in legal contemplation the Union is perpetual confirmed by the history of the Union itself. The Union is much older than the Constitution. It was formed, in fact, by the Articles of Association in 1774. It was matured and continued by the Declaration of Independence in 1776. It was further matured, and the faith of all the then thirteen States expressly plighted and engaged that it should be perpetual, by the Articles of Confederation in 1778. And finally, in 1787,

one of the declared objects for ordaining and establishing the Constitution was "to form a more perfect Union."

Fourth, Lincoln asserted that "if destruction of the Union by one or by a part only of the States be lawfully possible, the Union is less perfect than before the Constitution, having lost the vital element of perpetuity." Unless viewed through the lens of an ever-expanding empire, secession did not constitute the "destruction of the Union" but merely its downsizing. The Union was left intact among the States desiring to maintain it. That is why the nomenclature "civil war" is erroneous. The C.S.A. was not fighting to overtake and subdue the U.S. government; the C.S.A. was fighting a defensive war to preserve its independence from an imperialistic U.S. government.

And last, Lincoln concluded, "It follows from these views that no State upon its own mere motion can lawfully get out of the Union; that resolves and ordinances to that effect are legally void, and that acts of violence within any State or States against the authority of the United States are insurrectionary or revolutionary, according to circumstances." Such would "follow" if Lincoln's premises were analytically sustainable, but they are not. Consequently, the ordinances of secession were neither "insurrectionary nor revolutionary," and the war to subdue and reincorporate the Southern States back into the Union must have been, in the words of Chief Justice Chase, "a war for conquest and subjugation."[49]

Lincoln's first inaugural address, as well as his second, despite its gaping holes in historical fact, has been lauded as a great speech. Even a luminary such as Richard Weaver asserted that "one would go far to find a speech more respectful toward the established principles of American government—to defined and agreed upon things—than the First Inaugural Address."[50] Weaver was wrong and apparently carried away by Lincoln's argument from definition. Historian

Garry Wills approvingly acknowledged Lincoln's rhetoric for what it was, the displacement of the principles of 1789 with a new indissoluble and perpetual Union of States.[51] Never mind that Lincoln's *idée fixe* that the Union was sovereign and must be protected against all challenges was rejected by all the Southern States and probably most of the rest when it conflicted with their respective State interests.

The last point, State interests, is the key to understanding the clout Lincoln's *idée fixe* held over the nineteenth-century Northern ruling class. Lincoln's "Union" was essentially a means to a public-policy end, i.e., the economic subordination of the Southern States to the Republican Party's business constituents by any and all means necessary. In other words, a militaristic imperialism against an independent Southern confederacy was not off the table. Conveniently, Lincoln's unconstitutional imperialism against the Confederacy was rationalized and thereby made palatable by the "justice" of abolition. The convergence of ruling-class interests and abstract justice was the perfect storm directed against the states' rights embodied in the Constitution and Bill of Rights, a storm so potent that even if it made the attempt, the Supreme Court would have been blown into oblivion. That storm is still blowing in the minds of most Americans, keeping at bay a genuine recovery of the States' Tenth Amendment reserved powers.

Right Makes Might

Lincoln's *idée fixe* continues to shape the American mind and most certainly the U.S. Supreme Court. Consider President McKinley's war against Spain; although it was predicated on the Republican Party's long-standing policies of high tariffs,[52] protectionism for domestic manufacturers, and militarized imperialism, the legacy of Lincoln's *idée fixe* made the war palatable. An American-led "new birth of freedom" in Spain's colonial holdings was the auspicious rationale for the war, with economic exploitation of Spain's colonial holdings being the actual driving force. In its March 26, 1898, Ultimatum to Spain delivered to Stewart L. Woodford, the United States ambassador to Spain, the State Department expressed the American position regarding Cuba: "The President . . . suggests that if Spain will revoke the reconcentration order and maintain the people until they can support themselves and offer to the Cubans full self-government, with reasonable indemnity, the President will gladly assist in its consummation."

Spain responded by mitigating the savagery of its military governor and offering Cuba partial independence. But with the sinking of the U.S. battleship *Maine* and the stoking of anti-Spain passions by vested U.S. commercial interests, war was declared on April 25, 1898, and Spain soundly defeated by August 1898. The U.S. emerged from the war as an imperialistic world power.[53]

The new territorial acquisitions presented an opportunity to implement the war's presumptive purpose, i.e., self-government for the newly liberated colonies. In a number of U.S. Supreme Court cases, known as the Insular Cases, the Court grappled with political reality. It put its imprimatur on indefinitely delaying self-government for the former Spanish colonies. Conveniently, the delay, as was the case during Reconstruction, suspended fundamental rights in order to facilitate economic opportunities for the victors. Essentially the war replaced Spain with the U.S. as the economic dominant mother country.

McKinley's foreign policy has been correctly characterized as a "Lincolnian,"[54] but the transitional presidency of Wilson is typically singled out as being most, if not solely, responsible for operationalizing American militaristic imperialism on behalf of an *idée fixe*. Most would agree that "Wilson and the Progressives managed a virtuoso performance of the messianic theme and all its variations, harmonizing the Puritan errand, Enlightenment optimism, Hegelian dialectic, abolitionist crusading, Darwinian racism, and Social Gospel millennialism." On the domestic front, Wilson and his Progressive allies "rebuilt the nation's foundations according to a new blueprint of democraticism, egalitarianism, universalism, efficiency, and consolidation of power."[55] Like Lincoln, Wilson's appetite to remake the political landscape was insatiable; he was, indeed, a man on an imperialistic mission against states' rights domestically and Old World European nationalism internationally.

Fair enough, Wilson and his Progressive abbettors are guilty as charged, i.e., they took an ideological wrecking ball to traditional politics here in the U.S. and overseas.[56] Or is such a conclusion too simplistic? Where did this armed ideologue get the political weaponry to go on his imperialistic missions? What happened to the constitutional checks designed to withhold such formidable political powers from the ruling elites of the U.S. government?

President Wilson's imperialistic policies, domestic and foreign, would have been improbable without the centralization of power in the chief executive. Concentrated political power is what linked Wilsonian idealism with real-time opportunity. The president most responsible for the consolidation of executive power is Mr. Lincoln. Without Lincoln's legacy, the constitutional framework of decentralization and its progeny. a limited national government (or governments, if the Confederacy and/or states' rights had survived). would have denied Mr. Wilson the wherewithal to impose his political agenda on Americans and Europeans. His wild-eyed dream to remake the political landscape would have remained just that, the dream of a onetime professor of political science and jurisprudence.[57]

Mr. Wilson idolized Mr. Lincoln and in many ways viewed himself as a political heir destined to complete Lincoln's unfinished work. His visceral attachment to an idealized Lincoln stems from being either a crass politician set on manipulating the American people or a megalomaniac on a messianic mission to impose a socialistic democratic order worldwide. One thing is clear. Imperialism is incompatible with the traditional American constitutional rule of law and would have been recognized by the founding generation as tyranny. The very definition of tyranny, according to Madison, is the consolidation of legislative, executive, and judicial powers in the same hands, or in other words, consolidated political power.[58]

There is a corpus of evidence demonstrating the extent to which Mr. Wilson was enthralled by Mr. Lincoln's masterful consolidation of political power and shared Lincoln's weariness of the founding principles of decentralization. Acknowledging that he read just about every biography about Lincoln, Wilson, on September 4, 1916, a few months prior to the U.S. entry into World War I, gave a deifying address commemorating Lincoln's birthplace:

> I have come here to-day, not to utter a eulogy on Lincoln; he stands in need of none, but to endeavor to interpret the meaning of this gift to the nation of the place of his birth and origin. Is not this an altar upon which we may forever keep alive the vestal fire of democracy as upon a shrine at which some of the deepest and most sacred hopes of mankind may from age to age be rekindled? For these hopes must constantly be rekindled, and only those who live can rekindle them. The only stuff that can retain the life-giving heat is the stuff of living hearts. And the hopes of mankind cannot be kept alive by words merely, by constitutions and doctrines of right and codes of liberty. The object of democracy is to transmute these into the life and action of society, the self-denial and self-sacrifice of heroic men and women willing to make their lives an embodiment of right and service and enlightened purpose. The commands of democracy are as

imperative as its privileges and opportunities are wide and generous. Its compulsion is upon us. It will be great and lift a great light for the guidance of the nations only if we are great and carry that light high for the guidance of our own feet. We are not worthy to stand here unless we ourselves be in deed and in truth real democrats and servants of mankind, ready to give our very lives for the freedom and justice and spiritual exaltation of the great nation which shelters and nurtures us.[59]

Wilson's use of religious overtones (gift to the nation, altar, vestal fire of democracy, shrine, sacred hopes of mankind, self-denial, self-sacrifice, enlightened purpose, commands of democracy, great light, give our very lives, spiritual exaltation) and transnational scope (guidance of the nations, servants of mankind) may be dismissed as rhetorical window-dressing. But what if Wilson was convinced that he, like Lincoln, was destined to spread democracy? In his address to Congress seeking a declaration of war against Germany, he specifically referenced Lincoln in his rationale for going to war:

When I addressed myself to performing the duty laid upon the President by the Constitution to present to you an annual report on the state of the Union, I found my thought dominated by an immortal sentence of Abraham Lincoln's— "Let us have faith that right makes might, and in that faith let us dare to do our duty as we understand it." . . . We are now about to accept gauge of battle with this natural foe to liberty and shall, if necessary, spend the whole force of the nation to check and nullify its pretensions and its power. We are glad . . . to fight thus for the ultimate peace of the world and for the liberation of its peoples . . . for the rights of nations great and small and the privilege of men everywhere to choose their way of life and of obedience. The world must be made safe for democracy. . . . To such a task we can dedicate our lives and our fortunes, everything that we are and everything that we have, with the pride of those who know that the day has come when America is privileged to spend her blood and her might for the principles that gave her birth and happiness and the peace which she has treasured. God helping her, she can do no other.[60]

Contrast Wilson's rationalizing the terrors of the French Revolution with Lincoln's "drawn sword" against the C.S.A.: "Yet that Revolution was the salvation of France, and perhaps of Europe too. How else could the fetters that bound men to an antiquated and intolerable system of tyranny have been shaken off?"[61] For Wilson, England was righteous and France and the rest of the continent's monarchies were in need of purification, as was the South in Lincoln's mind.

By 1863, Lincoln's justification for his war policies was not the U.S. Constitution but the *idée fixe,* thereby spreading democracy in the undemocratic and inegalitarian Confederacy.[62] The religious overtones of his Gettysburg Address (consecration, world, unfinished work, new birth of freedom) and Second Inaugural ("yet, if God wills that it continue until all the wealth piled by the bondsman's two hundred and fifty years of unrequited toil shall be sunk, and until every drop of blood drawn with the lash shall be paid by another drawn with the sword, as was said three thousand years ago, so still it must be said 'the judgments of the Lord are true and righteous altogether'") are strikingly similar to Wilson's. Both viewed slavery and the divine right of kings as synonymous and themselves as divine instruments in "trampling out the vintage where the grapes of wrath are stored."[63]

Mimicking Lincoln's rhetoric, in 1917 Wilson told a Confederate veterans reunion that God was behind the Union victory so that "liberty is made secure for mankind." Moreover, the U.S. was prepared to sacrifice "its wealth and its sons' wealth 'for the service of mankind.'"[64] Conveniently, the "service of mankind" coincided with the imperial interests of the ruling class.[65]

Liberty or Despotism

Constitutional liberalism[66] is supposedly the bulwark against the emergence of despotical powers. Centralization was the primary concern for the framers because it provides the instruments of oppression that despots need. The Tenth Amendment was intended to be the fallback position for the States, when (not if) institutional checks and balances and separation of powers fail. Zealotry for the rights of the people has been historically the rhetorical materials to consolidate power. Publius acknowledged that the "road to the introduction of despotism" was constructed by men who began their careers "by paying an obsequious court to the people, commencing demagogues and ending tyrants."[67]

Consider Franklin Delano Roosevelt's role in dismantling American federalism in order to consolidate power and his revealing call for a "Second Bill of Rights" in his 1944 State of the Union Address:

> In our day these economic truths have become accepted as self-evident. We have accepted, so to speak, a second Bill of Rights under which a new basis of security and prosperity can be established for all—regardless of station, or race or creed.
>
> Among these are:
>
> The right to a useful and remunerative job in the industries, or shops or farms or mines of the nation;
>
> The right to earn enough to provide adequate food and clothing and recreation;
>
> The right of farmers to raise and sell their products at a return which will give them and their families a decent living;
>
> The right of every business man, large and small, to trade in an atmosphere of freedom from unfair competition and domination by monopolies at home or abroad;
>
> The right of every family to a decent home;
>
> The right to adequate medical care and the opportunity to achieve and enjoy good health;

> The right to adequate protection from the economic fears
> of old age, and sickness, and accident and unemployment;
> And finally, the right to a good education.
> All of these rights spell security.[68]

Under the guise of enforcing rights/entitlements that the framers put beyond the reach of the U.S. government, the reserved powers of the States have been usurped by the U.S. government. The Affordable Care Act, i.e., federally mandated universal healthcare, is simply the latest rendition of uncontrollable centralization put into motion by Mr. Lincoln.

In the American political tradition, constitutional liberalism is premised upon several key tenets: the rule of law, the institutional—legislative, executive, judicial—separation of powers, and states' rights. The rule of law and separation of powers were theoretically and historically the weakest bulwarks against the emergence of unitary national powers and began to collapse under the weight of Supreme Court-endorsed nationalism almost immediately. The strongest bulwark, states' rights, required the most persistently coercive efforts to extinguish liberty's last refuge from the omnipotence of what Bertrand De Jouvenel characterized as the City of Command, the venue and means through which centralized authority exercises its power.[69]

This is not hyperbole. The presence of tyrannical government does not have to be consciously experienced in order to be validated. One should not expect a servile, inattentive, and/or hyper-nationalistic people to either care about or object to a soft and presumably benevolent tyranny. The charges lodged against King George III in the Declaration of Independence pale in comparison to the current controversies swirling over tax rates, universal healthcare, bank bailouts, military deployments, budget deficits, and the national debt.

The only effective response is the reactionary imperative of states' rights, properly understood. What good is the Tenth

Amendment if its original meaning of states' rights has been replaced with a dominant nationalism by the very nationalistic forces it was designed to thwart? Worse yet, why rely upon those forces to restore the states' rights substance? Perhaps the States need to rely less upon the U.S. Constitution and more upon their respective State constitutions. A case in point is the State of Louisiana. Its Declaration of Rights stipulates:

§1. Origin and Purpose of Government
Section 1. All government, of right, originates with the people, is founded on their will alone, and is instituted to protect the rights of the individual and for the good of the whole. Its only legitimate ends are to secure justice for all, preserve peace, protect the rights, and promote the happiness and general welfare of the people. The rights enumerated in this Article are inalienable by the state and shall be preserved inviolate by the state. . . .
§26. State Sovereignty
Section 26. The people of this state have the sole and exclusive right of governing themselves as a free and sovereign state; and do, and forever hereafter shall, exercise and enjoy every power, jurisdiction, and right, pertaining thereto, which is not, or may not hereafter be, by them expressly delegated to the United States of America in congress assembled.[70]

Louisiana's constitutional language and mandates are clear. The States' reserved powers cannot be confused with minimal discretionary powers of States under unitary national government. This includes one in which the States obediently defer to the myths concocted to prop up a dominant national government and its agent, the U.S. Supreme Court. It manifests a bond that ties the States collectively together in an associational Union, which in turn is administered by the national government as the agent of the States. The nature of the bond is critical to understanding the nature of the Union and the legitimate powers of the U.S. government in relation to the association of States.

Within the scheme of republicanism, it is significant if the bond (the mortar of the Union, if you will) maintaining the association of States is primarily consensual or coercive. It is a self-evident truth—one that no intellectually honest person can deny—that the Constitution of 1789 would not have been ratified had the document specified that the Union would be coercively maintained against the will of one or more States. The prospect of applying coercion against a State (or States) or the citizens of a State was anathema to the political culture upon which the national government was established in 1789. The framers were focused upon ultimately holding the national government accountable to the member States.

Because the U.S. Supreme Court has consistently provided constitutional legitimacy to a unitary model of nationalism that the framers would find to be abhorrent, it would be the height of folly to trust that institution as an honest broker when adjudicating challenges to resurgent Tenth Amendment movements. In the words of Justice Benjamin Curtis—a Whig nationalist—"Let it be remembered, also, for just now we may be in some danger of forgetting it, that questions of jurisdiction were questions of power as between the United States and the several States."[71] As long as State supreme courts were co-equal with the U.S. Supreme Court, the States retained a measure of security against national coercion and constitutionally suspect intrusion into their internal affairs. But once the U.S. Supreme Court extended its jurisdiction to the point of subordinating State supreme courts,[72] a major bulwark of the federal component of checks and balances was removed.

If Tenth Amendment cases were still the domain of State high courts, the prospects of surviving a constitutional challenge would be substantially enhanced. Unlike U.S. Supreme Court justices who have lifetime tenure and are stakeholders in national power, State supreme court judges are products of the political environments of their respective States. Today, to place judges on their respective supreme courts, seven States use partisan elections, sixteen nonpartisan elections, twenty-four merit selection, two gubernatorial appointment, and two legislative appointments.[73] The charge that State judges are too politicized and that deferring to State supreme courts would result in a hodgepodge of precedent lacks credibility. Conceptually, federalism implies diversity and not mandated uniformity of case-law precedent.

Consider the following. First, the highly contentious nomination-confirmation processes, along with ideologically inspired decisions and opinions, make clear that the U.S. Supreme Court is a political branch of the national government. It would be difficult to substantiate the existence of a politics without a policy, or a policy not premised upon an ideology. To be politically motivated requires an ideology, simply defined as "knowledge of the ends to be pursued," a knowledge of what is to be done.[74] In other words, the justices know what they want to accomplish in the realm of public policy. They cleverly use the people's misplaced trust in their fidelity to the Constitution to disguise their political agenda. This sort of political trickery has the added downside that it is unaccountable to the people and the States over which it exercises jurisdiction, i.e., power. And second, a lack of uniformity is an acceptable outcome of federalism, because it reflects the will of the people in their respective States, i.e., the consent of the governed, as mandated in Article IV, section 4: "The United States shall guarantee to every State in this Union a Republican Form of Government."

The transition from states' rights to unitary nationalism, i.e., domestic imperialism, was the most significant development in American politics. This marks one of the worst fears of the framers coming to fruition, tyranny. Known as a "political truth" of "great intrinsic value" is the realization that "the accumulation of all powers, legislative, executive, and judiciary, in the same hands, whether of one, a few, or many, and whether hereditary, self-appointed, or elective, may justly be pronounced the very definition of tyranny." Moreover, "were the federal Constitution, therefore, really chargeable with the accumulation of power, or with a mixture of powers, having a dangerous tendency to such an accumulation, no further arguments would be necessary to inspire a universal reprobation of the system."[75]

The U.S. Supreme Court facilitated and is a partner in this tyrannical accumulation of powers to the national government. Is it far-fetched to anticipate that a State that takes its Tenth Amendment prerogatives seriously risks the fate of the Confederate South at the hands of modern-day Mr. Lincoln: compliance or death? To dismiss, mock, or ignore the question is to answer it. The fate of Tenth Amendment movements may decide the question. If the leaders of the Tenth Amendment movements are serious about restoring the original Tenth Amendment to its rightful place within the constitutional framework, they must be willing to assert genuine states' rights, the U.S. Supreme Court be damned. As Jefferson forewarned, "To consider the judges as the ultimate arbiters of all constitutional questions [is] a very dangerous doctrine indeed, and one which would place us under the despotism of an oligarchy. . . . The Constitution has erected no such single tribunal, knowing that to whatever hands confided, with the corruptions of time and party, its members would become despots."[76]

American Republicanism and the Forgotten Question of Size

Donald Livingston

When thirteen self-proclaimed American States seceded from Britain in 1776, Europe was dominated by large centralized monarchies. Republican government was to be found only in the Swiss federation. Americans were determined to establish a republican regime in the western hemisphere. They proclaimed themselves a federation of republics, and later Article IV of the Constitution would "guarantee to every State in this Union a Republican Form of Government." Today we have largely lost what could be called *republican* government. This claim will seem strange to many. Do we not have government by consent through our representatives? Do we not live under the rule of law? What else is demanded of republican government?

Before these questions can be answered, we need to look more closely at what a republic is. The republican tradition took root in the civilization created by the ancient Greeks. For over two thousand years, that tradition taught that three conditions were essential for republican government. First, citizens *make the laws* they are to live under. Second, it is not sufficient that these laws be authorized by a majority of the legislature; they must also be in accord with a more fundamental law that citizens *do not make* but that has its source in a common tradition or natural reason. And third, a republic must be *small* in respect to population and territory.

Today most everyone accepts the first two conditions, but the requirement of size has dropped out. We are disposed to believe that it makes no difference how large a republic is. Only the first two conditions are necessary: self-government

125

through a legislature of elected representatives and the rule of law through a judicial system. This judgment is mistaken because everything in reality that has a function has a proper size and scale beyond which or below which it becomes dysfunctional, and this is as true of political order as of anything else. Of course, there are different conceptions of what the *function* of political order is and, consequently, different conceptions of size appropriate to those functions. A highly centralized empire has been admired by many as the best form of political order. The functions appropriate to this kind of politics demand large size and scale. Even so there are limits, and Imperial overreach is a common vice of empires.

But we are concerned here only with the proper size and scale of that peculiar style of political association known as *republican*. This is not an easy question, because republics are historic entities that have changed and adjusted to a great variety of historical contexts, and so there is a certain relativity in size and scale to consider. Nevertheless, as we shall see, there are general limits to size and scale that must be satisfied by anything that could properly be called a republic.

In what follows, I want to explore some of the most important ways the republican tradition has tried to define the proper size and scale of republican politics, how Americans contributed to that effort, and how they eventually abandoned it.

The Classical Republic and Size

Any thinking about the proper size and scale of republican order must take its bearings from the republican tradition that stretches back to the ancient Greeks. When we do so, we must be astonished to find that for over two thousand years, republics seldom went beyond a population of 200,000 people, and most were considerably smaller. This was true of ancient Greek republics, as well as medieval and early modern republics. We must find this astonishing because we are disposed to think not only that republics *can* have populations in the millions, tens, and even hundreds of millions but that republics *should be* large if they are to satisfy the demands of political life, namely economic prosperity, justice, security, and a high culture of human excellence.

But historical experience shows otherwise. Greek civilization was an anomaly in the ancient world. The disposition of that world was to create large centralized empires, and the larger the better: the Egyptian, Hittite, Assyrian, Babylonian, Persian, Macedonian, and Roman. Greek civilization was different. It was composed of some 1,500 small republics. Athens, one of the largest, had a population of around 160,000. There was no central authority to this civilization of over a thousand republics. It was held together by a common language, cultural style, commerce, and competition among the republics for cultural and economic achievement. So great were the achievements of these small competitive republics in architecture, science, mathematics, literature, the arts, medicine, philosophy, and sports (the Greeks were the first to make games a serious matter) that we still take inspiration from them. The ancient Greek philosophers are read today not as curious relics but for the insights they provide and as part of an ongoing dialogue between generations. This shows conclusively that large centralized states comprising millions are *not necessary* for the cultivation of human excellence.

Nor are large states necessary for economic prosperity. That is achieved through trade. Economic integration does not require political integration. Singapore is a wealthy city state and is economically integrated with the entire world, but it is not politically integrated with other states. Switzerland, though landlocked in the center of Europe, is often ranked in the top-ten richest states in the world in terms of per-capita income. Its trade is global, but it is famous for its republicanism and political independence. Few large states are self-sufficient. Japan imports all of its oil and cannot feed itself, but it is one of the richest countries in the world. Of the ten wealthiest states in the world in terms of per-capita income, the great majority are small states.

What about defense? Can small states defend themselves against large centralized states? The answer is that defense is a highly contingent matter, dependent on such factors as time, circumstances, terrain, ingenuity, and political will. The short answer is that sometimes they can, and sometimes they cannot. But history abounds with David and Goliath stories of very small forces defeating much larger ones. Switzerland has maintained its independence for over seven hundred years in the heart of wartorn Europe. Nor are large centralized states always havens of safety, because they spark rivalry and war with opposing large states. The massive power concentrated in them makes war more intense and the scale of destruction greater. The clash of large states in World War I led to some 16 million deaths (military and civilian). World War II harvested some 60 million deaths (mostly civilians). Were the large states of Britain, France, Italy, Germany, and Russia safe places to live in the twentieth century? They were not, but Switzerland was.

Perhaps the most dramatic case of the small defeating the large is the failure of the Persian kings to conquer the Greek republics. The centralized Persian empire commanded the resources of some 42 million people. Greek decentralized civilization contained only 8 million, strung out from Naples to the Black Sea in 1,500 little quarreling republics. Yet the massive force of the Persians was repeatedly defeated. Eventually the Greeks themselves suffered the fate of centralization under one of their own, Alexander the Great, and became the center of an empire. Prior to Alexander, the Greeks had produced a unique, highly decentralized civilization that lasted several centuries—longer than many empires. After centralization, the little republics lost their independence along with their vitality and creativity, yet the legacy of the high culture they created lived on and spread throughout the Roman Empire.

The Federative Polity of Christendom and Size

With the collapse of the Roman Empire, an entirely new kind of civilization grew up in Europe. It resembled Greek civilization in being highly decentralized but differed in having no common language and in having over it a common religion, spiritually (but not politically) uniting thousands of independent polities. Although Christianity authorizes no particular form of political association, its universalist mission to spread the Gospel around the world enables Christians to be open to a larger form of political association. What emerged in Christian civilization was what I shall call *a federative polity*—a regime of divided authority in which a central authority was endowed with limited powers needed to perform special functions for itself and the good of the smaller units, while each small unit retained the powers needed to perform its own special functions.

Everywhere in Christendom, power was divided. Whereas in other large civilizations the religious authority was united with the political authority, in Christendom they were divided. The Papacy was independent of the Holy Roman Emperor. The Holy Roman Empire itself was composed of hundreds of small principalities and free cities that jointly delegated limited authority to an elected emperor. Kingdoms were also scenes of divided authorities with cities, the Church, dukes, lords, and knights retaining original powers—their titles rooted in the same moral tradition as that of the kings. Europe was a vast mosaic of independent and quasi-independent social authorities: kingdoms, small principalities, dukedoms, baronies, republics, bishoprics, Papal States, free cities, leagues of free cities, knightly estates, and combinations of these.

This order was held together by "compacts," "treaties," "contracts," "consent," and "oaths." Divided authorities, of course, would give rise to frequent disputes over whether one authority had encroached on the domain of another. Where does Papal authority end and Imperial authority begin? What rights do the barons have against the king or the duke over a "free city" in his domain? By the sixteenth century, this discourse of rights would extend to individual rights over the intrusion of collective authorities of all kinds. Our language of liberty, rights, and the limits of authority has its source in the civilization of medieval Christendom.

This widespread division of authorities meant there would be no centralized empire in Europe, though attempts would be made, notably by Charlemagne, Charles V, Louis XIV, Napoleon, Hitler, and today the bureaucrats of the European Union. It would also mean that large urban centers would be difficult to create. By 1400, one of the largest cities in Europe was Paris, with around 100,000. London was 50,000. Many of the great cathedrals were built in cities of 12,000 or so. This highly decentralized civilization produced the jury system, the ideal of the rule of law, the rudiments of capitalism, an ethic of individualism, the romantic ideal, the parliamentary system, federalism, and the universities.

The *federative polity* is Christendom's contribution to political philosophy. It combined the advantages of large scale with something of the Greek republican teaching that polities should be small. The small unit retained the original powers needed to perform the functions that preexisted formation of the federative polity. Catholic social teaching has continued to refine this medieval inheritance with its doctrine of "subsidiarity," taught by Pope Pius XI in the encyclical *Quadragesimo Anno:* "It is an injustice and at the same time a grave evil and disturbance of right order to assign to a greater and higher association what lesser and subordinate organizations can do." The larger unit is to assist the smaller in performing *its* functions "and never to destroy or absorb them."

The Catholic teaching on "subsidiarity" assumes a hierarchy of authorities, but by the time of the Reformation, a dissenting Protestant version of the federative polity emerged. This was nicely exemplified in the thought of the German philosopher Johannes Althusius, whose main work *Politica* was published in 1614. Althusius treats the family as the primordial political unit. This was different from Aristotle's republicanism, which treats the family as an economic not a political unit. For Althusius, it is political because it contains the relations of authority and subordination. Families federate to form villages; these federate into towns and cities. Villages and towns federate to form a provincial authority, and provinces federate to form a commonwealth. In addition, there are voluntary associations of all kinds formed by compact among individuals: universities, guilds, commercial associations, and the like. And finally there is the universal association of the Church, which gives a color and tone to the whole but which is distinct from secular political authority.[1]

The corporate entities (villages, cities, provinces) and the associations of individuals are united in a symbiotic relation with each other. An individual in an Althusian federation enjoys a heterogeneous range of associations and allegiances on a large scale unavailable to citizens of the ancient republics. As a Christian, he is united spiritually (though not politically) with the whole of Europe. As a member of a guild or university, he enjoys an identity that cuts across the provinces and even commonwealths. He may have an intense loyalty to his own city or province, as did the ancient Greeks. But if he does not, then, as a member of the commonwealth, he is free to move from one city or province to another if it will receive him. The relation the individual has to the whole is symbiotic. Accordingly, Althusius describes individuals who enjoy this kind of association as *symbiotes.*[2] These are not *citizens* as understood in the ancient republics, nor *subjects* as understood by monarchies. The symbiotes are a new kind of political being endowed with a larger sphere of action and a larger and more differentiated soul than that of the classical citizen, whose soul is limited by the public good of his small republic and its gods. And it is different from the soul of a subject under empire, whose end is to serve the good of the emperor and the empire.

Although the soul of the symbiote is more differentiated and expansive than that of the classical citizen, Althusius retains much of what was valuable in the classical republic. Each corporate entity in an Althusian federation has a *telos*, a thing of its own to enjoy and defend. Each, therefore, is morally intrusive to the individuals within it. An individual who enters a city or province in the commonwealth different from his own must conform to its moral code, which might be quite different from what he is used to. The symbiotic soul must be capable of tolerating great moral differences in the commonwealth.

Each city, province, and estate that makes up the commonwealth has a moral substance similar to that of an ancient republic. And this enables Althusius to teach that any unit in the federative polity capable of maintaining itself can *lawfully secede* from the federation and join another federative polity or exist independently: "One of the estates, or one part of the realm, can abandon the remaining body to which it belonged and choose for itself a separate ruler or a new form of commonwealth when the public and manifest welfare of this entire part altogether requires it."[3] And it can do this not only when oppressed by central authority but also to improve its general welfare.

How large can an Althusian polity be? Althusius provides no figure but says it should be of "medium" size—larger than a Greek republic but smaller than a European monarchy.[4] He gave Rome as an example: "When it was of medium size, it was free from many corruptions. When it grew to a great size . . . it abounded with corruptions."[5] Althusius favors the biblical Jewish federation of tribes over the isolated Greek republic or even the Roman republic. He thought that God had revealed this symbiotic, federative style of polity as the best for mankind. Consequently, he was sympathetic to federative polities such as the United Provinces of the Netherlands and the Swiss federation. But whatever Althusius meant by "medium" size, it is clear that an Althusian federation will always be of the right size, because if the federation grows so large that it no longer serves the interests of its federative units, they can lawfully secede.

Size, Secession, and American Republicanism

The American colonists who seceded from Britain were some 97 percent Protestant and had inherited the dissenting Protestant disposition of Althusius, but more directly from Scottish Calvinists such as George Buchanan, Samuel Rutherford, and Francis Hutcheson. These overlapped with the English "Commonwealth Men," especially John Trenchard and Thomas Gordon, whose *Cato's Letters* were published from 1720 to 1723. These essays had little influence in monarchical Britain but enormous influence in the American colonies, where Bernard Bailyn estimates that half the private libraries contained a copy.[6] In the last chapter of *A System of Moral Philosophy* (1755), Francis Hutcheson explained the conditions under which colonies may secede from the mother country. Hutcheson was a self-acknowledged influence on the great Scottish philosopher David Hume, who was almost alone among major British thinkers in supporting the right of the American colonists to secede. Writing in 1775, he said: "I am an American in my Principles, and wish we woud [sic] let them alone to govern or misgovern themselves as they think proper."[7]

By inheriting the Protestant version of the federative polity of Christendom, Americans also inherited the republican tradition of the ancient Greeks and especially of the Roman republic. They were educated in the Greek and Latin classics. They admired republican heroes such as Cato, Cicero, and king killers such as Brutus. They filled their public spaces with the names and architecture of republican Greece and Rome. They emulated what they imagined to be the style of ancient republican life and removed themselves as far as possible from monarchy and all its ways.

But Americans faced what seemed an insuperable problem. The republican tradition they inherited taught them that republics had to be small *and* that governing an extensive territory would *necessarily* require a centralized monarchy. The borders of the vast territory acquired from Britain had been drawn not by republican considerations but my monarchical ones. And so it seemed that Americans were doomed, by the sheer size of the territory they occupied, to end up with some version of a centralized monarchy— despite their republican dispositions. What could be done?

A solution was suggested by colonial experience. America was a vast but sparsely populated territory. As a region filled with people and became strong enough to form a political society, it could secede just as the colonies had seceded from the mother country. In the undeveloped, expansive territory of America, Althusian secession and republican self-government went hand in hand. This disposition was strengthened by the dissenting Protestant character of the settlers and by the fact that the British sovereign, except for regulations on commerce, had left Americans pretty much to themselves. And so the Scottish philosopher David Hume could make a note to himself in the 1730s that "the charter governments in America are almost completely independent of England."[8]

This meant that though under British sovereignty, the colonists had in effect long practiced republican self-government. They had cleared the forests, fought off natives as well as the Spanish, built societies, and established governments on their own. Their obligations to the Crown were mainly of a commercial character. All of this, they thought, gave them a title to rule themselves. Moreover, their political experience was shaped in small Protestant communities on a scale actually smaller than that of the ancient Greeks. As of 1776, few Americans lived in urban centers. The largest of these was Philadelphia, with around 30,000 people. New York did not reach the size of ancient Athens, at around 160,000, until about 1830.

Although these factors encouraged the cultivation of republican dispositions, so vast was the territory Americans acquired that the temptation to monarchy remained. A memorable instance of heroically resisting that temptation is provided by Virginia. The republic of Virginia had conquered from Britain the vast Northwest Territory, comprising the present States of Ohio, Indiana, Illinois, Wisconsin, and Michigan. There was fear that Virginia would in effect create a monarchy by gaining control of the central government and dominating the Union. Virginia statesmen argued that Virginia could not both be a republic *and* rule territory of such size and urged that the Northwest Territory be ceded through treaty to the Confederation as common property. So Virginia escaped monarchy by *division.*

Shortly after this act of republican magnanimity by Virginia, the Constitution was ratified, and Article IV guaranteed to each State "a Republican Form of Government." But a problem remained, because the States themselves were too large to claim republican government as classically understood. The remedy was *secession* in the direction of a more human scale of political order. So the western counties of Virginia seceded and formed the State of Kentucky. Maine seceded from Massachusetts. Western counties of North Carolina failed in their attempt to form the State of Franklin, but out of that movement came the State of Tennessee, carved from the western part of North Carolina. The Republic of West Florida seceded from Spanish rule but was annexed by the United States in 1810. This act of secession was long a source of republican inspiration for those in the South and Southwest. The flag of the West Florida Republic was a single white star on a blue ground. This would later be incorporated into the Texas flag, which was flown when Texas seceded from Mexico and then from the United States, and it is still flown today. Memory of the West Florida Republic inspired a Confederate song to its blue ensign with a single star called "The Bonnie Blue Flag," which celebrated republicanism *via* secession. The song was popular throughout the Confederacy, and that flag became a national symbol. It is still flown in the South today. North Carolina also placed a single star on a blue ground in its ensign, which is still in use.

But even allowing division by secession, the States were still too large by classical republican standards, when we recall that for two thousand years republics seldom were larger than 200,000 people. As a remedy, Thomas Jefferson proposed dividing the counties of his own State of Virginia into what he called "ward republics." Each "ward republic" would be "a small republic within itself."[9] Jefferson compared them to New England towns, many of which had political identities older than the New England States. These little polities had nullified Jefferson's embargo on trade with Britain and would later nullify Madison's war of 1812. Jefferson did not like their policies, but he admired their spirit of independence. Writing to Joseph Cabell on February 2, 1816, he said, with some admiration: "I felt the foundations of the government shaken under my feet by the New England townships. . . . As Cato then concluded every speech with the words, *'Cathago delenda est'* so do I every opinion with the injunction, 'divide the counties into wards.'"[10]

To take a contemporary example, Jefferson's "ward republics" were to function somewhat like Swiss cantons, each having considerable autonomy over education, morals, welfare, voting, and its own militia. He wrote John Tyler on May 26, 1810, that "these little republics would be the main strength of the great one."[11] Of these small republics federated—in the manner of Althusius—into a larger polity, Jefferson wrote to John Cartwright in 1824 that "the wit of man cannot devise a more solid basis for a free, durable well-administered republic."[12]

In Jefferson we have all the elements of an Althusian federative polity cast on a scale much larger than what Althusius proposed but compatible with his teaching. Althusius theorized in a fixed and immobile world of European polities and social authorities. Jefferson theorized in a dynamic world of large unexploited territories and expanding populations. To get a picture of what a developed "Althusian America" might have looked like, suppose the territory of the United States had remained that of the original thirteen States. Suppose further that the Jeffersonian vision of republicanism, through division of States into smaller States, had continued. Then the original thirteen States, through repeated secessions, could have given birth to thirty or even fifty States, as we have today. And each of these could be further divided into Jeffersonian "ward republics" in the manner of Swiss cantons. Switzerland is a little over half the size of South Carolina, with twenty-seven little states and four languages. And it should be stressed that Swiss cantons are *states* and not comparable to American *counties,* which are mere administrative units of State legislatures.

If the logic of Jeffersonian republicanism had been followed, the original thirteen States could have spawned a large number of Swiss-style federative States. But that did not happen. America went in a different direction and in time would collapse into a greater centralization of power than anything eighteenth-century European monarchs could have imagined. We have inherited that massively centralized regime, but it is important to understand that nothing in the American founding made it inevitable, nor does it have to continue.

Paradoxically, this regime might not have come about had it not been for Jefferson's Louisiana Purchase, which more than doubled the size of the Union. This greatly strengthened the temptation to monarchy and seemed to confirm the darkest suspicions of New England Federalists, who believed there was a Virginia conspiracy to consolidate power, "a deliberate plan to govern & depress New England."[13] New England Federalists did not want to expand beyond the size of the original thirteen States (what they called the "good old United States"). We should recall that the original Union was more interested in moral consensus than in sheer size. Article VII of the Constitution requires ratification by only *nine* States, leaving the other four to remain under the Articles of Confederation or to form a Union of their own. Only nine States were needed to form the United States, not thirteen and much less fifty.

Though Jefferson unwittingly laid the groundwork for the centralization that was to come, he was not a centralist and denied that such vast territory would lead to centralization of the Union. Like his Virginia colleagues who ceded the Northwest Territory to the Union, he offered secession and division of territory as a means of blocking the drift to monarchy. As people went west, he argued, they would reenact the primal experience of the English colonists. They would clear land, build societies, and form States, and when a number of these were developed enough to govern themselves, they would secede from the Union and form federations of their own. In a letter to Joseph Priestly on January 29, 1804, Jefferson said he would be happy to have a Mississippi Confederacy on the western banks of the Mississippi alongside the old Atlantic Confederacy. And he even imagined a Pacific federation, comprised, he said, of "free and independent Americans, unconnected with us but by the ties of blood and interest, and employing like us the rights of self-government."[14]

Sen. Thomas Hart Benton of Missouri and other Jeffersonians had the same vision. Benton told the Senate in 1825: "In planting the seed of a new power on the coast of the Pacific Ocean, it should be well understood that when strong enough to take care of itself, the new Government should separate from the mother Empire as the child separates from the parent at the age of manhood."[15] Daniel Boorstin observes, "Jefferson propagandized for an independent Pacific republic, and in the 1820s many leading Americans—including Albert Galatin, James Monroe, William H. Crawford, Henry Clay, Thomas Hart Benton, and possibly James Madison—shared the vision."[16] Boorstin concludes that the Jeffersonian vision of "the United States as a planter of new nations had an appeal we have long forgotten."[17]

The Jeffersonian vision of westward expansion would yield what Jefferson called an "empire of liberty." It would be continental in scale but not the centralized empire that the American regime has become today. It would be a voluntary association not merely of States but of American *unions of States*. The States in each American federation of States would have the right of secession. And if Jefferson had his way, these would themselves be divided—not into counties but small republics on the Swiss model, each having considerable autonomy over its own affairs.

To sum up, the republican tradition for over two thousand years taught that republics should be small, in the range of 200,000 or so. The Greek, Roman (before it became an empire), medieval, and early modern republics hovered in this range. The republic in Rousseau's famous *Social*

Contract is modeled on his beloved Geneva, which had around 25,000 people. Republics of this size have generated an astonishing level of high culture. And some have outlasted large empires. Venice, "the Serene Republic," lasted some 1,200 years before being conquered by Napoleon.

The federative polity that emerged from Christendom as articulated by Althusius provided new opportunities for republican life. Small republican polities as well as other forms of independent social authority could enjoy the benefits of large-scale symbiotic association while retaining the right of self-government within their own sphere. Should the central authority intrude into the functions of the smaller polity, or should its happiness require it, the polity could *lawfully* secede from the federation.

America from the settlement at Jamestown, Virginia until the war of 1861-65 to suppress Southern secession was virtually an Althusian polity writ large. Jefferson's "empire of liberty" simply republicanized it throughout. The Althusian federative polity itself was of "medium" size, which I have taken to be roughly the size of Switzerland. However, all but nine American States today are considerably larger in territory than Switzerland (though not in population). So is Jefferson's "empire of liberty" simply too large to preserve a republican style of politics? It is not if the States themselves enjoy the right of secession and are ordered internally by a system of Jeffersonian "ward republics," each of which enjoys a high degree of self-government over the things that are the essence of republican life, namely morals, religion, education, voting, social welfare, and the like. From the republican point of view, the larger the polity, the greater the moral weight to the right of secession. This explains why Jefferson thought it natural that America would evolve not into a single large-scale federation—much less a unitary state—but into a number of federations.

Can a Large Modern State Be a Republic?

Although an Althusian federative polity ordered in the right way can provide the advantages of large scale *and* preserve the values of republicanism (as long as there is a right of secession), such a polity is not itself a republic. It is a federation. A republic has plenary powers directly over individuals—and is small. A federation is a voluntary symbiotic relationship between sovereign States, a central authority, and individuals—and is large. So the question remains whether a republican style of politics could be enjoyed in a large state that was *not a federation*. This is precisely what was claimed in the French Revolution. The French state that emerged was called a *republic*, but it was large and centralized; and since it was said to be "one and indivisible," secession was ruled out absolutely.

Here for the first time in history, the question of size and scale was disconnected from republicanism. The centralized French state ruled directly over some 28 million *individuals* instead of over a federation of symbiotically related individuals and political societies as in Althusius and Jefferson. The French Revolutionary idea of a large republic ruling directly over millions of individuals quickly spread throughout Europe and has become the dominant model in the world. Though advocated by would-be nationalists such as Alexander Hamilton[18] and later by Justice John Marshall, Justice Joseph Story, and Daniel Webster, it did not become established in America until after Lincoln's successful war to prevent eleven American States from seceding and forming a federation of their own—the very thing provided for both in Althusius's "medium"-size federation and in Jefferson's "empire of liberty."

In *Yankee Leviathan: The Origins of Central State Authority in America,* Richard Bensel explained how the North's invasion destroyed the federative polity of the founders and created a consolidated nationalist regime. This was just the sort of regime that drove the colonists to secede in 1776. It most likely would not have lasted had it not been for the Spanish-American War, World War I, World War II, and the Cold War, which transformed America from a federative polity into a unitary welfare-warfare state. But the process of centralization took time. It was not until 1937 that Congress approved a national anthem for the new kind of monster state that had been in progress since 1865. And the pledge of allegiance to its flag was not approved by Congress and codified until 1942.[19]

It should be noted that the "pledge of allegiance to the flag" imitates the French "republic" in describing the regime as "one nation indivisible." Althusian and Jeffersonian secession are ruled out absolutely as treason. Since we have all inherited this language, we need to keep in mind that prior to the war to prevent secession of the Southern States, the Stars and Stripes was not perceived as a *national* flag. It was a flag identifying the office of the central government in a federation, much in the way Europeans view the European Union flag today. It was not even carried in battle until the Mexican war. It did not take on a "national" character until Lincoln's successful war to prevent secession, and then it was the flag only of the North. It was not perceived by most Southerners as *their* "national" flag with any enthusiasm until early in the twentieth century.

Today the French Revolutionary model of a "republic" with plenary powers ruling directly over millions of individual has a global purchase. We speak without embarrassment of the French Republic, the American Republic, and the People's Republic of China. But all of these fall well outside the size and scale of the republican tradition. To this one might object that traditions evolve and change over time. Why cannot the republican tradition of self-government and rule of law be expanded to include a centralized unitary state ruling millions in a vast territory?

That is a fair question. But in answering it, we must keep in mind the constraints of size and scale demanded by the republican tradition. One can increase the size of something just so far without destroying what makes it valuable. A jury of 12 if expanded to 1,200 would lose what makes the jury system valuable. A charming English cottage and garden if expanded to four times its size would not only lose its charm, it would be a monstrosity. Why should we think that republican values of self-government and rule of law can be preserved in an American unitary state of 305 million people? Why should not size and scale matter in political things (and especially in republics) as well as in everything else in nature?

To appreciate just how *unrepublican* these post-French Revolution "republics" are, it will be helpful to compare them with the first model of a *large republic* ever proposed. This model was sketched out in David Hume's essay "Idea of a Perfect Commonwealth," published in 1752. Althusius and Jefferson seek to preserve human-scale republican values in a *federative polity*. Hume does not. He seeks to expand the size of the population and territory of a *unitary state* but in such a way as to preserve the human scale demanded of republican self-government. And the question is whether this can be done.

David Hume's Vision of a Large Republic

Hume agrees with the republican tradition that "a small commonwealth is the happiest government in the world within itself," but "it may be subdued by great force from without." The solution would be a large republic ordered in such a way as to "have all the advantages both of a great and a little commonwealth." The thesis of the essay is that the large republic Hume proposes not only continues the republican tradition—unlike the later French or post-Lincolnian American "republic"—but would be the best form of political association.[20] The question, though, is whether Hume can expand the size of the republic without destroying those values unique to republican government (self-government and rule of law) that require a human scale.

He asks us to imagine a large republic the size of Britain or France divided into 100 small republics. Each of these is divided into 100 parishes. The members of each parish meet annually to elect 1 representative. This yields 100 representatives in each small republic's legislature. The legislature selects from among its members 10 magistrates to exercise the executive and judicial functions of the republic and 1 senator to represent the republic in the national capital. That yields 100 senators, from among which 10 are chosen to serve as the national executive and judiciary.

Laws are normally proposed by the national senate and passed down to the provincial republics for ratification. Each republic has one vote regardless of population, and the majority rules. To free the provincial legislature from having to vote on every trivial law, a bill can be sent instead to the ten provincial magistrates in each republic for ratification.[21]

Let us now compare Hume's large republic—in respect to self-government—with the highly centralized regime the United States has become today. Hume's republic has 100 senators in the national capital representing the individual States, as we do. But the legislative body representing the nation of individuals is located in the several capitals of the provincial republics. This has four advantages. First, it provides a better (and more republican) ratio of representation to population. Hume's republic is the size of Britain, which in his time had some 9 million people; yet his regionally dispersed legislatures jointly yield 10,000 representatives. By contrast, the United States has not 9 million but 305 million people. Its representative body contains not 10,000 representatives but only 435—a number Congress capped by law in 1911. Hume's large republic provides a ratio of 1 representative for every 900 people and so is of a *republican scale*. The United States yields a ratio of approximately 1 representative for every 700,000 people, which is not remotely within a republican scale.

Nor can this unrepublican character of the United States be remedied by increasing the size of the House of Representatives. Judging by the size of legislatures around the world, 435 is about the right size for a lawmaking body. Or to put it another way, the ratio of representatives to population at the first Congress was about 1 for every 60,000 people. Madison thought that was an inadequate ratio for nearly 4 million people. But if that inadequate ratio were used today, there would be over 5,000 members in the House of Representatives. This would be impossibly large for a lawmaking body. Size as such does matter.

But if the number of representatives in Washington *cannot be increased* as the population expands, then we have evidently reached the point where talk of republican self-government is utterly meaningless. In the not too distant future, the population of the United States will reach 435 million. This would yield one representative for every million persons. Who could hear this regime described as a republic where the people enjoy self-government and the rule of law without breaking out into laughter? Our condition today in all essentials is no different. Yet we continue to talk as if we enjoyed "republican" government.

Near the end of a long career of service to his country, George Kennan, at the Institute for Advanced Studies at Princeton University, and called by some "the conscience of America," argued the Aristotelian point that States can simply become too large for self-government: "There is a real question as to whether 'bigness' in a body politic is not an evil in itself, quite aside from the policies pursued in its name." Though known for his moderation and realism in international affairs, Kennan described the United States as having developed into "a monster country . . . along with others such as China, India, the recent Soviet Union, and Brazil." If the United States has indeed reached the point of political obesity, then the only remedy would be to downsize it through secession and division (in the spirit of Jefferson's "empire of liberty") into a number of federative units on the continent forming a voluntary commonwealth of American federations. And this is in fact what Kennan proposes.[22]

Suppose, however, that we reject dividing the Union into distinct territorial jurisdictions but nevertheless insist that its politics conform to a republican scale. In that case we should adopt some such model as Hume's large republic. This would require abolishing the House of Representatives in Washington and transforming the State legislatures into a joint national legislature. The Senate would propose legislation to be ratified by a majority of the States, each State having one vote.

Consider trying to enact the unpopular recent legislation in Hume's large republic. A strong majority of Americans opposed the bailouts for the monster banks whose corrupt policies caused the financial meltdown in 2009; the economic stimulus packages; and Barack Obama's healthcare plan of some two thousand pages, rushed through with publically acknowledged privileges given to some States and not others and admissions by its leading supporters that they had not read it. To this should be added that many believe that Congress has no constitutional authority to impose a healthcare plan, whether or not the plan is a good one. The Constitution leaves healthcare to the States. But putting aside the merits of these unpopular acts of legislation, had they been sent down to the legislatures of Iowa, South Carolina, Wyoming, etc., for debate and ratification, as required by Hume's large republic, their defeat would have been so certain that they probably never would have been proposed in the first place.

The second advantage offered by Hume's model is that by dispersing the national legislature among the provincial republics, he has eliminated the corruption that inevitably comes from putting the House of Representatives and the Senate in the *same place*. The number of representatives in Washington is 435 in the House, 100 in the Senate, and one president—a grand total of only 536 lawmakers. A majority of this number is only 269. This small number rules 305 million people. And the majority can be less, since both houses can lawfully, and often do, operate with a mere quorum. A quorum majority of both houses of Congress is only 135.

But the matter is worse than that. Most of the regulations we live under are not passed by Congress at all but spring from executive bureaucracies under the Imperial presidency. Agencies with Orwellian names such as the IRS, FDIC, FSEC, FDA, EPA, FCC, and FTC (not to mention the many presidential "czars") make laws and regulations that can skirt the will of Congress or frustrate it.

As if this were not enough, the Supreme Court, through the power of "judicial review" (which is nowhere found in the Constitution), has usurped the "police powers" of the States over law enforcement, morals, speech, religion, education, health, and voting—the very essence of republican life. Nine unelected Supreme Court justices with life tenure, sometimes by votes of five to four, make major social policy for 305 million people. Political issues that are reserved to the States, such as abortion, have been taken out of the *policy arena* and magically transformed into "constitutional rights." This means, in effect, that the Court can rewrite the Constitution at will, entirely bypassing the amendment process, which requires ratification by three-fourths of the States.[23] To speak of republican self-government and rule of law in such a regime is Orwellian.

The federal budget is some $3.55 trillion, which is more than the entire gross domestic product of Germany. Add to this the projected deficit of more than $1 trillion, and we have an amount greater than the gross domestic product of Japan. This vast sum is voted on by a majority of only 269 in Congress (and a mere 135 if a quorum is used). And if that is not enough, this small number can borrow money or inflate the currency simply by printing money out of thin air (to the devastation of the poor and thrifty). Is it any wonder that Congress has become a frenzied scene of pork spending and regulations benefitting favored groups at the expense of others?

Corruption, of course, would also exist in Hume's large republic but not at the scale, intensity, and utter impenetrability that exists in Washington. Hume's national legislature sits jointly in the provincial capitals, of which there are 100. So a lobbying interest must deploy a much greater number of lobbyists and over greater distances. In addition, it would be much more difficult for representatives to coordinate with each other to buy and sell votes, as is routinely done in Congress today. Moreover, in Hume's large republic there are 10,000 dispersed representatives who live in the same neighborhood with their constituents and would have to answer to them. If we had Hume's large republic, could public funds be used so easily to shamelessly buy, for example, the votes of Sen. Mary Landrieu of Louisiana and Sen. Ben Nelson of Nebraska to pass Obama's healthcare bill? Would State legislatures approve public funds to benefit the States of Louisiana and Nebraska at their expense merely to pass a healthcare bill that a large majority of Americans say they do not want? This is so unlikely that the Senate under an Americanized version of Hume's large republic would never have proposed such things.

Third, Hume provides a number of checks to prevent a faction from dominating the whole. If the senate rejects a proposed law, only *10 senators* out of 100 are needed to veto that decision and forward the bill to the republics for consideration. Laws thought to be trivial can be sent from the senate to the ten magistrates of the republic for ratification instead of calling on the whole legislature. But only *5* out of 100 provincial representatives are needed to veto this and call for a vote of their legislature. Each republic can veto legislation of another republic and force a vote on the matter by all the republics.

Finally, Hume's constitution wisely prohibits expanding the *size* of the republic by conquest. Yet he dryly observes, "Republics have ambition as well as individuals, and present interest makes men forgetful of their posterity."[24]

Is the American "Republic" Really a Monarchy?

Hume gave us the first theory of a large republic that respects the republican tradition's insistence on human scale. Though greatly expanded in size, it is still recognizable as a republic. Eighteenth-century Americans were the first to attempt a republican style of politics in a vast territory. Some historians have seen Hume's essay as a model that inspired Federalists such as James Madison and Alexander Hamilton, who wanted a large centralized regime on the model of Britain.[25] But this is to misread both Hume's essay and the Constitution ratified by the States in 1789. Hume's polity is a republic (though a large one), but the American polity of 1789 was not a republic. It was a *federation of republics*. A federation of republics is not itself a republic, any more than a federation of country clubs is a country club. Each American State could be viewed as a large Humean republic, but a federation of such States could not be.

Under the Constitution of 1789, the central government could rule over individuals but only under the powers delegated to it by the sovereign States. All other powers of sovereignty belong to the States. What was not prohibited to the States by the Constitution was reserved. Given this framework, the final safeguard for republicanism in America was and could only be some form of lawful State interposition, nullification, or secession.

These constitutional remedies were regularly invoked in antebellum public discourse and greatly constrained the central government. As of 1860, the central government was nearly out of debt and imposed no inland taxes. It lived simply off a tariff on imports and land sales. The Supreme Court was tightly constrained in the exercise of judicial review. It challenged the constitutionality of acts of Congress only twice: *Marbury v. Madison* and *Dred Scott v. Sandford.* The right of State interposition and nullification was exercised in every section of the Union during the antebellum period. The Wisconsin legislature and State Supreme Court nullified judgments of the Supreme Court in 1854 and 1859.[26] Secession was also invoked in every section of the Union.[27] Both of these constitutional remedies were casualties of the Union's successful war to prevent eleven American States from forming a federation of their own—acts authorized by natural law, according to Althusius and Jefferson.

From 1865 on, no American State would any longer enjoy the republican form of government guaranteed in Article IV of the Constitution. Lincoln denied that the States were or had ever been sovereign political societies. He said they should be thought of as counties in a unitary state.[28] If so, a revolutionary paradigm shift in political language would have to occur (and did occur). The traditional republican ideals of self-government and rule of law would still be invoked and celebrated as unique American possessions, but they would no longer be tethered to requirements of human scale and size as insisted on by the republican tradition for over two thousand years. Centralized regimes ruling tens and even hundreds of millions would now, without embarrassment, be called republics: the French republic, the American republic, the People's Republic of China, and many others. But not one of these regimes is a republic—not even a large Humean republic.

But if they are not republics, what are they? The answer was given by Alexis de Tocqueville, who argued that the French

Revolution, which was supposed to have overturned the monarchy, fundamentally changed nothing.[29] What he meant by such a seemingly absurd claim was this. Medieval Europe was composed of thousands of independent and quasi-independent polities and social authorities. For some four hundred years, monarchs, through conquest and other means, had been crushing independent social authorities such as the Church, small principalities, free cities, republics, and the nobility into larger and fewer states. To rule this deracinated and heterogeneous mass, the kings created an administrative system seeking a monopoly on coercion over individuals. This coercive system was thought of as the king's property to be passed on to his heirs. But it eventually took on a life of its own, symbolized in the doctrine of the two bodies of the king and in the declaration upon a king's death: "The king is dead; long live the king." The first body of the king was the flesh and blood king. The second body was the artificial corporation, with a would-be monopoly on coercion over individuals in a territory.

This artificial corporation was called not a monarchy but "absolute monarchy." David Hume judged in the 1750s that absolute monarchy was only three generations old. It was the rise of absolute monarchy (a relatively new system in 1776) that brought forth resistance by the American colonists and led to the discourse on "liberty" that we have inherited.

When Tocqueville said the French Revolution fundamentally changed nothing, he meant that all it did was kill the first body of the king. It left the second body of the king intact, merely changing its name from the "Crown" to the "Republic." That artificial corporation with a would-be monopoly on coercion over individuals created by the king was now said to represent not the flesh and blood king but the French people. The revolution merely replaced the person of the king with a fictitious "nation-person." The administration of coercion not only remained but was vastly expanded beyond anything the monarchs could have imagined. In short, what emerged after the French Revolution was an absolute monarchy without the monarch, a regime that had all the major defects of monarchy but none of its benefits.[30]

What was bad about monarchy was its disposition to centralize power by consolidating hitherto independent social authorities under the will of the second body of the king. Its major benefit was that its authority rested on the same footing as that of the independent social authorities it sought to dominate, so there was a limit as to how far the king could go without subverting his own authority. The post-French Revolution era of "republics" would increase centralization beyond the wildest dreams of monarchs. The German economist Hans Hoppe estimates that, before the mid-nineteenth-century, monarchs—bad as they might be—were never able to extract more than 5 to 8 percent of the GNP, whereas mass "republics" have been able to exploit over 60 percent.[31]

In his war to prevent secession, Lincoln and the perversely named "Republican" Party destroyed the two American institutions that had made republicanism possible in a regime of continental scale, namely State nullification and secession. Without these acknowledged rights, there could be no practical check to centralization. From the very beginning, there was fear that the second body of the king would be resurrected in America under the republican name. Thinkers as different as George Mason, James Madison, the Jeffersonians, New England Federalists, and others accused each other of policies leading to "monarchy." Jefferson described centralists such as Hamilton as "monocrats." In America, that meant consolidation of State and local government under central control. After Lincoln's war to prevent secession, the second body of the king, against which the colonists seceded, was resurrected and (as in France) was called a *republic*, "one and indivisible." From then on, anti-monarchical discourse dies out in the United States. Americans were reconciled to monarchy as long as it was called a "republic."

The Indian Summer of American Republicanism

Today it is widely assumed that the "checks and balances" in the American system are those between the president, Congress, and the Supreme Court. The checks from the States on central authority in the form of interposition, nullification, and secession are ruled out. But this is just another way of saying that the central government can define the limits of its own powers. And *that* is what the American colonists and ratifiers of the 1789 Constitution meant by *absolute* monarchy.

The framers of the Articles of Confederation were so fearful that the second body of the king would be resurrected that they refused to allow the central government to impose taxes or conscript troops. The framers of the U.S. Constitution were also fearful and incorporated the Bill of Rights, not to protect individuals from the States (as the Supreme Court perversely interprets the Bill of Rights today and which massively centralizes power) but to protect the States (where alone republican life could be enjoyed) from the central government.

The third constitution Americans made for themselves was the Constitution of the Confederate States of America, which is very much a Jeffersonian legacy and goes even further to protect against centralization.[32] It is essentially the U.S. Constitution *reformed* to prevent unauthorized centralization. The Great Seal of the Confederacy bore an equestrian statute of George Washington, and there was strong support for naming the new nation "Washington," indicating its allegiance to the founding *federative* republicanism. Among the most important of these reforms are restrictions placed on how the central government can raise and spend money. Without patronage, centralization cannot occur.

First, a spending bill required the high bar of a two-thirds vote of both houses of Congress. Second, federal subsidies for commercial enterprises were prohibited.[33] There was no corporate welfare in the Confederacy. Third, every spending bill had to be for one and only one item as described in its title. This rules out the practice of buying and selling votes by tacking on pork spending amendments having nothing to do with the purpose of the bill. Fourth, the central government could not spend on internal improvements. These were left to private enterprise and the States. The only exceptions were facilities to encourage commerce, such as lighthouses, harbors, and the like. In those cases, the government was to be reimbursed by a fee paid by users of the facility. Fifth, the central government could not make contracts that allowed it to pay for cost overruns. Sixth, the president had a line-item veto and served only one six-year term. These reforms would limit the central government's ability to expand by dispensing patronage and would keep wealth in the States and local communities without which a republican style of life is impossible.

Other reforms sought to prevent factions from controlling the central government. First, a two-thirds vote of both houses of a State legislature could impeach any federal official in its territory. Second, and most important, the amendment process began with the *State legislatures,* not Congress. If any three States agreed on an amendment, Congress would have to call the States in convention to vote on it. And only two-thirds of the States were needed to ratify it, instead of three-fourths as demanded by the U.S. Constitution. ·

In the U.S. Constitution, if two-thirds of the States concur, Congress must call a Convention of the States to propose amendments. This condition has never been met, not only because the two-thirds requirement is a high bar to reach but also because it opens the door to uncertain constitutional change and because Congress could exercise undue control over the process. The other avenue of amending the Constitution is to receive a two-thirds vote of both houses of Congress.

So practically speaking, all amendments must pass through the gate of Congress. How likely is that? Since 1790, over 10,000 amendments have been proposed to Congress. Only 30 have left the gate, and 27 have been ratified. It is nearly impossible today for the people to amend the U.S. Constitution on any serious matter. This was not so in the Confederate Constitution, where the gatekeeper for putting an amendment to the vote was not Congress but an agreement between only three State legislatures.

Finally, the Confederate Constitution allowed the entrance of non-slaveholding states, abolished the slave trade, and, unlike the U.S. Constitution, required Congress to pass laws enforcing the ban. There was no danger that the Confederate Union would become too large and unworkable because, in addition to various forms of State interposition and nullification, it allowed the secession of a State.[34] It should be noted that Pres. Ronald Reagan affirmed the Confederate view in his first inaugural by declaring that the central government did not create the States, the States created the central government. This raised quite a murmur among the nationalists. It was these reforms that enabled Lord Acton to say that the Confederate Constitution was the best attempt so far to remedy the defects to which vast-scale republican governments give rise.[35] Whether or not that is true, it was certainly the most thoughtful attempt by *Americans* to preserve a republican style of politics on a continental scale.

This, of course, is not how we have been trained to think. The post-Lincolnian story of America has been a celebration of the unitary state, "one and indivisible," that was forged out of war and on the ruins of the federative polity of the ratifiers. In this story, the Confederate Constitution can only be viewed as a barrier to the creation of such a unitary state. But it is important to see that the Confederate Constitution was an American constitution—the legacy of the Anti-Federalists, who defended human-scale republicanism and warned against adopting the Constitution on the grounds that it would inevitably centralize power and destroy State and local sovereignty, and of the Jeffersonians, who held up State interposition, nullification, and secession as remedies to creeping monarchy (under whatever name).

With the collapse of the Confederacy, State nullification and secession were declared heresies by the new nationalist historians. If this were believed, there would be no effective barrier to a revival of the second body of the king in the form of a consolidated leviathan, with the States reduced to the status of the counties Lincoln said they always were. In this regime of continental scale, comprising a mass of 305 million, the central government would be able to define the limits of its own power. The only check left to the people would be the ritual of national elections, rendered meaningless, among other things, by the unrepublican ratio of representatives to population and managed by two "national" political parties whose nourishment is drawn from centralization.

American Republicanism Suppressed but Not Defeated

Yet the republican disposition, best exemplified in Jefferson's "empire of liberty" and his teaching about "ward republics," has not died out. Although Americans are no longer Althusian *symbiotes* in a voluntary federation of republics, but are now taxpaying *subjects* of the second body of the king, they continue to describe themselves in republican language, with its favorable connotations of human scale—even though that language systematically *misdescribes* their experience. Lincoln described America as our *homestead* and a *family* and the States as *counties*. Bill Clinton held *town hall* meetings through satellite aimed at some 300 million Americans—as if such a mass could be considered a town. Franklin Roosevelt held cozy *fireside* chats on radio before millions. All of this warm, human-scale republican language hides from us our true condition as subjects of the second body of the king and reconciles us to it.

But the persistence of this language also shows that the historic memory of republican liberty is deep and haunts American political discourse at every turn. The regime cannot describe itself without stealing the favorable human-scale connotations of republican language and painting itself as something it is not. And this suggests that Americans are still open to authentic republican speech and conduct. If that tradition is to be revived, it must be by thinking through its insistence—from Aristotle to Althusius, Hume, and Jefferson—that republics should be small or, if large, should conform to the presumption of human scale either through federation, with the right of lawful secession, or in some such way as sketched out in Hume's large republic.

That the republican tradition's insistence on size and scale is not dead is suggested by Kennan, who, as we have seen, argued that America had grown simply too large for the purposes of republican self-government and that we should begin a public debate on how to divide it in the direction of a more human scale. He asked us to imagine a number of federal unions on the continent, forming an American commonwealth of federations of States. Though this will cause some to panic, Kennan was proposing nothing new. What he suggested was simply a recasting in contemporary terms of Jefferson's "empire of liberty."

To appreciate Kennan's point, we should pause to consider just how large the United States is. If California were an independent country, it would have the eighth largest GDP in the world; that of Texas slightly less than Russia's; that of Florida equal to Mexico's; and New York State roughly half of Great Britain's. And there are *forty-six* other States to consider, each of which could easily be an independent country. Contrary to Lincoln, the American States do not look like "counties" but more like *countries*, and some quite large ones at that.[36]

Or to put the matter of size and scale in a different light, suppose the Union were divided into a number of federations, as Jefferson and Kennan imagined. The South (if Oklahoma were included) would have the third-largest GDP in the world, after Japan and China. The North would rank fifth, a fraction below Germany . The West would be in seventh place, slightly after France. The Midwest would rank eighth, followed by Great Britain. The Northwest would be slightly below Russia and above Mexico and Australia. Four of these federations would be in the top-ten largest GDP states in the world. These federations would not only be able to govern themselves; they would be major players in the world.

Division of the Union in the direction of a more human scale is a genuine political possibility open to Americans. That the lives and fortunes of 305 million Americans should be the playthings of an oligarchy in Washington that can act by a majority in Congress of only 269 (and 135 if acting by a quorum) and that the essence of republican life—religion, morals, education, marriage, voting rights, law enforcement, and social welfare—should be decided by nine unelected Supreme Court justices is something no free people whose souls are attuned to the republican tradition would tolerate.

The current Tea Party movement is animated by a dim historic memory of this republican tradition. Yet probably most of its members think that gaining control of Congress, the presidency, and the Supreme Court is the solution. They have for so long absorbed the post-Lincolnian myth of an "indivisible" Union that they have difficulty thinking of State interposition, nullification, and secession as policy options. Instead, they hope to gain control of the second body of the king themselves, so that they can do unto others what has been done unto them.

They think this way because they have forgotten the republican tradition's teaching about the necessary connection between self-government, the rule of law, and a human scale to political order. The Tea Party movement should recall the forgotten question of size and scale and heed Kennan's suggestion that we begin a public debate on how to divide into distinct territorial jurisdictions that unmanageable and out-of-scale artificial corporation known as the United States, which has grown too large for the purposes of self-government.

Tea Party members praise the Constitution and rightly demand that usurpations by the central government cease, but they do not ask themselves at what *scale* the Constitution can effectively operate and protect republican self-government. Article VII stipulates that only *nine* States were needed to ratify the Constitution. Thirteen States were not needed to form the United States, much less fifty. This also implies that even *four* States were sufficient to form a federation, because if the four had not ratified the Constitution, they would have remained under the Articles of Confederation. Alexander Hamilton and John Jay in *The Federalist* observed that those opposed to the new Constitution preferred "three confederacies; one consisting of the four northern, another of the four middle, and a third of the five southern states."[37] New Englanders in 1804 wanted to limit what they called the "good old United States" to the original thirteen States and threatened secession over expanding its size. In an article published in the *New York Herald* on August 18, 1812, Gouverneur Morris, architect and signer of the Constitution, urged secession and the formation of a federation comprising New England and New York.

The first work on the Constitution was *A View of the Constitution of the United States* (1803), by St. George Tucker, known as the "Blackstone of America." It served as a handbook on the Constitution for the first fifty years of its life. Tucker, like Jefferson, held that the right of secession followed from the fact that the Constitution was a compact between sovereign

States, and he laid out the conditions under which a State could lawfully secede from the compact.[38]

The next early work on the Constitution of national importance was *A View of the Constitution of the United States* (1825), by William Rawle, a leader in the Pennsylvania Bar, friend of George Washington and Benjamin Franklin, and early abolitionist. Rawle too believed that the Constitution was a compact between the States and that, consequently, a State could secede: "The secession of a state from the Union depends on the will of the people of such state. The people alone, as we have already seen, hold the power to alter their constitution."[39] Like Tucker, Rawle carefully laid out the conditions for lawful secession. His work was West Point's text on the Constitution from 1825 to 1840. It was reviewed by Boston's prestigious *North American Review* in 1826 and pronounced "a safe and intelligent guide" to the Constitution. The reviewer found no difficulty with the argument that secession is constitutional, which dominates the last chapter, titled "Of the Union."[40] This should not be surprising, since from 1804 to 1814 New Englanders seriously considered secession. In the 1850s, there was a movement among mid-Atlantic States to form a "Central Confederacy" distinct from the radicalism of both New England and the Deep South. It would include the mid-Atlantic States, Southern border States, and contiguous States to the west.[41]

From the 1830s on, abolitionists argued for secession of the North from the Union. The American Anti-Slavery Society passed the following resolution: "That the Abolitionists of this country should make it one of the primary objects of this agitation to dissolve the American Union."[42] This was also the view of the *Douglass Monthly*, printed by Frederick Douglass. Abolitionist Horace Greeley, editor of the *New York Tribune*, wrote on February 23, 1861, after the Confederacy was formed: "We have repeatedly said . . . that the great principle embodied by Jefferson in the Declaration of Independence, that governments derive their powers from the consent of the governed is sound and just; and that . . . if the cotton States, or the gulf States only, choose to form an independent nation, they have a clear moral right to do so. Whenever it shall be clear that the great body of Southern people have become conclusively alienated from the Union; and anxious to escape from it, we will do our best to forward their views."[43]

These Americans did not think that the Union was "indivisible." And it had already divided into two federations when Greeley wrote the words just quoted. If nine States were sufficient to form the United States in 1789, why were not eleven States sufficient to form the Confederate States in 1861? These are questions about size and scale that have long been suppressed by the post-Lincolnian myth of an "indivisible" unitary American state—a legacy not of the framers but of emulators of the French Revolution.

Republicanism and Secession, or How Big Is Too Big?

Size and scale, however, did attract attention during the George W. Bush administration, when its spokesmen talked of forming a North American Economic Union. The fear was similar to that of the Anti-Federalists who opposed the Union of 1789, namely that economic integration would eventually lead to political integration. Mexico has thirty-one states, and Canada has ten provinces. A union of the two would be forty-one states. Why not integrate these with the fifty American States to form a North American Union dedicated to liberty, prosperity, justice, and human rights for all? How could Americans object to this, especially if we suppose that its constitution would be exactly the same as the U.S. Constitution, the only difference being that instead of fifty States there would be ninety-one? And if it is said that this would be too large and unwieldy, is this not also true of the current Union of fifty states? How many States beyond the original nine required by the Constitution can one include without practically transforming the Constitution into an anti-republican instrument? Has it not already been so transformed? There either is a limit or there is not. If there is, it should be an important part of current political discourse. But it is not.

When the League of Nations was formed, it was a club to which only large states could belong. Today that attitude has changed. The United Nations recognizes small states because so many have been produced since World War II by secession. Of the states recognized in the world today, over half are five million or less, a third are one million or less, and the rest are 500,000 or less. Fifty-two are 100,000 or less, twenty-four are 10,000 or less, and thirteen are smaller than the territory of Washington, D.C. One is smaller in area than the Washington Mall: the Vatican.

Today there is hardly a limit on how small a state can be. Indeed international commerce and advances in transportation and communication make it easier, and more rational, to have small states than ever before. There is no reason why an order of states, even at the size of the illustrious classical Greek, ancient medieval, and early modern republics, could not flourish today. Those small republics were in the range of 200,000 or so. It might be desirable that their contemporary counterparts be larger, either in the manner of a medium-size Althusian federation of republics or a large republic as sketched out by David Hume. But the point is there is no necessity that they be larger than the ancient republics.

As late as the 1850s, Fernando Wood, the mayor of New York, argued that New York should secede and declare itself a free city and free-trade zone: "As a free city, with but nominal duty on imports, the local Government could be supported without taxation upon her people. Thus we could live free from taxes, and have cheap goods nearly duty free."[44]

At that time, New York's population was 800,000. Today it is some 8 million. In 1969, twice Pulitzer Prize-winning author

Norman Mailer ran for mayor of New York on a platform of seceding to form the fifty-first State in the Union. He argued that the city could be divided into a number of Swiss-type cantons with considerable autonomy over local affairs. Some of these, for example, might require religious attendance; others might exclude any religious establishment in their jurisdiction. Mailer described himself as a "left conservative." But what he was actually defending was the ancient republican tradition in its Jeffersonian idiom.

What he did not fully appreciate is that the power currently concentrated in post-Lincolnian Washington makes it practically impossible that any State (including Mailer's would-be City State of New York) could be so divided as to enjoy the local autonomy Mailer had in mind. Such a division would be struck down as unconstitutional by the Supreme Court's fanciful reading of the Fourteenth Amendment.[45] To enjoy this kind of republican liberty, the States themselves, acting in their sovereign capacity, would have to recall, through acts of interposition and nullification, those reserved powers under the Tenth Amendment they have allowed to slip out of their hands.

Nor should we exclude secession from the Union, which would enable a State to have a fresh start. If Switzerland can be a flourishing federation of 27 cantonal states with 7 million people, why cannot a City State of New York with 8 million? The Canadian federation has a population of 34 million, divided into ten provincial states, each of which has the right of state nullification in the area of civil rights and the right of secession.[46] Why cannot California with 37 million be an independent State and divided into a Canadian-type federation of provincial states, each with the right of nullification and secession? The American Union of States is not and never was intended to be an end in itself. Indeed no political association could be an end in itself. The Union was, and should be, an instrument for the benefit of republican liberty in the States and local communities.

The question is whether it could possibly perform that task at the current size and scale. If the answer is no, as Kennan suggests it is, then the burden of proof is on the Union to justify itself. Such arguments might or might not be forthcoming, but the point is that the question has been suppressed for over a century. Kennan is right in urging that it be revived.

It is said that secession must be ruled out absolutely because it causes war. But that is not true. Norway peacefully seceded from Sweden in 1905. Singapore peacefully seceded from the Malaysian federation in 1965 and declared itself a free city of the sort envisioned by New York's Fernando Wood in the 1850s. Fifteen states peacefully seceded from the "indivisible" Soviet Union. And many other examples could be given. Secession does not cause war. War is typically caused by one section of a polity using violence to prevent another section from governing itself.

Secession should once again be considered an option available to an American State and more so today than ever before. It might be that no American city, State, or federation of States wants to withdraw from the Union. But if we retain any allegiance to the values of the republican tradition, we must at least revive the constitutionalism of State interposition and nullification, as a means whereby a State can protect its citizens from unconstitutional acts of the central government, as Thomas Woods has recently urged in *Nullification: How to Resist Federal Tyranny in the Twenty-First Century*. Or we should perhaps consider restructuring the Union in line with something like Hume's large republic, where the State legislatures would jointly act as a national legislature. And if it is said (and I think rightly) that Hume's large republic fits only the size of an American State and would be inapplicable to a federation of continental scale with fifty States, then we should consider Kennan's suggestion of dividing the Union into a number of federations of States, forming an American commonwealth of federations with a central authority hedged in by an explicitly acknowledged right of nullification and secession. In short, revive Jefferson's "empire of liberty."

In any case, it is important for Americans to understand that republicanism and secession (along with interposition and nullification) went hand in hand for the founding generation and continued up to the resurrection of the second body of the king after the war to suppress secession. That is the most noble part of the American political tradition—at least it is for those whose souls are attuned to the republican tradition, which is deeply rooted even today in American history, law, memory, and language. That tradition can be recovered and made topical again whenever Americans choose to do so.

The republican tradition prior to the French Revolution spoke with one voice that *size as such* matters. Aristotle, the first great philosopher of the republican tradition, said, "A great state is not the same as a populous one."[47] This followed from his teaching that everything in nature has a size appropriate to its function: "To the size of states there is a limit, as there is to other things, plants, animals, implements, for none of these retain their natural power when they are too large or too small, but they wholly lose their nature or are spoiled."[48] When a healthy cell grows too large, it divides into two cells. It is the cancerous cell that no longer knows how to stop growing. That artificial corporation, created by the States over two centuries ago, called the "United States" has, over time, metastasized into a cancerous growth on a federation of continental scale, sucking republican vitality out of States and local communities. The natural chemotherapy for this peculiar condition is and can only be some revived form of State interposition, nullification, or secession. If these are rejected out of hand as heresies (as our nationalist historians have taught since the late nineteenth century), then we can no longer, in good faith, describe ourselves as enjoying a republican style of government, whether of the form advocated by Aristotle, Althusius, Jefferson, or Hume.

"To the Size of States There Is a Limit": Measurements for the Success of a State

Kirkpatrick Sale

Yes, Aristotle declared there to be a limit to the size of states: "a limit, as there is to other things, plants, animals, implements; for none of these retain their natural power when they are too large . . . , but they either wholly lose their nature, or are spoiled," so he said.[1] But really, what the hell did he know? He lived at a time when the entire population of the world was somewhere around 120 million people. The population of the Greek-speaking city states, which were *not* united in a nation, in all may have been 8 million, and Athens, where he lived, considered a large city, would have been around 160,000 people. Limits? He couldn't even *imagine* a world (ours) of 6.8 billion, a nation (China) of 1.3 billion, or a city (Tokyo) of 36 million. How is he going to help us?

It is because, firstly, he *did* know that there are limits: "Experience shows that a very populous city can rarely, if ever, be well governed; since all cities which have a reputation for good government have a limit of population. We may argue on grounds of reason, and the same result will follow: for law is order, and good law is good order; but a very great multitude cannot be orderly."[2] And it doesn't matter if that city is 1 million or 36 million—political entities at such sizes could certainly not be democratic in any sense, could not possibly function with anything approaching efficiency, and could exist only with great inequities of wealth and material comfort.

And because, secondly, he *did* know that *human beings* are of a certain limited size of brain and comprehension and that putting them in the aggregate does not make them any smarter—or as another philosopher, Lemuel Gulliver, once said, "Reason does not extend itself with the bulk of the body." There is a human scale to human politics, defined by human nature, that functions well only in such aggregations as do not overstress and overburden the quite capable and ingenious but limited human brain and human capacity.

Aristotle thought mostly in terms of cities, not knowing nations, but even if we may extend those units with the experience of 2,000 more years to larger units such as nations, they have to be limited: limited by human nature and human experience. And it is with that maxim of Aristotle's that we now may start contemplating what in today's world would constitute the ideal, or let us say the optimum, size of a state, with these two overriding criteria: "sufficient," in Aristotle's words, "or a good life in the political community"—that would be some form of democracy—and "the largest number which suffices for the purposes of a good life"[3]—that would be efficiency. Democracy and efficiency.

And mark well—this is not some sort of idle philosopher's quest. It is, or could be, the foundation of a serious reordering of our political world, and a reordering such as the process of secession—indeed, *only* the process of secession, as I see it— could provide. We have abundant evidence that a state as large as 305 million people is ungovernable. Did not Katrina and the BP oil disaster prove that, or runaway health costs and broken borders, or the failure of education, alternative energy, climate change, housing, job creation, and a thousand other social ills unmet? Bloated and corrupted beyond its ability to address, much less solve, any of the problems as an empire it has created, it is a blatant failure. So let us be bold to ask, what could replace it, and at what size? The answer, as will appear, is the independent States, that is to say nations, of America.[4]

Let us start by looking at real-world figures of modern-day nations to give us some clue as to population sizes that actually work.

Of all the world's political entities—there are 223 of them, counting the smallest independent islands—45 are below 250,000 people, 67 below 1 million, and 108 below 5 million. *In fact, 50 percent of nations are below 5.5 million,* and a full 58 percent are smaller than Switzerland's population of 7.7 million.[1] Obviously, most countries in the world function with relatively small populations. And looking at the nations that are recognized models of statecraft, there are eight of them even below 500,000—Luxembourg, Malta, Iceland, Barbados, Andorra, Liechtenstein, Monaco, and San Marino. The example of Iceland, with the world's oldest parliament and an unquestioned beacon of democracy (banking troubles aside), suggests that 319,000 people is all you would need. Going up a bit in size, there are another six models of good governance below 5 million: Singapore, Norway, Costa Rica, Ireland, New Zealand, and Estonia.

Next, let us look at the size of the most prosperous nations ranked by per-capita GDP.[6] (Parenthetically let me say that I realize GDP is a crude and entirely uncritical measure of economic worth and reflects all kinds of growth, much undesirable, but until we have nations devoted to steady-state economies instead, this is the best way to gauge economic performance.) Eighteen of the top twenty by GDP rank (a total of twenty-seven countries because of ties) are small, under 5 million, and all but *one* of the top ten are under 5 million (that's the U.S., at tenth place, the others being, in order, Liechtenstein, Qatar, Luxembourg, Bermuda, Norway, Kuwait, Jersey, Singapore, and Brunei). The average size of those nine is 1.9 million. The average size of all twenty-seven of the top economic nations, excluding the U.S., is 5.1 million.

You are beginning to get the picture.

Let us take another measure—freedom, as reckoned by three different rating sources, Freedom House, the *Wall Street Journal,* and *The Economist,* using measures of civil liberties, open elections, free media, and the like.[7] Of the fourteen states reckoned freest in the world, nine of them (64 percent) have populations below Switzerland at 7.7 million and eleven below Sweden at 9.3 million, and the only sizeable states are Canada, the United Kingdom, and Germany, the largest, at 81 million.

There is one other measure of freedom put out by Freedom House, ranking all the nations of the world according to political rights and civil liberties, and there are only forty-six nations with perfect scores.[8] The majority of those are under 5 million in population, and indeed seventeen of them are even under 1 million. That is rather astonishing in itself. And only fourteen of the forty-six free nations are over 7.5 million. Excluding the United States, whose reputation for freedom is fully belied by its incarceration of 2.3 million people, 25 percent of the world's prisoners, and excluding the United Kingdom, Spain, and Poland, *the average population of the free states of the world is approximately 5 million.*

Let me finally take several other national rankings. Literacy: of the forty-four countries that claim a literacy rate of 99 or better (I say claim, since it is hard to verify), only fifteen are large, while twenty-nine (66 percent) are below 7.5 million.[9] Health: measured by the World Health Organization, twelve of the top twenty are under 7 million, none over 65 million.[10] In a recent ranking of happiness and standard of living by sociologist Steven D. Hales, the top nations were Norway, Iceland, Sweden, the Netherlands, Australia, Luxembourg, Switzerland, Canada, Ireland, Denmark, Austria, and Finland, all small but Canada and Australia.[11] And a "sustainable society index" created by two scholars, adding in environmental and ecological factors, ranks *only* smaller countries in the top ten—in order, Sweden, Switzerland, Norway, Finland, Austria, Iceland, Vietnam, Georgia, New Zealand, and Latvia.[12]

Enough of that—the point, I trust, is well and simply made. A nation can be not only viable and sustainable at quite small population sizes, a model of more-or-less democratic and efficient government, but in fact can provide all the necessary qualities for superior living. Indeed, the figures seem to suggest that, though it is certainly possible to thrive at sizes under a million people, there is a more-or-less optimum size for a successful state, somewhere in the range of 3 to 5 million people.

Next, let us take a quick look at *geographic* sizes of successful nations.[13] A great many nations are surprisingly small— underlining the point, often missed by critics of secession, that a nation does not have to be self-sufficient to operate well in the modern world. In fact, 85 of the 223 political entities counted by the United Nations are under 10,000 square miles— that is to say, the size of Vermont or smaller—and they include Israel, El Salvador, the Bahamas, Qatar, Lebanon, Luxembourg, Singapore, and Andorra.

And if we go back to that measure of economic strength, the GDP per capita, small nations prove to be decidedly advantageous. Of the top twenty ranked nations (twenty-seven in all including ties), all but eight are small in area, under 35,000 square miles, the global median (the size of South Carolina), and two of those eight are Norway and Sweden, technically large but effectively small when excluding their empty northern areas. In other words, 77 percent of the prosperous nations are small. And most of them are quite small indeed, under 10,000 square miles (Liechtenstein, Qatar, Luxembourg, Bermuda, Kuwait, Jersey, Singapore, Brunei, Guernsey, the Cayman Islands, Hong Kong, Andorra, San Marino, the British Virgin Islands, and Gibraltar).

All this is proof positive that economically successful nations need not be large in geographic size In fact, it is strongly suggestive that large size may be a hindrance. The reason for this is that administrative, distribution, transportation, and similar transaction costs obviously have to rise, perhaps exponentially, as geographic size increases. Control and communication also become more difficult to manage over long distances, often to the point where central authority and governance become nearly impossible, and as all the lines and signals become more complex, the ability to manage efficiently is severely diminished.

Small, let's face it, is not only beautiful but bountiful.

Once that important idea is understood, a further logical argument can be derived from it: that in many cases a smallish nation might find it desirable to divide up even further so as to take advantage of smaller areas for more efficient economic functions. This might be outright secession in some places, where it would simply be good economic sense—and good political and cultural sense as well. But it might also take the form of economic and political devolution, giving smaller areas autonomy and power without outright secession, much as Switzerland is the model of.

In fact, I wish to propose, out of these figures and even more so out of the history of the world, that there is a Law of Government Size, and it goes like this: *Economic and social misery increases in direct proportion to the size and power of the central government of a nation.*[14]

In testing this law in history—Sale's Law, as I like to think of it—let me begin with Arnold Toynbee's great and justifiably classic study of human civilization, whose primary conclusion is that the next-to-last stage of any society, leading directly to its final stage of collapse, is "its forcible political unification in a centralized state," and he gives as evidence the Roman Empire; the Ottoman, Bengal, and Mongol empires; the Tokugawa Shogunate; and ultimately the Spanish, British, French, and Portuguese empires. The consolidation of nations into powerful empires leads not to shining periods of peace and prosperity and the advance of human betterment but to increasing restriction, warfare, autocracy, crowding, inequality, poverty, and starvation.

The reason for all this is not mysterious. As a government grows, it expands both its bureaucratic might over domestic affairs and its military might over external ones. Money must be found for this expansion, and it comes either from taxation, which leads to higher prices and ultimately inflation—result, as Mr. Micawber might say, social misery—or from printing new money, which also leads to higher prices and inflation—result, again, social misery. Wealth is also thought to come from conquest and colonization, enlarging spoils through warfare, but it comes at the price of imposing increased government control, military conscription at home ("war is the health of states," as Randolph Bourne put it), violence, bloodshed, and misery for one's own army and civilians and opposing forces abroad. Result, economic and social misery.

I have detailed much of this in my book *Human Scale,* but let me just give a capsulated version here, concentrating on Europe. There have been four major periods of great state consolidation and enlargement in the last thousand years:

1. From 1150 to 1300 AD, royal dynasties replaced medieval baronies and city states in England, Aquitaine, Sicily, Aragon, and Castile, resulting in rampant inflation of nearly 400 percent and almost incessant wars, with increasing battle casualties from a few hundred to more than 1 million.

2. From 1525 to 1650, with the consolidation of national power through standing armies, royal taxation, central banks, civilian bureaucracies, and state religions Europe saw an inflation rate of more than 700 percent in just 125 years and an unprecedented expansion of wars, a war intensity seven times greater than Europe had seen before, with warfare casualties increasing to maybe 8 million, maybe 5 million in the Thirty Years War alone.

3. From 1775 to 1815, the period of modern state government over most of Europe, including national police forces, conscripted armies, and centralized state power a la the Code Napoleon, there was an inflation rate of more than 250 percent in just forty years, in 1815 the highest at any time until 1920s, with war casualties up to 15 million (maybe 5 million in the Napoleonic Wars) in that short period.

Finally, in period 4, from 1910 to 1970, familiar to us, all European nations consolidated and expanded power, known in many places as totalitarianism (known in the U.S., though we had all the components of totalitarianism—consolidated central power, a national bank, income tax, national police, conscription, imperial presidency—as freedom and democracy), resulting in the worst depression in history and inflation of 1,400 percent and, of course, the two most ruinous wars in all human history contributing to casualties, mostly deaths, of 100 million or more.

The inevitable conclusion is that the larger the state, the more economic disasters and military casualties: the Law of Government Size.

Now that we have established the virtue of smallness worldwide, let us apply these figures to the United States and see what they tell us.[15]

Of the fifty States, just over half (twenty-nine) are below 5 million people. Half the population lives in forty States that average out to 3.7 million people; the other half is in the ten largest States. In the 3-to-5-million population class, there are ten States and one colony that I am suggesting would be ideal secession candidates—Iowa, Connecticut, Oklahoma, Oregon, Puerto Rico, Kentucky, Louisiana, South Carolina, Alabama, Colorado, and Mississippi. Another thirteen between 1 to 3 million would be ideal—Montana, Rhode Island, Hawaii, New Hampshire, Maine, Idaho, Nebraska, West Virginia, New Mexico, Nevada, Utah, Kansas, and Arkansas. Another eight below a million but larger than Iceland would also be ideal, and that includes beloved Vermont. In other words, thirty-one of the States (plus Puerto Rico) fall in a range where similar sizes in the rest of the world have produced successful independent nations. Those are the candidates for successful secession.

Add to that the lessons from geographic size. We have already seen that eighty-four political areas in the world are smaller than Vermont, the second smallest U.S. State. Now let us see how the States measure up to the world figures.[16] The median U.S. State area is roughly 58,000 square miles—twenty-five States are smaller than that, twenty-five bigger. If all of those under 58,000 were independent, they would match seventy-nine other nations in the world, among them Greece, Nicaragua, Iceland, Hungary, Portugal, Austria, the Czech Republic, Ireland, Sri Lanka, Denmark, Switzerland, the Netherlands, and Taiwan. In other words, size is no hindrance whatsoever to successfully operating as a nation in the world—and, as I have suggested, small size seems indeed to be a virtue.

It need not be all about population or geographic sizes—one might factor in cultural cohesion, developed infrastructure, historical identity, and suchlike—but that certainly seems to me to be the sensible place to start when considering viable States. And since the experience of the world has shown—indeed, over and over again in the formation of nations since the nineteenth century—that entities in the 3-to-5-million range may be optimum for governance and efficiency, and some within a 1-to-3-million range, that is how to begin assessing bodies for their secessionist potential and their chances of national success.

I hope all this Aristotelian examination is not regarded as a mere academic exercise, though a great deal of exercise, I assure you, has gone into it. I believe that it establishes an impetus for Americans who understand that their national government (no oxymoron intended) is broken and cannot be fixed (there were 86 percent of them in a national poll not long ago)[17] and who realize that the *only hope* to reenergize American politics and recreate the vibrant collection of democracies that the founding generation of the eighteenth century envisioned is to create truly sovereign States through peaceful, popular, powerful secession.

Let me underscore that conclusion: the *only* hope is secession.

Too Big to Fail?
Lessons from the Demise of the Soviet Union

Yuri Maltsev

The dispute between the market order and socialism is no less than a matter of survival. To follow socialist morality would destroy much of present humankind and impoverish much of the rest.

—Friedrich August Von Hayek

The fall of the Berlin Wall, followed in 1991 by the collapse of Europe's last major empire, the Union of Soviet Socialist Republics, changed the course of world history to an extent not yet fully understood today. That collapse exposed the total bankruptcy of big governments based on central planning and an overregulated command economy: the U.S.S.R. was too big *not* to fail. It should teach us the lesson that any centralized tyranny—whether it emanates from Moscow or Washington, D.C.—leads to corruption, violations of property and other human rights, misery, murder, and eventually dismal failure. Hence it provides a better perspective on our own situation, on the dangers of our own big and out-of-control government pursuing socialist schemes.

Let us look at a little history.

Political Economy of the U.S.S.R.

Kremlin leaders realized from the first that the only way of managing an economy under socialism was not with "worker self-management" and the like but with direct government coercion based on mass murder and forced labor. The absolute command economy and the monstrous "killer state" were created. Management of production and distribution was performed by the central government, enforced by mass deportations and the slaughter of "bourgeois intellectuals" and the natural elite.[1] By secret decrees of Vladimir Lenin and Josef Stalin, clergy, "capitalists" (whatever that meant), military and police officers, as well as most politicians (including even those who supported socialism and the Soviets) were designated either for an immediate slaughter or slow death in the dreadful concentration camps of the Gulag. The ultimate human toll of Soviet socialism is estimated at over sixty million who perished in the Gulag system during Stalin's collectivizations, purges, campaigns against "unearned" incomes, and other devilish experiments.

The system that replaced the market was that of central planning, with rationing of means of production as well as of housing, education, healthcare and consumer goods, and the creation of non-economic institutions of compulsion to work based on slave labor in gulags, collective farms, and industry.

Western historians focus on the terror against intellectuals and political opponents, but over half of all executions took place in the countryside. The "liquidation of the kulaks" (relatively wealthy peasants) ended up in 10 million of them deported to Siberia with their families, where most died of starvation and hypothermia. In Ukraine, Stalin starved to death over 7 million peasants, and similar famines with catastrophic results were organized in the Volga region and South Russia. Local bureaucrats also deported orphans, the elderly, and the handicapped to their deaths in the Gulag system.

Russian socialists were the first to abolish property rights, which were declared "a sanctification of capitalist oppression and exploitation." They pursued the expropriation of private property with fanatical zeal and unprecedented brutality. Like the other versions of socialism—Italian Fascism and

German National Socialism—Soviet communism provides credible evidence that the abolition of private property leads to the extinction of other personal rights and freedoms, as well as the creation of monstrous centralized tyrannies and killer states.

It is still common in academia to identify the socialists as the Left and the Nazis as the extreme Right, as if they stood on opposite ends of the ideological spectrum. But in fact, under both fascist and socialist regimes, government bureaucracy completely controls the production. It decides what shall be produced, how much, for whom, when, and how. The difference between the systems is that the German and Italian patterns did indeed allow—or, more accurately, tolerated—private property. However, it was "property" in a restricted sense— not the unrestricted private ownership of Roman law and nineteenth-century Europe but rather conditional possession, under which the state, the owner of last resort, reserved to itself the right to interfere with and confiscate assets that, in its judgment, were unsatisfactorily used. And the governments of fascist Italy and Nazi Germany directed production decisions, curbed entrepreneurship and the labor market, and determined wages and interest rates by centralized authority similar to that in the socialist states.

The United States is very close today to this model, as indeed are most centralized Western welfare states with confiscatory taxation, nationalization of major industries and the financial sector, affirmative-action policies, environmental regulations, and other policies undermining property rights.

With the end of private property, the price system, necessary for an efficient economy, ceased to exist in the Soviet official economy, although in hiding there was a fiercely prosecuted black market. Efficient allocation of resources became not even theoretically possible. Karl Marx's goal of the social regulation of production upon a definite plan was finally achieved, but it led to a colossal waste of resources, shortages of almost everything, and the greatest loss of human life in history.

This system survived relatively intact until the economic reforms of the 1960s associated with Nikita Khrushchev's campaign of "destalinization." Economic discussion encouraged by this campaign led to proposals by such reform-minded economists as A. M. Birman, E. G. Lieberman, and L. V. Kantorovich, who persuaded the Communist Party leadership to understand the necessity of reforming the Soviet economic order on principles of decentralization, shifting responsibilities from federal authority to localities. Younger participants in this conversation—L. I. Abalkin, A. G. Aganbegyan, N. I. Petrakov, B. V. Rakitsky, and others—twenty years later would become close confidants of Mikhail Gorbachev and the economic architects of *perestroika*. Instead of the complete overhaul of socialist slavery, they proposed a series of measures to introduce an oxymoronic "market socialism," including profit, reorientation of the incentive system to indicators measuring sales, abandonment of centralized direct funding of enterprises, and the introduction of self-governance and self-financing. But even so, in an economy under total government monopoly with no private property, there could be no means of rational economic calculation. (Providing opportunities for secession of republics or a market-price system were not even mentioned in these discussions.)

These piecemeal measures exposed the futility of reforming socialism, the absurdity of a "third way" between slavery and freedom that still occupies many minds in Western academia. They made clear the analysis of Ludwig Von Mises, who wrote in *Human Action:*

Private ownership of the means of production (market economy or capitalism) and public ownership of the means of production (socialism or communism or "planning") can be neatly distinguished. Each of these systems of society's economic organization is open to a precise and unambiguous description and definition. They can never be confounded with one another; they cannot be mixed or combined; no gradual transition leads from one of them to another; they are mutually incompatible.[2]

By creating a system that redistributed resources between the small number of firms that were profitable (whatever this means under central planning) and the vast majority that were unprofitable, the Soviet party and government *apparatchiks* suppressed any attempt by the enterprise managers to become less dependent on the state planning mechanism. The system punished efficient enterprises and supported the losers. However, it was the masses, not the bureaucrats, who bore the brunt of the resulting state waste, as the bureaucrats set the price of labor in the U.S.S.R. at a bare subsistence level.

The absurdity of the system was clearest with the introduction of the concept of profit. Profit under these "reforms" became a planned category, calculated as a normative percentage of the costs. This "high cost-high profit" approach was one of the catalysts for the total collapse of the system during Gorbachev's *perestroika*.

For a while, huge losses in the system were covered by foreign currency obtained from the sales of oil, gas, and other natural resources and credits readily provided by Western governments and banks. Since the mid-1970s, over $300 billion was spent in this way. The Kremlin bureaucrats, who had to purchase grain in the world market in order to make up for domestic production failures, used these hard-currency reserves to feed the population. Russia and Ukraine—"breadbaskets of Europe" before the First World War—became the world's largest importers of grain.

By the mid-1980s, the deterioration of the Soviet economy reached a critical point. More than half the state business enterprises were failing and survived only because of huge government bailouts and handouts. The agricultural sector, with a collective farm system based on state ownership of land and forced labor, required an infusion of more than 100 billion rubles a year to support.

With the election (by eleven Politburo members) of Gorbachev as general secretary of the Communist Party in March 1985, reformers got a new hope. Gorbachev, without knowing or wishing it, gave the process of change a powerful impulse, which determined the future development not only of his own country but also of other states and nations enslaved in the world socialist empire. Being a devoted socialist, Gorbachev was trying to solve the problems of declining productivity and negative economic growth in the 1980s by introducing reforms that would put the U.S.S.R. on par with the developed market economies of the West.

This system, *perestroika*, was the last and most far reaching attempt to reform Soviet-type socialism while preserving its fundamental features. "The socialist choice of the people," as Gorbachev in his time liked to say, "should be cherished and preserved." But in fact, *perestroika* led to a breakthrough out of socialism and laid the foundations for the post-socialist development of the country. This breakthrough had nothing to do with the ill-devised and badly implemented economic reforms. The true reason for the demise of socialism and the Soviet empire was the weakening of political control and removal of coercion from a system that had been glued together only by coercion. With *perestroika*, the ailing regime lost its repressive impetus, and the socialist economic mechanism, built upon repression, fell like a house of cards.

The Empire Unravels

The centralized empire began to unravel in the 1980s and the Soviet republics began considering full independence from

Moscow, while the autonomous republics of Russia and Russian regions demanded more autonomy. At first the leaders of the republics and regional autonomies of the U.S.S.R. were thinking of nullification as an acceptable legal measure by which the states could protect their citizens' rights. Even pro-Union, pro-Gorbachev politicians considered nullification as a possible safety valve for preventing complete secession, for they saw that if there was to be no escape from onerous and destructive Moscow authority within the Soviet Union, then the only way to escape it was to secede.

The Baltic States were the first to announce withdrawal from the Soviet Union, as their parliaments became radical enough and tired enough of repeated acts of nullification of laws and decrees emanating from the Kremlin. Lithuania, which had suffered a Moscow-staged bloodbath in January 1990 when twenty-six Lithuanians were mowed to death by Soviet tanks in Vilnius, was the first republic to declare its independence, on March 11, 1990. Signed by all members of the formerly rubber stamp Lithuanian Supreme Soviet, the Lithuania Independence Act (*Aktas del Lietuvos nepriklausomos valstybes atstatymo*) emphasized "restoration and legal continuity of the old Lithuania nation, which was illegally occupied by the Soviet Union in June 1940 as a part of the criminal Molotov-Ribbentrop Pact." Another Baltic state, Estonia, began the process of secession in mid-1988 by the nullification of Soviet legislative acts and other government orders coming from Moscow. Again, a formerly rubber stamp body, the Estonian Supreme Soviet on February 23, 1989, ordered the hammer-and-sickle flag of the Estonian S.S.R. replaced with the blue-black-white flag of independent Estonia.

With the decline of the Estonian Communist Party in the late 1980s, other political movements, groupings, and parties moved to fill the power vacuum. The first and most important was the Estonian Popular Front, established in April 1988 with its own platform, leadership, and broad constituency, followed by the Greens and the dissident-led Estonian National Independence Party. By 1989, the political spectrum had widened and new parties were formed and re-formed almost daily.

The republic's Supreme Soviet transformed itself into an authentic representative body. It passed an early declaration of sovereignty (November 16, 1988), a law making the Estonian language the official language of the country (January 1989), a law on economic independence (May 1989) confirmed by the U.S.S.R. Supreme Soviet that November, and local and republic election laws stipulating residency requirements for voting and running for office (August, November 1989).

Although the majority of Estonia's numerous Russian-speaking Soviet-era immigrants did not support full independence, they were divided in their goals for autonomy from Moscow. In March 1990, 18 percent of Russian speakers supported the idea of a fully independent Estonia, up from 7 percent the previous autumn, and by early 1991 only a small minority of them was opposed to full independence.

The first freely elected parliament during the Soviet era in Estonia passed a Sovereignty Declaration on November 16, 1988, and independence resolutions on May 8, 1990, and renamed the Estonian S.S.R. the Republic of Estonia. On August 20, 1991, the Estonian parliament issued a Declaration of Independence from the Soviet Union, recognized on September 6, 1991, by the Supreme Soviet of the U.S.S.R. In 1992, Heinrich Mark, the prime minister of the Republic of Estonia in exile, presented his credentials to the newly elected president of Estonia, Lennart Meri.

It was the defeat of the coup in August 1991 in Moscow that led to the total collapse of the U.S.S.R. Boris Yeltsin, president of the Russian Federation, should be credited with a major contribution to its final demise, because immediately after the failed coup he signed a "Decree on Dissolution of Activities" of the governing bodies of the Communist Party. As a result, Gorbachev, leader of the party, represented only himself.

In December 1991 in Minsk, leaders of Russia, Ukraine, and Belarus, the founding countries of the U.S.S.R., met and terminated the Union Treaty of 1922 engineered by Stalin and declared their intention to establish a Commonwealth of Independent States (CIS), a loose international organization modeled after the British Commonwealth. Eleven of the fifteen former Soviet Republics decided to join. Only Lithuania, Latvia, Estonia, and Georgia declined. Later that month, Gorbachev resigned and the Soviet Union formally ceased to exist.

Thereafter, the process of disintegration and secession spread over the Russian Federation itself. Tartastan and Chechnya came up with declarations of independence and sovereignty. In 1992-93, Vologda, almost 100 percent ethnic Russian, declared its independence from Russia, and the Moscow Regional Council declared an independent Republic of Moscovia. In Chelyabinsk, the Regional Council returned the city and the region to their pre-revolutionary name, Yekaterinburg (after Empress Catherine I), and proclaimed an independent Ural Republic. Secessionist movements were also very strong in oil-and-mineral-resources-rich Siberia and the Far East.

Lessons Learned

The major lesson to be learned from the spectacular failure of the Soviet command system is that it failed due to internal contradictions, not human error. Some observers, attracted by the appealing but illusory features of the statist command system—equality, job rights, and managed growth—may conclude that the system itself was sound but simply could not succeed because of some technical or cultural factors. Both scientific apologists and lay sympathizers of socialism in the West have tried to persuade us that the collapse of communism resulted from human error rather than a systemic failure. (The radical Left even questions the very existence of socialism in Russia during the twentieth century, calling it rather "State Capitalism," according to which it was capitalism that "failed again.") But that simply is not true, and we should all be thankful to the Soviets that they proved conclusively that socialism does not work. No one can say they did not have enough power or enough bureaucracy or enough planners or they did not go far enough.

The "most audacious attempt in human history to abolish private property has ended in disaster," the scholar Richard Pipes declared. "It is unlikely to be repeated as long as the memory of that calamity remains fresh."[3]

Unfortunately, despite the collapse of socialism and communism in Russia and Eastern Europe, socialism as a theory is still alive and growing in Western academia. The existence today of a dozen American Marxist journals and more than four hundred American university courses given per semester on Marxism prove that, for some, "the only lesson of history is that it does not teach us anything." Thousands of Western academics belong to a thriving industry of Marxist studies. The gap created by the collapse of communism in the East, which put a screeching halt to Marxist studies in Eastern Europe and Russia and disbanded numerous institutions of Marxism-Leninism there, was immediately filled by Marxist scholars of the West. Another sad legacy of Marxism is the mindset of certain people both in the East and West who still believe that only the Big State could cure economic ills and achieve social justice.

Post-Communist Transition

The major prerequisite for a successful transition from a command economy to economic freedom and efficiency is private property and private decision-making in the allocation of resources. There can be no suspicion on the part of prospective buyers and investors that any industry is being propped up through subsidies or special privileges that distort the prices of shares, products, or services. And an intensive and extensive economic exchange cannot exist or last very long without confidence in the stability and reliability of legal institutions.

The widespread frustration with the "free market" reforms of Yeltsin's and then Vladimir Putin's governments in Russia led to the situation where every new announcement of impeding reform caused perverse public response and where new legislation that was passed ostensibly to increase freedom only increased opportunities for fines and bribes. All economic and fiscal legislation in this period was absolutely inconsistent with legality. Every law that has promised stability in taxation and established rules of economic conduct has been overtly revoked so as to preserve willful government expropriations. Even with the introduction of a 13 percent flat tax in Russia in 2000, there was little tax relief when payroll and other taxes constituted over 50 percent of the national income.

The new class of Russian entrepreneurs is on its way to becoming a rent-seeking private bureaucracy. The source of the bureaucratization of private enterprise in Russia is the same as everywhere else: the destruction of the profit motive by government regulations and taxation. Current economic and political developments in Russia are taking the path towards even more government intervention—away from the Russian but toward the German pattern of socialism, so well described by Von Mises[4]—coupled with a totalitarian political regime of ex-K.G.B. officer Putin.

It has long been a tenet of the Austrian school of economists that there can be no gradual transition between two such distinctively different systems as communism and socialism, and today it has become obvious—even to the World Bank bureaucrats—that they were right. According to the World Bank's study of eight formerly communist states—Estonia, Kyrgyzstan, Latvia, Lithuania, Moldova, Russia, Ukraine, and Uzbekistan—"the countries that have been the most successful in reorienting trade and stabilizing the downward spiral in trade and output are those that reformed the fastest (such as the Baltics)." It is also obvious from the experience of three others—Russia, Byelorussia, and Kazakh—that *gradual* "reform" only provides a convenient excuse to the vested interest of the bureaucrats to change nothing at all; huge government, and industrial and agricultural bureaucracies together with their counterparts in organized crime, are the true beneficiaries of gradual change. As a result, Russia and Kazakhstan experienced "shock without therapy" and became major recipients of the international welfare system run by the U.S. government under the aegis of the World Bank, the International Monetary Fund, and the United Nations and all its sixteen "sister" organizations. It is not surprising that the World Index of Economic Freedom put Russia in 134th place out of 181 countries.

One of the main reasons for Russia's failure under Putin is that the numerous programs for "privatization" did not lead to private property, or to private ownership, but were intended to create "mixed" collective-property ownership, essentially leaving property rights as a monopoly of the state. Some of these "privatization programs" were aimed at providing the opportunity for a workforce to obtain 51 percent of the shares of its enterprise virtually without paying, but the net result was an accumulation of equity and power by the managers of the enterprise, many of whom became the real owners of Russian industry. Other programs intending to promote a balance "between economic efficiency and social justice" (whatever that means in Russian bureaucratic jargon) led to the squandering of state assets by bureaucrats. Even a "radical reformer" such as Yegor Gaidar, while at the helm of the Russian government, repudiated privatization as "unnecessary": "We cannot link the restructuring of regulatory mechanism to full-scale privatization. If we did, we simply wouldn't live enough to see it." Thus years after announced economic reforms, Russia continues to possess the largest and most ineffective public sector in the world, the chief cause of its low standard of living.

A second related reason for Putin's failure is the high level of militarization of the Russian economy and society. The government, by wasting scarce resources on the development of highly sophisticated systems of weapons and on space exploration, completely ignores the basic human needs of its citizens.

Western Investment

Western economic-aid transfers are essentially non-economic in nature and represent purely political decisions motivated by both open and hidden agendas of the donor countries. Private foreign investors in the previous Soviet sphere should look, at a minimum, for these signs: extensive and radical transition plans, provisions for repatriation of earnings, complementary institutional infrastructures, mutually acceptable prices and terms of contract, the prospects of satisfactory financial and economic results, and favorable cultural environment. The more successful a transition economy is in solving the tasks of quickly reforming the economy, the higher the level of investment, including foreign investment, will be. It is no surprise that the leaders in terms of foreign direct investment per head of population are

Estonia and Hungary, countries that succeeded most in freeing their economies.

The short-term possibilities for foreign investment in the Russian economy remain quite limited. The business climate will remain risky as long as investors need to worry about economic instability, lack of reliable currency, political conflicts, and uncertainty about the future of the Russian empire. It is evident that the ways to enhance the dynamic economic development of Russia are to attract foreign capital and secure access to the modern knowhow and methods of management.

In the long run, there are objective prerequisites for foreign capital investment: a skilled labor force and an abundance of natural resources and land. Foreign investments are more likely to be made in economies that are market oriented and genuinely desire direct foreign investment. Tough competition on the world market for foreign capital among both developed and developing market economies has already prompted liberalization of tax and investment regimes, tax holidays, the sharing of risk capital by way of joint-venture arrangements, etc.

A Clear Alternative

The experiences of political and economic transitions in the formerly socialist states unequivocally point to the fact that the Austrian school of economics was absolutely right in defining secured property rights and the rule of law as necessary to achieve a successful transition to a market economy. Success stories can be found in Central and Eastern Europe: Hungary, Poland, Slovenia, the Czech Republic, Estonia, Latvia, and Lithuania are now economically free nations. Moreover, the Balts, Poles, and Slovenians expanded considerably faster than the 2-percent-to-3-percent-a-year global average. Major ingredients of success were radical privatization and an end to sending financial and other resources to Moscow or Belgrade or some other imperial capital. These small countries spectacularly outperformed large ones such as Russia, Ukraine, and Kazakhstan, multinational states with bloated bureaucracies disrespecting property rights, huge public sectors, confiscatory tax systems, expensive military and other wasteful government expenditures, and widespread nepotism, crime, and corruption. There is a strong correlation between economic freedom and rates of economic growth: the free economies of Estonia, Latvia, Lithuania, and Slovenia boast the highest growth rates in Europe, while the overregulated statist regimes of Ukraine, Belarus, and Tajikistan show negative growth rates of -25, -17.1, and -15 percent respectively.

In fact, Estonia was recently ranked fourth in the world in terms of its economic freedom by the World Index of Economic Freedom. This small Baltic country surpasses most of the free world in providing markets with an established rule of law, as well as an overall stable legal environment. Lithuania and Latvia are both following the Estonian example. Even though statists in the West criticize these countries for "undue tax advantages" and "unyielding macroeconomic policies," the fact is that all three Baltic countries have the highest rates of economic growth and lowest inflation rates in Europe.

Conclusions

A market economy cannot function without a legal structure that is consistent with its underlying institutions of private property and freedom of contract. A developed market economy must evolve on the basis of the institutionalization of the rule of law, where the legal code is primarily directed towards defending person and property against invasion, either by the state or private parties.

Governmental decisions must be rooted in the consensus of the governed, acting through structures designed to prevent individual oppression or political tyranny, and procedures that are subject to appraisal by an independent judiciary rendering judgments based on law. That stands in contrast to decisions based on arbitrary fiat of power, political rent-seeking, or personal gain. Thus, a government maintains a framework of security and order within which liberty can be secured. Individual rights of person and property are treated as normatively prior to the government's, and as standards take precedence. Governments are instituted among people so as to secure and protect those rights.

Obviously not only the U.S. government but the governments of a majority of modern states are as far from this ideal as can be imagined. Limitations of property rights are imposed in these nations by welfare-state policies and regulatory requirements. The true burden of these requirements is shared jointly by owners in the form of the reduced market value of their property, by employees of the regulated industries in the form of lower real wages, and by customers in the form of higher prices and fewer choices. Indeed, the entire economy is harmed to the extent that regulation reduces natural comparative advantage and the real growth potential of the economy. The assault on property rights, points out Von Mises, is not always apparent, because it is carried out in the name of "common good" or "social interests," "converting them into a critique of the capitalist system or of the conduct of entrepreneurs."[5]

Complying with regulatory requirements entails both explicit and implicit costs. Explicit costs include the resources used to comply with the regulations, such as the costs of hiring additional employees to process government paperwork. Implicit costs are much higher, involving the lost opportunities from diverting resources into less efficient activities. Both of these regulatory costs are often overlooked in the fog of newspeak rhetoric generated by vested interests, using (and abusing) words such as "social justice," "compassion," "greed," "environmental quality," "wildlife conservation," and "consumer protection."

The most fundamental institution of the market economy is a regime of private property rights. Property rights are moral and legal sanctions to own, control, and possess wealth created by human effort. Without property rights, economic growth and human progress are impossible. The linkage between human effort, the resulting product, and well-being must be secure and stable for economic activity to flourish.

Economic and political systems of nations differ in the amount of planning they do and the extent to which they restrict private ownership of property. Wherever you see shifting, arbitrary, or unstable property rights, you see such poor decimated societies as Belarus, Moldova, and Turkmenistan. The absence of property rights, the "mother" of human rights, inevitably leads to negation of every other right, starting with the first right, a right to life. The utmost importance of property rights for human dignity and prosperity cannot be overestimated. Unfortunately, it is still far from being understood by the majority of people.

Most Likely to Secede:
U.S. Empire and the Emerging Vermont Independence Effort

Rob Williams

> You can't bloat a modest republic into a crapulent empire without sparking one hell of a centrifugal reaction.
> —Bill Kauffman, *Bye Bye Miss American Empire*

> The Gods of the Empire are not the Gods of Vermont.
> —Dennis Steele; 2010 Vermont independent gubernatorial candidate

> Secession is every American's birthright.
> —*Vermont Commons: Voices of Independence* news journal

What's the dirtiest word in U.S. politics? A few hints. It begins with an *s* and, in its verb form, sounds like "succeed." It is a word that even many well-educated Americans have trouble pronouncing, let alone spelling.

It is the founding principle of the United States as a political creation. With help from Benjamin Franklin, John Adams, and the first Continental Congress, Thomas Jefferson enshrined this key political concept as the first action verb—"dissolve"—in the 1776 Declaration of Independence.

It was a constitutionally legitimate and widely affirmed concept, publicly agreed upon by political leaders from both Northern and Southern States, during the first seventy years of the U.S. republic. Numerous new nineteenth-century American States, from Maine to Kentucky, employed it in separating from existing States.

Now mistakenly remembered as an exclusively Southern invention, it was first championed as a regional movement by nineteenth-century New Englanders. And since Pres. Abraham Lincoln's victory over the Southern States in the so-called "Civil War," it has been largely forgotten.

The dirtiest word? Secession.[1]

A little revisionist history is useful.

The eighteenth-century American "revolution," really an English colonial struggle to secede from the British Empire and establish "free and independent states," was built on the secession principle, and both nineteenth-century Northern and Ssouthern political leaders alike embraced the concept. During the early 1800s, New Englanders talked openly for decades about secession, in response to federal abuses of power involving war, militarism, territorial expansion, and immoral confiscation of escaped slaves. And Lincoln's "War to Prevent Southern Secession," popularly but mistakenly remembered as the "Civil War," linked this legitimate nineteenth-century political concept of secession forever to the South, slavery, and racism, largely erasing it from our twentieth-century cultural and historical memory.

These days, the concept of secession is now deemed too "radical," even "treasonous," to be discussed in mainstream political, media, and news circles—until now. Secession, the *s* word, the dirtiest word in U.S. politics, is ready to reenter U.S. political conversation as an old idea, rediscovered, the next big thing, which is funny because secession is about smallness, decentralization, devolution not revolution. And there are signs that Americans of all political stripes are interested.

"Secession is the next radical idea poised to enter mainstream discourse—or at least the realm of the conceivable," writes Empire State denizen Bill Kauffman in his book, *Bye Bye Miss American Empire: Neighborhood Patriots, Backcountry Rebels, and Their Underdog Crusades to Redraw America's Political Map.* "The prospect of breaking away from a union once consecrated to liberty and justice but now degenerating into imperial putrefaction will only grow in appeal as we go marching with our Patriot Acts and National Security Strategies through Iraq, Iran, Afghanistan, and the frightful signposts on our road to nowhere."[2]

Secession's signposts, meanwhile, are popping up all over the United States.

• More than thirty of our fifty States in the U.S. Empire are home to active secessionist organizations.[3]

• In recent years, the country has witnessed three national conferences organized around secession—the first (Burlington, Vermont in 2006) and the third (Manchester, New Hampshire in 2008) both taking place in New England. The second, held in Tennessee, produced a document called the Chattanooga Declaration, which declared, "The deepest questions of human liberty and government facing our time go beyond right and left, and in fact have made the old left-right split meaningless and dead. The privileges, monopolies, and powers that private corporations have won from government threaten everyone's health, prosperity, and liberty, and have already killed American self-government by the people."[4]

• In a July 2008 national Zogby Poll, approximately 20 percent of American adults agreed that "any state or region has the right to peaceably secede from the United States and become an independent republic."[5]

• Even venerable national newspapers and magazines of record—the *New York Times*, the *Wall Street Journal*, and *TIME* among them—have begun covering the "secession story."

Why Secession? The U.S. as Empire

Why nonviolent secession? Two reasons:

Our "global village" of 7 billion human inhabitants faces an unprecedented two-headed planetary challenge, in the form of Peak Oil—the end to our "petroleum man" century of cheap and abundant fossil-fuel energy—and its more publicized sister, climate change, which is ushering in a new and more unstable "Eaarth," as Vermont environmentalist Bill McKibben explains in his book of the same title. Peak Oil and global climate change are poised to clean planetary house and dramatically destabilize our world as we know it.

In the face of this unfolding global crisis, the United States has morphed in troubling ways over the past several decades, emerging as an aggressive global player competing for the world's remaining geostrategic fossil-fuel energy reserves. Simply stated, the U.S. is no longer a self-governing republic responsive to the needs and concerns of its citizens but an uncontrollable Empire governed by an unholy alliance of transnational corporations and a federal government bought and paid for by the same, with profit *über alles* as their primary goal.

The United States is an "Empire"? What is this—*Star Wars?*

Like blind men with the elephant, both liberal and conservative critics alike recognize portions of this troubling reality. Blue Staters rightly complain about Big Business monopolies and corporate personhood and lament the coming of what they see as anthropomorphic climate change. Red Staters, generally more skeptical of climate change as a human-induced phenomenon, rightly bear witness to Big Government excess and intrusion into the lives of ordinary citizens. And everyone rightly worries about inexorably rising energy prices.

In truth, both liberals and conservatives are partly right. In the face of Peak Oil and climate change, the twenty-first century United States, it is fair to say, is governed by neither a republican form of government nor organized around a capitalist form of economic life. Instead, "fascism" rules the day, as observed by *Il Duce* himself, good Italian Benito Mussolini, who defined the term as "a monopolistic merger of Big Business and the power of the State." "This left/right thing has got to go," explains *Vermont Commons: Voices of Independence* news-journal publisher emeritus Ian Baldwin. "We're decentralists and we're up against a monster."[6]

The cofounder of Chelsea Green publishing company, and one of the wisest Vermonters engaged in Vermont's emerging independence effort, Baldwin's influence permeates the pages of *Vermont Commons*, the Green Mountain's only Statewide independent news journal. Drawing on philosophical strands from the anti-imperialist, decentralist, "green," libertarian, paleo-conservative, progressive, and mutualist traditions, Baldwin and his editorial board defined a two-part mission for *Vermont Commons* from the outset: economic re-localization (popularly referred to by the now-clichéd term "sustainability") and political decentralization (sovereignty in the short term, with secession as an end goal). The journal has published writers from across the political spectrum who offer critiques and solutions to the problem of Empire. More about *Vermont Commons* later.

Sightings of Baldwin's "monster," the United States of Empire, have been reported by observers from across the political spectrum for decades now. On the domestic front, the news is deeply troubling. "Of all western democracies, the United States stands near dead last in voter turnout, last in health care, last in education, highest in homicide rates, mortality, STDs among juveniles, youth pregnancy, abortion and divorce," explains journalist Christopher Ketcham in *GOOD* magazine, summarizing his conversations with retired international businessman and Duke University economics professor emeritus Thomas Naylor, cofounder of the secessionist think tank the Second Vermont Republic. "The nation has trillions in deficits it can never repay, is beset by staggering income disparities, has destroyed its manufacturing base, and is the world's most egregious polluter and greediest consumer of fossil fuels." The nation is also inhabited by "some 40 million

Americans living in poverty, tens of millions more in a category called 'near poverty,' and a permanent underclass trapped by a real unemployment rate of 17 percent."[7]

This depressing demographic data would be somewhat easier to confront if one assumed that the United States government is at all interested in solving the myriad problems that bedevil its citizens. Or that the current average size of U.S. congressional districts—a whopping 647,000 citizens per representative, larger than the entire population of the State of Vermont—creates any sort of possibility for democratic discussion and representative government.

Instead, however, the evidence seems to indicate that Washington, D.C. has allied itself with large corporations to strip away both decision-making control and resources from ordinary Americans in almost every conceivable way. Libraries of books have been written on stupendous financial skullduggery and Wall Street's fleecing of Main Street, U.S. war-making and arms dealing globally, multinational corporations' monopolistic control of our nation's food and energy supply, massive electoral fraud, and the impending bankruptcy of the U.S. government, beholden to the Wall Street banksters, Goldman Sachs and their ilk, and the so-called Federal Reserve (which is neither).

It is no wonder that the United States military-industrial complex, in the throes of what Yale historian Paul Kennedy dubbed "imperial overstretch" in his 1987 book, *The Rise and Fall of Great Powers*, strives to maintain a policy of "full spectrum dominance" in an effort to control the world's remaining easily recoverable fossil-fuel energy reserves. Or that the United States seeks to bolster what retired policy analyst Chalmers Johnson calls a global "empire of bases" (as many as 1,000, by best estimates) in more than 130 countries around the world—the best defense is a good offense. Or that the United States promotes what former Wall Street financial analyst and Bush I regulator Catherine Austin Fitts calls a "tapeworm economy," in which small groups of large corporations make obscene amounts of money by blowing up stuff (and people—"collateral damage"), rebuilding what they've destroyed with taxpayer and borrowed money paid to "contractors," and then privatizing once publicly held assets (oil and much more). Look no farther than the lengthy U.S. occupation of Iraq as a case study in how the "tapeworm economy" works.[8]

In the face of what James Howard Kunstler called this "Long Emergency," what options do we as Vermonters, as Americans, have? Let's be honest. After all, although 20 percent of the respondents in a 2008 nationwide Zogby Poll said they would support a secessionist movement in their State, 70 percent expressed opposition to secession. What are our other options? "The only ones I can envision are: denial, compliance, political reform, implosion, rebellion, and dissolution," writes Naylor, in his 2008 book, *Secession: How Vermont and All the Other States Can Save Themselves from the Empire.*

In the passage below, Naylor briefly describes each of these options and concludes that nonviolent secession "represents the only morally defensible response to the U.S. Empire."

DENIAL: Most Americans—including our government, our politicians, corporate America, Wall Street, the Pentagon, and the media—are in complete denial of our perilous plight. In spite of all of our obvious problems, they seem oblivious to the cataclysmic risks we are facing. But, obviously denial does not solve problems, and it seems clear that these problems will not simply vanish or solve themselves. So we reject this option.

COMPLIANCE: Many armchair environmentalists, pacifists, democratic socialists, and simple-living adherents are all too aware of the risks facing the Empire, but feel completely powerless at the feet of corporate America and the U.S. government to do anything about them. So they talk about how bad things are and they try to live their personal lives in positive ways, but in relation to our government they do nothing but naively hope for the best. For them the name of the game is compliance. Since that gets us nowhere, we reject this option, too.

REFORM: The real Pollyannas are liberal Democrats who believe that all we need do is elect the right Democrat president and all of our problems will be solved. They see political reform (such as campaign finance reform) as a panacea, failing to realize that, so long as the Congress is controlled by corporate America, there will never be any meaningful campaign finance reform. Since we have a single political party disguised as two, it matters not whether the president calls himself a Democrat or a Republican. The results will be the same. So, again, we reject this option.

IMPLOSION: When Soviet Leader Mikhail S. Gorbachev came to power in 1985, who could have imagined that the Soviet Union would soon implode and cease to exist? The United States seems to be well on its way to replicating the experience of its former archenemy in an American setting. So, do we want to sit by and wait for that to happen? Again we reject this option.

REBELLION: Just as armed rebellion gave birth to the United States in 1776, so too could some combination of stock market meltdown, economic depression, crippling unemployment, monetary crisis, skyrocketing crude oil prices, double-digit interest rates, soaring federal deficits and trade imbalances, curtailment of social services, repeated terrorist attacks, return of the military draft or environmental catastrophe precipitate a violent twenty-first century revolution against corporate America and the U.S. Government. However, we also reject this option, because we are opposed to all forms of violence.[9]

There is, Naylor and other Vermont secessionists conclude, just one viable option: peaceful dissolution of the U.S. as Empire—secession, in a word.

Secession: Why Vermont?

What could be more absurd than tiny Vermont, the second least populous State in the United States of Empire, confronting the largest, wealthiest, most powerful, most materialistic, most environmentally destructive, most militaristic Empire of our era? A February 2008 poll conducted by the University of Vermont's Center for Rural Studies found that 77 percent of eligible Vermont voters thought the U.S. government had lost its moral authority, while nearly 50 percent believed the United States had become unsustainable (politically, economically, militarily, and environmentally). Many others found it to be ungovernable and, therefore, unfixable. Given this troubling situation, Vermont's only morally defensible response to the U.S. Empire, Green Mountain secessionists suggest, is nonviolent secession. And although Vermont is home to one of the most active independence efforts in the country today, there is absolutely nothing new about the notion of secession in Vermont, as the historical record illustrates.

First consider Vermont's political origins and culture. Vermont is the only State to exist prior to the creation of the United States as its own independent republic, for fourteen years, to be exact: from 1777 to 1791. "Only in Vermont was the concept of a state as self-constituted political community fully and radically tested," writes historian Peter Onuf in his book *The Origins of the Federal Republic.* "In this sense, Vermont was the only true American republic, for it alone has created itself."[10] (The Lone Star Republic of Texas and the Bear Flag Republic of California were both wrested from Spanish Mexico by force.)

The State of Vermont, moreover, was front and center throughout nineteenth-century New England's secession conversations related to militarism, war, and expansion. Vermont was the first State to outlaw slavery within its borders; and Vermonters today still speak out against tyranny of all kinds—nuclear war, GMO seeds, the unlawful conscription of National Guard troops by the U.S. government for foreign invasions—every March during our annual town-meeting day.

Despite Vermont's long history of independent thinking and action, few Vermonters today realize that calls for nonviolent secession represent a return to Vermont's early-nineteenth-century roots, when New England secessionists led the opposition to the 1803 Louisiana Purchase, the national embargo of 1807, and the War of 1812. New England secessionists also expressed their opposition to a military draft at Connecticut's regional Hartford Convention in 1814, where New England abolitionists urged Northern States to disengage from the new U.S. republic. During January 1815, Vermont joined other New England States in signing the report of this Hartford Convention in opposition to the proposal of the U.S. secretary of war to implement a military draft for continuing the mismanaged War of 1812 with England. This report was nothing less than a declaration of the right to secede.

Even during the post-Civil War era, marked by the triumph of federal over State power and the economic and political consolidation of the United States as a corporate-friendly industrial Empire, the spirit of Vermont independence never left the Green Mountains. In 1928 and 1929, for example, a quirky little Vermont literary magazine known as *The Drift-Wind* published a series of tongue-in-cheek articles by Arthur Patton Wallace and Vrest Orton, calling for Vermont independence. According to Orton, the purpose of such a movement would be "to constitute an Arcadia for persons of free thought, active mind, high standards, and aspirations and cultural imagination." Orton was the founder of one of Vermont's most visible commercial retail enterprises, the Vermont Country Store, which still carries on a thriving global business through tourist visits and online sales.

Four years after the appearance of *The Drift-Wind*, radical economist and political dissident Scott Nearing and his partner, Helen Knothe, moved to the Pikes Falls region in Vermont's southern Green Mountains. Near the town of Jamaica, they organized a community known as the Forest Farm experiment, committed to simple living, self-sufficiency, sustainable agriculture, cooperation, mutual aid, and an ascetic lifestyle. The Forest Farm complex included eight stone houses and a 4,000-tap sugar bush that Helen and Scott Nearing transformed into a self-sustaining maple-candy business, with the help of their Vermont neighbors.

On August 6, 1945, the day the U.S. government dropped the first atomic bomb on Hiroshima and ushered in the "nuclear age," Scott Nearing wrote to Pres. Harry S. Truman that "your government is no longer mine." Biographer John Saltmarsh described Nearing as "a complete secessionist from capitalist cultural hegemony," observing:

> Nearing moved through a series of secessions—from Christianity, from politics, and finally from American society itself. The secessions in Nearing's life were progressive repudiations of American canons of moral conduct, as well as indications of Nearing's perception of the fragmented, segmented, discontinuous nature of U.S. society. Only in Vermont's isolated private sphere provided by homesteading could a radical resistance and constructive challenge to capitalist culture be nurtured."[11]

It is not surprising, then, that when the Second Vermont Republic minted their first Vermont independence coin in 2009, they selected Scott Nearing's visage to represent the silver "face" of the independence effort.

More recent secession expressions in Vermont are also notable. In 1973, Chicago-based economist David Hale, who grew up in the Vermont town of St. Johnsbury, called for Vermont independence in a provocative *Stowe Reporter* piece entitled "The Republic of Vermont: A Modest Proposal." His essay won the New England Press Association Award that year.[12] In their 1990 town meetings, seven of seven independent-minded Vermont communities, including the Vermont State capital of Montpelier and St. Johnsbury, voted overwhelmingly to secede from the United States. Few Vermonters seemed surprised. A few years earlier, when most Americans supported Pres. Ronald Reagan and his Cold War "evil empire" saber-rattling, more than 180 Vermont towns defied him and demanded a nuclear freeze. University of Vermont political scientist Frank Bryan, who has flirted with the idea of Vermont secession for years, has famously observed, "Vermont is just obstinate. We'll do anything to be on the wrong side."[13] But is Vermont on the wrong side, or is the United States?

Consider the Iraq War (2003-11), the longest-running military conflict in U.S. history. When the U.S. government decided to invade and occupy Iraq in March 2003, all three members of Vermont's congressional delegation voted against the White House-backed resolution giving Pres. George W. Bush the U.S. Congress's blessing to pursue military action against Iraq. Vermont was the only State in which every member of the delegation rejected the resolution. Sen. Patrick J. Leahy explained, "This resolution permits the president to take whatever military action he wants, wherever he wants, for as long as he wants. It is a blank check . . . and this Vermonter does not sign blank checks."

Almost exactly two years later, in 2005, during Vermont's annual town-meeting day, fifty Vermont towns passed resolutions calling for the president and Congress to take steps to withdraw all American troops from Iraq. Two years later, both houses of the Vermont legislature passed resolutions calling for the immediate withdrawal of all troops from Iraq—the first State legislature to do so. Thirty-six Vermont towns passed nonbinding resolutions in their 2007 town meetings demanding that President Bush and Vice Pres. Dick Cheney be impeached. Clearly, Vermonters have an independent streak—and our annual town-meeting days are but one way in which Vermont citizens express their collective will.

Founding SVR and Galvanizing the Secession Idea

Triggered by the many grievances associated with President Bush's war on terror, a hearty group of Vermont patriots launched the Second Vermont Republic in October 2003. SVR defines itself as "a nonviolent citizens' network and think tank opposed to the tyranny of Wall Street, Corporate America, and the U.S. Government, and committed to the return of Vermont to its status as an independent republic and more broadly to the dissolution of the Empire." According to Naylor, SVR supporters "subscribe to the following beliefs: political independence, human scale, sustainability, economic solidarity (buying locally), power sharing, and community."[14]

A former international businessman, Duke University economics professor, and author of more than one dozen books, Thomas Naylor has played a central role in birthing the Vermont independence effort. His main premise is that the United States of Empire, like the Soviet Empire before it, will ultimately collapse due to a failure of moral authority, provided enough U.S. citizens can reimagine what he has called an UNtied States, with Vermont as leading the way. His work in his "retirement" has consisted of planting the seeds of Vermont independence, and the first several years of energy for the Vermont secession effort stem from his tireless efforts, which began even before he moved to the Green Mountains.

In October 1990, the *Bennington Banner* published an essay by Naylor entitled "Should the U.S. Be Downsized?" Four years later in *Challenge*, Naylor, newly relocated to Vermont, wrote that "the time has come both for the individual states and the federal government to begin planning the rational downsizing of America" and suggested that Vermont might lead the way by helping "save our nation from the debilitating effects of big government and big business" and by "providing an independent role model for the other states to follow." In 1997, Naylor coauthored a book entitled *Downsizing the U.S.A.*, which not only called for Vermont independence but the peaceful dissolution of the U.S. Empire. "In the book, we argued that the U.S. government had become too big, too centralized, too powerful, too undemocratic, too militaristic, too imperialistic, too materialistic, and too unresponsive to the needs of individual citizens and small communities," he explained. "However, since we were in the midst of the greatest economic boom in history, few Americans were interested in downsizing anything."[15]

It wasn't until after the events surrounding September 11, 2001, that the idea of Vermont independence began to emerge full flower. On March 5, 2003, two weeks before the second war with Iraq began, Naylor spoke at an antiwar rally at Johnson State College and decided, as he remembered, to "test-market" the idea of an independent Vermont. "Basically, my pitch to the students was 'if you want to prevent future wars in places such as Afghanistan and Iraq, we have no choice but to break up the United States into smaller regions, and that process should begin with Vermont declaring its independence from the United States,'" Naylor remembers. "They were stunned, but they got it. Their positive response literally provided the energy to launch the Second Vermont Republic."[16]

Ten days after the U.S. began bombing Baghdad, Naylor sponsored the first of four monthly meetings at the Village Cup in the town of Jericho to discuss how such a Vermont independence effort might evolve. Early on, Naylor recalled, "we decided not to become a political party but rather a civic club." The small group who attended the meeting decided to register the name "Second Vermont Republic" with the secretary of state on June 19, 2003. Despite Naylor's decision in "retirement" to not personally engage with the Internet, SVR did launch a Web site the following January, and the site has served as an archive and clearinghouse for the idea of Vermont independence ever since.

SVR "Street Theater" Secession Strategy: Building Support for Vermont Independence

Early on, SVR began to attract influential allies—both in Vermont and internationally. Over a July lunch in the backyard of Vermont's Bread & Puppet Theater Museum, located in the town of Glover, Vermont artist/icon Peter Schumann and his famous puppeteers agreed to help the Second Vermont Republic promote Vermont independence through their theatrical performances. That October, with the release of Naylor's book *The Vermont Manifesto*, the first Statewide meeting of the Second Vermont Republic was held in the New Building of Bread & Puppet Theater. Fifty people attended. "From the standpoint of puppeteers and their subversive papier-mâché," explained Schumann, "the Second Vermont Republic sounds like a very good idea to fight the megalomania of the globalizers."[17] Using puppets to promote secession may seem silly, but Naylor always understood the importance of "street theater" as an attention-getting medium. "The Second Vermont Republic confounds those who would analyze it using the language of practical politics," explains Kauffman. "It pursues with humor and a dogged optimism a goal that seems manifestly impossible. It speaks radical notions with a conservative diction."[18]

And it wasn't just puppets who came on board to support "radical notions" of secession. More influential figures from across the political spectrum began lending their support to the idea of Vermont independence as well. Of the idea, U.S. foreign-policy analyst and consummate "realist" George F.

Kennan commented, "I see nothing fanciful, and nothing towards the realization of which the efforts of enlightened people might not be usefully directed."[19] Left-leaning Harvard economist John Kenneth Galbraith, meanwhile, wrote, "I must assure you of my pleasure in, and approval of, your views of the Second Vermont Republic."[20] And George Mason University professor of economics Walter Williams, a high-profile libertarian and public intellectual, has also supported SVR's cause. Clearly, the idea of secession is one that transcends dualistic political categories.

SVR used a wide variety of public "secession street theater" events to promote the cause of Vermont independence. In June 2004, SVR and the Bread & Puppet Theater held a parade in downtown Montpelier, beginning in front of the firehouse and proceeding six blocks to the steps of the State House. Nearly 350 people attended the rally, with highlights including a performance by Bread & Puppet, live music, and a dozen speakers calling for Vermont independence. John Remington Graham, author of *A Constitutional History of Secession*, keynoted the event, which ended with the reading of the Vermont Declaration of Independence and distribution of a new thirty-two-page, glossy *Journal of Vermont Independence*. (Nearly a year later, this journal evolved into *Vermont Commons: Voices of Independence*, under Ian Baldwin's leadership.)

The following March (2005), Ben Matchstick of Bread & Puppet Theater and near-mythical Vermont Green Mountain Boy general Ethan Allen (played by Calais actor/historian Jim Hogue) led a "memorial service" at the Langdon Street Café commemorating the day in 1791 when Vermont joined the United States. The service included a reading from Ecclesiastes with Chopin's "Funeral March" playing in the background. A funeral procession with a New Orleans-style funeral band carried a flag-draped coffin containing the deceased First Vermont Republic to the State House, where it was placed at the foot of the statue of Ethan Allen. That same summer also marked the beginning of an annual July tradition involving Vermont independence supporters participating in Fourth of July parades (2004 saw marchers in Barton, Cabot, and Warren). The politically radical, funky, grassroots, seat-of-the-pants Warren parade attracts as many as 20,000 people each year to the Mad River Valley. The parade's homemade floats, held together by duct tape, nails, and baling twine, combine New England Americana with vintage Vermont culture and the residual effects of 1960s hippie living. Since 2006, the Warren and then Montpelier parades have become annual events in which to promote Vermont independence, with secession supporters reminding their neighbors to celebrate Vermont independence on July 7, as part of their patriotic festivities. (The very first Vermont Constitution was agreed upon on July 7, 1777, in the town of Windsor, still widely remembered as the "birthplace of the Vermont Republic.")

SVR: National and State Secession Conferences

Along with his Middlebury Institute colleague Kirkpatrick Sale, Naylor has also used SVR to spearhead a number of national conferences to explore the idea of secession. On November 5-7, 2004, forty people from eleven States and England attended a conference at the Middlebury Inn cosponsored by SVR and Wessex, England-based Fourth World (publisher of *Fourth World Review* magazine) entitled "After the Fall of America, Then What?" The Fourth World defined itself as being "committed to small nations, small communities, small farms, small shops, the human scale, and the inalienable sovereignty of the human spirit," and the conference's underlying premise dovetailed with much of Naylor's SVR work. The United States, attendees agreed, had become unsustainable, ungovernable, and unfixable. If that were indeed the case, then do individual States, as Naylor likes to say, "go down with the *Titanic*," or do they "seek other alternatives?" The conference also included a mock town meeting open to the public, with guest appearances by Ethan Allen (Hogue again) and Thomas Jefferson (Thetford actor and citizen activist Gus Jaccaci).

At the conference's close, more than half of the delegates signed "the Middlebury Declaration," which called for the creation of a movement that would "place secession on the national agenda, encourage secessionist organizations, develop communication among existing and future secessionist groups, and create a body of scholarship to examine and promote the ideas and principles of secessionism." Coinciding with Bush's controversial reelection, the Middlebury Conference received considerable State, national, and international media attention, with the Quebec newspaper *Le Devoir* publishing a front-page article on it. In April 2005, with the active support of the Second Vermont Republic, both houses of the Vermont legislature passed a unanimous resolution naming January as Vermont history and independence month. U.S. senator Jim Jeffords (a Republican turned Independent), Burlington mayor Peter Clavelle (a Progressive Party leader), and Lt. Gov. Brian Dubie (a Republican) all supported the resolution.

The next three years saw continuing interest in Vermont independence, as well as the beginnings of a national conversation about the idea of nonviolent secession, carried on over a series of three conferences, two of which took place in New England. On November 3-5, 2006, the Middlebury Institute hosted the first North American Secessionist Convention in Burlington, Vermont. Delegates from eighteen States attended, including representatives from Texas, Alaska, Louisiana, Hawaii, California, New Hampshire, and Tennessee. The Middlebury Institute's Kirkpatrick Sale served as both the keynote speaker and facilitator. On October 3-4, 2007, the Second North American Secessionist Convention took place in

Chattanooga, Tennessee. It attracted delegates representing secessionist organizations in thirty-six States. The convention received worldwide media attention as a result of an Associated Press story that described the meeting as bringing "the far left and the far right of American politics together."[21]

By this time, Vermont independence supporters had received some flak in the left-leaning Vermont blogosphere for engaging with Southern secession supporters who possessed different political perspectives, but the A.P. story had it right: secession was emerging as a national political idea that transcended traditional Red/Blue divisions. The following year saw a Third North American Secessionist Convention unfold in Manchester, New Hampshire on November 14-15, at which it became clear that the Vermont independence effort represented perhaps the most organized nonviolent independence effort in the United States.

In Vermont, the idea of nonviolent secession was gaining traction at the State level as well. On October 28, 2005, SVR held the first Statewide secession convention in the United States since North Carolina voted to secede from the federal republic on May 20, 1861. The daylong event took place in the House Chamber of the State House in Montpelier, and perhaps only in Vermont would such a meeting be possible. More than three hundred attendees heard keynote speaker James Howard Kunstler, author of *The Long Emergency*, warn that "the end of the cheap fossil-fuel era will lead to the most serious challenge to our collective identity, economy, culture, and security since the Civil War." The objectives of the convention were twofold, as Naylor remembers. "First, we ought to raise the level of awareness of Vermonters of the feasibility of independence as a viable alternative to a United States that had lost its moral authority and is unsustainable," he explained. "Second, we wished to provide an example and a process for other states and nations that may be seriously considering separatism, secession, independence, and similar devolutionary strategies." The delegates approved two resolutions. Naylor explained, "The first called for Vermont to return to its status as an independent republic as it had between January 15, 1777 and March 4, 1791. The other called for the Second Vermont Republic to seek membership in the Unrepresented Nations and Peoples Organization."[22]

On November 7, 2008, SVR sponsored a Second Statewide Convention on Vermont Independence in the House Chamber of the State House in Montpelier. The convention took the form of an all-day circus and medicine show entitled "The Vermont Village Green: Alternative to Empire." Consisting of a potpourri of radical music, art, theater, circus, conversation, politics, and community aimed at fomenting a Genteel Revolution against the American Empire, the conference was attended by trends forecaster Gerald Celente, New Mexico writer Chellis Glendinning, Alaskan Independence Party leader Lynette Clark, Bread & Puppet Theater, Vermont folk musician Pete Sutherland, Peak Oil writer James Howard Kunstler, Rural Vermont leader and citizen activist Amy Shollenberger, outspoken University of Vermont student Tyler Wilkinson-Ray, and Kirby businessman Dennis Steele, who would play a more high profile role in the Vermont independence effort just a few years later.

Secession: Branding Vermont, Standing for Office

As more Vermonters became interested in the secession question, the Vermont independence effort began harnessing a wide variety of media to promote vigorous discussion about the independence mission and to, as I like to say, "make secession sexy—an attractive political option." One of the more important symbolic decisions made was to adopt the distinctive eighteenth-century flag of Ethan Allen and the Green Mountain Boys (GMB), now the flag of the Vermont

National Guard, as a symbol of choice for the emerging Vermont independence effort. The GMB symbol is now affixed to bumper stickers, flags, buttons, and T-shirts. Nonviolent secessionists have also developed a bimonthly Statewide news journal entitled *Vermont Commons: Voices of Independence*, which circulates 10,000 copies of a now-forty-page journal in 350 locations all over Vermont. In the world of digital broadcasting, meanwhile, Dennis Steele launched RadioFreeVermont.org, an Internet radio station featuring Vermont music and Vermont independence politics. The station plays music from more than 300 Vermont musicians and has listeners in nearly 150 countries worldwide. To push Vermonters towards thinking about financial independence, SVR recently issued its own silver "Freedom and Unity" token bearing the image of Scott Nearing. The coin contains one ounce of silver, and SVR plans to issue a second token commemorating Revolutionary War general Seth Warner.

The real breakthrough moment for Vermont independence, however, came with the arrival of citizen candidates willing to throw their hats into the State electoral arena. For the first time in more the 150 years, secession was front and center in a Statewide New England political campaign. On January 15, 2010, Vermont Independence Day, a slate of nine Vermont independence advocates announced their candidacy for Statewide office at the Capitol Plaza Hotel in downtown Montpelier. The secession ticket included candidates for governor, lieutenant governor, and seven State Senate seats, and all the candidates shared a commitment to work to bring home the Vermont National Guard troops from Afghanistan and Iraq immediately, as well as a desire to return Vermont to its status as an independent republic. That year, gubernatorial candidate Dennis Steele and his campaign manager, Matthew Cropp, ran a tenacious Statewide campaign with very little money, challenging the two major-party contenders to a series of debates (one of which was broadcast on Vermont Public

Television). While Steele garnered less than 1 percent of the votes on an election day marked by the tightest major two-party gubernatorial contest in decades, he succeeded in raising nonviolent secession as a serious Statewide political issue. Other openly secessionist candidates polled as high as 15 percent of the popular vote (such as Montpelier High School valedictorian James Merriam, who ran for a house seat in Montpelier).[23]

Nonviolent Secession: The Soviet Empire and Eastern Europe as Case Studies[24]

Where the 2010 Vermont independence electoral foray goes remains to be seen. But Naylor harbors no illusions. "Secession is a hard sell, and at the end of the day, comes down to a question of popular will," he explains, drawing on his experiences in Eastern Europe and the Soviet Union to make one of his favorite analogies about the possibility of Vermont independence. "The six Communist regimes in Eastern Europe and the Soviet Union were all brought down by a common nonviolent strategy, namely by demonstrating unequivocally that the leaders of these regimes had lost their moral authority," Naylor observes. "The Communist government of Poland was not toppled in 1989 by Solidarity leader Lech Walesa whispering sweet nothings in the ear of President Wojciech Jaruzelski. Rather it, as well as the five other Eastern European Communist governments, were brought down by a sophisticated mixture of confrontation, negotiation, and testing of limits spread out over several years."

The hard question, as Naylor sees it, involves citizen engagement and moral courage. "Ultimately, the Soviet Empire's collapse involves a contest of political wills. The political will of the people trumped the will of the government to stay in power," he explains. "The Emperor was found to have no clothes both in the Soviet Union as well as in its Eastern European satellites." And Naylor does not mince words when it comes to Vermont independence as an expression of popular public will. "If a Second Vermont Republic is to prevail," he concludes, "citizen supporters of an independent Vermont must challenge the moral authority of the U.S. government, and the Vermont Congressional delegation . . . as well as their supporters in Vermont's Democratic and Progressive parties."

While Naylor's "take no prisoners" rhetoric has alienated many would-be supporters of Vermont independence in the short term, his uncompromising vision has catalyzed spirited debate within the Vermont independence community about emerging strategy and tactics, and Naylor himself happily acknowledges his role as a gadfly, a citizen willing to speak what he believes are uncomfortable truths.

Secession: Vermont's Radical Imperative

To outsiders today, it seems easy to pigeonhole tiny Vermont. The national corporate commercial "news" media think they have Vermont pegged as the bluest of Blue States, chock-full of "Obama-loving, latte-drinking, Prius-driving, Birkenstock-wearing, trust-fund babies." It is true that we have more than our fair share of sometimes-smug Prius drivers on Vermont roads and that 70 percent of the Vermont electorate voted for Mr. Obama in the 2008 presidential election (if electronic voting machines, which even tiny and independent-minded Vermont possesses in some of our towns, are to be believed). It is also true that Vermont political trends are not so easily understood. To wit: we were the first State to bless civil unions for gay couples, *and,* as a State of hunters and farmers, we have the most open and progressive gun-carry laws of any State in the country.

Rather than Red versus Blue, "radical" is our term of choice. "Arguably, Vermont is the most radical State in the Union, in terms of its commitment to human solidarity, sustainability, direct democracy, egalitarianism, political independence, and nonviolence," writes Naylor.[25] Culturally, historically, and politically, Vermont, with its commitment to "live and let live tolerance" promotion of individual rights, and attention to the common good ("Freedom and Unity" is our State's current motto), is a natural starting place for considering any State's nonviolent secession. Etymologically, the word "radical" means simply "getting to the root cause of a thing."

And, secessionists continually suggest, this thing called "the United States" is simply too big, too centralized, too corrupt, too inefficient, and too impossible to govern anymore. "If something is wrong, it is too big," wrote Leopold Kohr in his 1957 book, *The Breakdown of Nations*, which has emerged as a bible of sorts for secessionists everywhere. "Instead of Union, let us have disunion now. Instead of fusing the small, let us dismember the big. Instead of creating fewer and larger states, let us create more and smaller ones."[26] If Vermonters heed Kohr's advice, Vermont can help reinvent the United States as the UNtied States—decentralized, relocalized, and supportive of what E. F. Schumacher called a "small is beautiful" paradigm, in his 1973 book of the same title.

Nonviolent Secession in Vermont: Three Big Questions[27]

Given the traction already gained by the Vermont independence effort, more and more questions are being asked about secession. The three most asked include: Is it constitutionally possible for a State such as Vermont to secede from the United States? Would it be politically feasible? Could Vermont survive economically as an independent nation? Let's consider them one at a time.

When Americans think of secession, what usually comes to mind is the series of events leading up to what Americans typically refer to as the "Civil War" of 1861-65. Did the Confederacy's eleven States have the right to secede? In an article entitled "The Foundations and Meaning of Secession," Pepperdine University law professor H. Newcomb Morse provides convincing evidence that individual American States do indeed have the right to secede and that the Confederate States did so legally.[28] A close consideration of Morse's case is in order.

First, Morse argues that numerous States throughout both the South and the rest of the nation had nullified acts of the central government judged to be unconstitutional long before the people of South Carolina voted in convention to secede on December 20, 1860. Some of these acts of nullification took place in Kentucky (1799), Pennsylvania (1809), Georgia (1832), South Carolina (1832), Wisconsin (1854), Massachusetts (1855), and our own Vermont, which nullified the Fugitive Slave Act in 1858. According to Morse, "nullification occurs when the people of a state refuse to recognize the validity of an exercise of power by the national government which, in the state's view, transcends the limited and enumerated delegated powers of the national constitution."[29] Those numerous historical instances where individual States nullified national laws give credence to the view that the "compact" (as Thomas Jefferson and others called it) forming the United States had already been breached and that the citizens of the Confederate States were morally and legally free to leave the United States if they so chose.

Second, and most importantly, the U.S. Constitution does not forbid withdrawal from the United States. According to the Tenth Amendment of the Constitution, "the powers not delegated to the United States by the Constitution, nor prohibited by it to the States, are reserved to the States respectively, or to the people." Stated alternatively, that which is not expressly prohibited by the Constitution is allowed, and nowhere in the U.S. Constitution is secession expressly prohibited. The States delegated powers to the national government, not sovereignty. By international law, sovereignty cannot be surrendered by implication but only by an express act. Nowhere in the Constitution nor in the State ratification documents is there any expressed renunciation of sovereignty. Because sovereignty remains, all powers delegated can be recalled.

Third, Morse points out, while the Confederate States were in the process of taking leave of the United States, three amendments to the Constitution were presented to the U.S. Congress placing conditions on the rights of States to leave. Then on March 2, 1861, after seven States had already left, a Constitutional amendment was proposed that would have outlawed their departure entirely. Although none of these amendments was ever ratified, Morse asks, "Why would Congress have even considered proposed Constitutional amendments forbidding or restricting the right to withdraw from the United States if any such right was already prohibited, limited or non-existent under the U.S. Constitution?" An illustrative question.

Fourth, Morse notes, three of the original thirteen States—Virginia, New York, and Rhode Island—ratified the U.S. Constitution only conditionally. Each of these States explicitly retained exit rights. By the time South Carolina split in 1860, a total of thirty-three States had acceded to the federal republic. By accepting the right of Virginia, New York, and Rhode Island to withdraw, had they not tacitly accepted the right of a State to leave the United States?

Fifth, according to Morse, following the "Civil War" the United States government removed its occupying armies from Arkansas, North Carolina, Florida, South Carolina, Mississippi, and Virginia only after coercing these former Confederate States into enacting new constitutions containing clauses prohibiting secession. But again, why would this have been deemed necessary if these States never had the right to secede in the first place? In addition, in the eyes of most legal scholars, agreements of this sort made under duress are voidable at the option of the aggrieved party; thus, there is absolutely nothing to prevent these six States from amending their constitutions again.

Sixth, Morse argues that the proper way for a State to leave the United States is through a State convention of delegates elected by the people of the State to decide one and only one issue, namely, the right of self-determination. According to Morse, every Confederate State properly utilized the convention process, rather than a legislative means to withdraw, and thus followed the process that was understood and agreed upon to be correct.

The Political Feasibility of Nonviolent Secession

In the end, it comes down to one thing: political will.

Ultimately, as was the case with the American Revolution of 1776 (a "War of Secession" from the British Empire), whether or not a State is allowed to secede is neither a legal nor a constitutional question but rather a matter of political will. The ultimate test of sovereignty lies with the citizens themselves: how strong is the will of the people of the departing State to be free and independent of the control of the larger nation it was a part of? One of the questions raised most often in conversations about the idea of Vermont secession and the Second Vermont Republic is, "How would the United States respond to an attempt by Vermont to secede from the Empire?" The deeper and more troubling question behind the question is, "Would the world's largest superpower send troops to Vermont?"

Perhaps in contemplating these questions, Vermonters can learn a lot from Eastern Europe's experience with Václav

Havel's idea of the "power of the powerless." Within a matter of a few weeks in 1989, the iron-fisted communist regimes in Bulgaria, Czechoslovakia, East Germany, Hungary, and Poland were replaced by more democratic governments with little or no violence involved in the transition. Only Romania was a bloody exception to this rule.

The 1989 election of Solidarity leader Lech Walesa proved the climax of a bitter eight-year struggle to bring down the repressive Polish communist government. During martial law, several hundred Solidarity leaders were imprisoned for relatively short periods of time. But amazingly, only a handful of Poles were actually killed during this entire period. Czechoslovakian playwright Václav Havel's so-called "velvet revolution" also brought down communism in Czechoslovakia nonviolently.

Contrary to popular belief, nonviolence is not a passive approach to conflict resolution but rather a proactive approach that goes right to the crux of power relationships. It demands strength and courage, not idle pacifism. It can undermine power and authority by withdrawing the approval, support, and cooperation of those who have been dealt an injustice. In addition, it elicits external support by drawing on the very real power of powerlessness.

Many American Sovietologists were surprised that the Soviet Union did not intervene militarily in Poland in the 1980s, as it had done in Budapest (1956) and Prague (1968). But Poland had many influential friends and supporters, not the least of which were the United States and Western Europe. Certainly, the Soviets could have snuffed out Solidarity, but just as certainly this action would not have played well in London, Paris, or Washington.

A secessionist Vermont could also find a lot of good friends—within the United States, in Canada, in Europe, and in the rest of the world. So it is not a foregone conclusion that the United States government would intervene militarily in

Vermont. Part of Vermont's strength lies in the absurdity of its confronting the most powerful nation in the world. If Vermont attempted to secede, it would undoubtedly attract sympathy from within the United States and abroad simply by virtue of its role as an underdog.

Conquering Vermont, moreover, might feel very much like invading Liechtenstein or one of the more rural Swiss cantons. Besides the ridiculous power disparity, there is also Vermont's almost complete lack of strategic and military importance. The United States would not have much to lose by letting Vermont go. In 1775, Ethan Allen took Fort Ticonderoga without firing a single shot. If Vermont can succeed in undermining the moral authority of the United States and convince the rest of the world that the United States government is corrupt to the core, then it too may be able to escape from the United States without ever firing a shot. That is the essence of what Naylor calls "Vermont's genteel revolution."

The Economic Viability of Nonviolent Secession

Could Vermont or any other State survive economically over the long haul as an independent republic? Many supporters of Vermont independence believe that the answer is decidedly yes: not only would Vermont survive; it would thrive.

For starters, Vermont's size in and of itself does not pose an economic problem. Of the globe's 223 countries, nearly 67 have populations that are smaller than Vermont's 623,000. Some of them include Andorra, Aruba, the Bahamas, Belize, Brunei, Grenada, Kiribati, Malta, Qatar, St. Lucia, and Tonga. Ten of the richest countries in the world each has a population smaller than Vermont and a higher per-capita income. San Marino and Monaco are smaller than Vermont yet have comparable income levels.

Some critics claim that Vermont is so dependent on the federal government financially that it could never make it on its own, but this is a highly debatable assertion. Based on research conducted by University of Vermont political scientist Frank Bryan, for every dollar Vermonters pay to the U.S. government in taxes, they get back on average seventy-five cents.[30] Plus, many federal projects come with all sorts of strings attached and rules as to how federal funds may actually be used, and they often oblige a State to commit its own funds to projects that are of little benefit to the State. The No Child Left Behind Act is an egregious example of such a federal program.

A question raised frequently by Vermonters concerning the economic implications of secession is, "What about Social Security and Medicare?" If Social Security remains intact, then the U.S. government has a contractual obligation to pay recipients according to the prevailing payment schedule, no matter where they happen to live. That is, whether you live in England or the independent republic of Vermont, you are still entitled to receive the benefits that you have earned. Given the U.S. government's massive debt, the long-term future of Social Security, meanwhile, remains somewhat unclear.

Since there are few benefits paid by Medicare for services rendered outside the United States, Medicare recipients might be among the short-term losers if Vermont were to secede from the United States, unless Vermont could compensate Medicare recipients for these lost benefits. Indeed, Vermont, like Massachusetts, would need to invent its own healthcare system (based, perhaps, on some viable healthcare reform initiatives already under way in the Green Mountains).

Even though most Vermonters are opposed to the war in Iraq and many of the Pentagon's policies, Vermont's *pro rata* share of the annual "Defense" budget at present levels amounts by some estimates to over $1.5 billion. For those who oppose America's policies of full-spectrum dominance and imperial overstretch, this is a bitter pill to swallow, especially when one considers how else that $1.5 billion could be used, in the service of healthcare, renewable energy projects, Statewide job creation, and the like.[31]

Would an independent Vermont necessarily have to have its own standing army or defense capability? Costa Rica, for example, has survived since 1948 without any military force whatsoever. Liechtenstein has been neutral since 1866 and has no standing army. NATO provides for the military defense of Bermuda and Iceland. If Vermont felt a need for some form of military support to protect itself from attack by the United States, it could always appeal to Canada, NATO, or the United Nations for protection.

Other skeptics of Vermont independence equate secession with economic isolationism and ask, "Where will Vermont get its food and energy, if it secedes?" The answer is, "Presumably from the same sources that it currently does." Extensive trade with countries outside the United States is a very important aspect of the Vermont economy. Imports amount to around $3 billion annually, and exports are a little less than that figure. Per-capita exports in Vermont are the third highest in the nation, behind Washington and Texas. More than six hundred firms export nearly 25 percent of Vermont's gross State product, the value of goods and services produced in the State, and the rate of exports has been growing rapidly in recent years. There is no reason why this pattern should not continue after Vermont splits with the United States. While the U.S. government might try to impose a trade embargo on a seceded Vermont, it seems quite unlikely that Canada would abide by it, since Canada is Vermont's leading trading partner. Canada never honored the American-imposed embargoes on either China or Cuba.

And while it is true that Vermont is not self-sufficient, few countries are. For example, the second-largest economy in the world, Japan, has only limited supplies of strategic mineral resources and imports most of its food and all of its oil.

A free and independent Vermont, most importantly, could trade with whomever it pleased. It might belong to a trade and economic compact involving other independent States, similar to the European Union. Vermont would not necessarily have to have its own currency. For example, tiny Liechtenstein uses the Swiss franc and Ecuador the U.S. dollar. Vermont could simply adopt the Canadian or U.S. dollar, or possibly the currency of Quebec or New York, if either was independent and had its own currency, or, as many Vermont independenistas have advocated, create its own parallel or complementary currency.

A Nonviolent Secession Process for Vermont (and All Other States)[32]

Because secession has been viewed as a political impossibility by most Americans since the "Civil War," no mechanism exists in our government to deal with this subject. Constitutional though it may be for a State to take leave of the United States of Empire, there are no guidelines to facilitate negotiations between separating States and the federal government with regard to government property, relocation costs, federal debt, and net worth. The unofficial policy of the U.S. government concerning secession is one of complete denial.

In order to achieve its objective of breaking away from the United States of Empire, then, a second Vermont republic would need to invent its own rules for secession, giving attention to four different constituencies: (1) the citizens of Vermont, (2) the U.S. government, (3) citizens in other American States, and (4) global public opinion.

With these constituencies in mind, Naylor's Second Vermont Republic sees the act of secession itself as involving three very important steps:

1. Approval by a Statewide convention
2. Recognition by the U.S. government and other States
3. Diplomatic recognition abroad

First, the Vermont legislature must be persuaded to convene a Statewide convention of democratically elected representatives to consider one and only one issue—secession. Such a convention might include 180 delegates, the combined membership of the Vermont House of Representatives (150 seats) and the Vermont Senate (30 seats). To be credible at the State, national, and international levels, at least a two-thirds majority vote would be required to move the process forward.

Second, once the articles of secession have been approved by the convention, the governor of Vermont would be empowered to deliver this document to the president, secretary of state, Speaker of the House, chief justice of the Supreme Court, and anyone else in a position of authority in the U.S. government who would be willing to receive it. What follows would be a period of constructive engagement by the Vermont governor with the U.S. government, modeled closely after the strategies successfully employed by Lech Walesa and Václav Havel in Poland and Czechoslovakia respectively, to free their countries from Soviet rule in the late 1980s. The aim of these negotiations is recognition of Vermont as an independent republic by the U.S. government.

Simultaneously, Vermont would need to seek diplomatic recognition from Ottawa, London, Paris, Berne, Stockholm, the United Nations, and other influential players on the international stage. The Second Vermont Republic has already laid the groundwork, attracting substantial international media attention, particularly in Brazil, Canada, England, Germany, Italy, Switzerland, and Spain.

The moment of truth for the Second Vermont Republic will come when the citizens and government of Vermont start behaving as though Vermont truly were an independent nation. At that point, federal taxes will no longer be paid, federal-revenue flows into Vermont will cease, federal laws will be ignored, and the Vermont legislature will begin the process of reinventing Vermont as an independent republic.

As for life and politics in the new Vermont, will it be business as usual? Or could Vermont become a libertarian State, like that proposed by the New Hampshire Free State Project, or maybe a democratic socialist State modeled after Sweden? At that fateful moment, of course, these would be questions for the citizens of Vermont to decide.

Secession as Ideology, Journalism as Public Conversation

"Ideology of any sort . . . is a road without end that carries the enthusiast far from anyplace resembling home," Bill Kauffman writes in *Bye Bye Miss American Empire*. "A healthy secessionist movement must be founded in love: love of a particular place, its people (of all ethnicities and colors), its culture, its language and books and music and baseball teams, and yes, its beer and flowers and punk rock clubs."[33] I would add love of its journalism as well.

The Vermont independence movement's Statewide news journal, *Vermont Commons: Voices of Independence,* quietly marked its fifth year in publication in April 2010. As the founding editor and current publisher, I have worked with the editorial board to co-create a particular set of values that may help reinvent journalism in this new century. Through an organic process shaped by experimentation, adaptability, and close monitoring of the larger "landscape of crisis" that has characterized the national (read: "imperial") news arena, we've developed a set of principles I'll briefly mention here. The most important thing I have learned as both a writer and Vermont independence supporter is the vital importance of public discussion and debate. In our more optimistic moments, we like to think that we are helping to pioneer a more sustainable model for twenty-first-century journalism, based on a not-for-profit, participatory, solutions-oriented, old+new news model with a Commons focus that tempers a fierce subjectivity ("Free Vermont!") with a commitment to nonpartisanship ("Let's get everyone around the table.").

Our news journal makes no pretense towards "objectivity," which, as many media scholars have pointed out, is often synonymous with a "Big Business/Empire friendly" lens. Instead, we've made a conscious decision to model *Vermont Commons: Voices of Independence* after the fiercely subjective nineteenth-century republican newspapers in the newly created United States. That is to say, we at *Vermont Commons* begin with a distinct and subjective point of view. We also try to balance this viewpoint with a nonpartisan approach, seeing our news journal as a "big tent" for a variety of voices from a wide range of political perspectives—liberal, conservative, progressive, libertarian, and decentralist/mutualist among them. Our Web site's mission statement captures all of these characteristics in a single sentence: *Vermont Commons* is "solutions-oriented, non-partisan, and interested in promoting ongoing and vigorous debate about a more sustainable future for the once and future republic of Vermont, and the world." Vigorous debate, after all, leads to action.

Conclusion: Nonviolent Secession and the Vermont Village Green

Naylor is fond of a metaphor to replace that of U.S. Empire—the "Vermont Village Green." His thinking is compelling, because anyone who has ever visited Vermont knows that living in the Green Mountains often feels like living in a tiny European country. "Vermont is smaller, more rural, more democratic, less violent, less commercial, more egalitarian, more humane, more independent, and more radical than most states," Naylor explains. "Vermont provides a communitarian alternative to the dehumanized, mass-production, mass-consumption, narcissistic lifestyle which pervades most of America. In the Green Mountains," Naylor concludes, "the politics of human scale always trumps the politics of money, power, size, speed, greed, and fear of terrorism."[34]

And ultimately, what secession means for Naylor is tied to Vermont's survival as being a place and a culture that is uniquely "Vermont." "Fundamental to what it means to be a Vermonter is the right of self-preservation," he explains. "If Vermont is to remain true to its beliefs it has no choice other than to maintain a commitment to a human scale lifestyle. To remain small, rural, radical, clean, green, democratic, and nonviolent, Vermont must continue to resist being subsumed by an undemocratic, materialistic, militaristic, megalomaniac, robotic, imperialistic, global empire of which it is a part," Naylor concludes.

So here, one last time, is the ultimate question about Vermont's radical imperative.

Does Vermont really have any other choice than to extricate itself from the United States of Empire?

Living out the answer to this question is what we in the Vermont independence community are committed to doing, each in our own ways, working together as best we can.

And we are under no illusions. The road ahead for the citizens of the United States of Empire will be long and difficult. The twenty-first-century world is shaping up to look little like the twentieth, and we need to prepare ourselves for the changes ahead. "Every empire, every too-big thing, fragments or shrinks according to its own unique character and to the age of history to which it belongs," explains Paul Starobin, author of *After America: Narratives for the Next Global Age*, in a recent *Wall Street Journal* editorial entitled "Divided We Stand." "America's return to its origins could turn out to be an act of creative political destruction, with 'we the people' the better for it."[35]

Here in the Green Mountains, we're more interested in creation than destruction. In addition to the Second Vermont Republic, *Vermont Commons*, our Radio Free Vermont station, and our ongoing projects focusing on re-localized production of finance, fuel, food, and other resources, we take heart in the courage of our neighbors who have just stood for Statewide office, including our gubernatorial candidate, Dennis Steele, and our lieutenant gubernatorial candidate, Peter Garritano, and welcome thoughtful questions, continued dialogue, fierce debate, and, above all, enthusiastic participation as we explore what it might mean to reinvent Vermont as an independent republic again. While we don't pretend to have all the answers, the twenty-first-century Vermont independence movement, full of questions, ideas, impulses, and entrepreneurial energy, is well under way.

Of all fifty States, then, Vermont may be the one "most likely to secede."

Free Vermont! Long live the UNtied States.

Notes

Introduction

1. George Kennan, *Around the Cragged Hill* (New York: W. W. Norton, 1993), 143. See the chapter "Dimensions," 144.

2. Ibid., 145.

3. Raoul Berger, *Government by Judiciary* (Indianapolis: Liberty Fund, 1997).

4. Ibid., 145.

5. Ibid., 146.

6. Ibid., 148.

7. Ibid.

8. Ibid., 150.

9. Ibid.

Secession: A Constitutional Remedy that
Protects Fundamental Liberties

1. Robert Schlesinger, "Texas Secession? Perry, One Third of Texans Are Wrong: Texas Can't Secede," http://politics.usnews.com/opinion/blogs/robert-schlesinger/2009/04/17/texas-secession-pe . . .

2. Jay Bookman, "When Secession talk is in the air, the nation has lost its bearings," http://blogs.ajc.com/jay-bookman-blog/2010/07/26when-secession-talk-is-in-the-air-then . . .

3. "Health Care Law: 58% Favor Repeal of the Health Care Law, 36% Are Opposed," http://www.rasmussenreports.com/public_content/politics/current_events/healthcare/health-care-law.

4. Resolutions nullifying the federal healthcare reform act have been introduced into the legislatures of nearly every State in the Union. As of September 2010, resolutions have passed the legislatures and have been signed by the governors of Utah, Wyoming, Mississippi, Alabama, Maryland, Tennessee, Virginia,

and Louisiana. Resolutions have passed both houses of the State legislatures of Arizona, Missouri, Nebraska, Kansas, South Carolina, North Dakota, South Dakota, Idaho, and Oklahoma. Resolutions have passed one or more houses in Texas, Indiana, Michigan, Ohio, and Georgia. Resolutions were on the November 2010 ballot in Arizona, Colorado, and Oklahoma. http://www.tenthamendmentcenter.com/ nullification/10th-amendment-resolutions/. Gun control has also contributed to increased State activity confronting federal power. Editorial, "States Tell Obama to Take a Hike," http://www. washingtontimes.com/news/2010/sep/15/states-tell-obama-to-take-a-hike/.

5. Michael Boldin, "Nullification Movement Gains Steam: Missouri Rejects Healthcare Mandates," http://www.tenthamendmentcenter. com/2010/08/03/nullification-movement-gains-steam-missouri-rejects.

6. Michael Cheek, "Mullen: National Debt is a Security Threat," http://www.executivegov.com/2010/08/mullen-national-debt-is-a-security-threat/

7. "Dem. Pete Stark at Town Hall: 'The federal government can do most anything in this country,'" http://ironicsurrealism.blogivists. com/2010/08/02dem-pete-stark-at-town-hall-the-federal- . . .

8. Jacob E. Cooke, ed., *The Federalist* (Middletown, CT: Wesleyan University Press, 1961), 256 (Madison, Federalist No. 39).

9. Zachariah Chafee, Jr., and Sidney Post Simpson, *Cases on Equity: Jurisdiction and Specific Performance*, 2 vols. (Cambridge, MA.: n.p., 1934), 1:2; Edward D. Re and Joseph R. Re, *Cases and Materials on Remedies, 4th Ed.* (Westbury, NY: Foundation Press, 1996), 19-20.

10. Ibid.

11. Simpson, *Cases on Equity*, 1:3; Re, *Cases and Materials on Remedies*, 21.

12. Simpson, *Cases on Equity*, 1:4; *Cases and Materials on Remedies*, 21.

13. Simpson, *Cases on Equity*, 1:4-7; *Cases and Materials on Remedies*, 21-23; George B. Adams, "The Origin of English Equity," *Columbia Law Review* 16 (1916): 87, 90-92, 97.

14. Walter W. Cook, "The Powers of Courts of Equity," *Columbia Law Review* 15 (1915): 106-7.

15. Joseph Story, *Commentaries on Equity Jurisprudence as Administered in England and America, 13th Ed.*, 2 vols. (Boston: Little, Brown, 1886), 1:52-56.

16. *Williston on Contracts, 3rd Ed.*, 18 vols. (Mt. Kisco, NY: Baker, Voorhis, 1957), 1:1. Because the law of contracts has remained virtually unchanged since the early eighteenth century, the author relies upon the most popular American treatise on the subject, *Williston on Contracts*.

17. Ibid., 1:1-30.

18. Ibid., 11:2-3.

19. Ibid., 11:204-5.

20. Ibid., 11:644-64.

21. Ibid., 11:664-77.

22. Ibid., 12:9-14.

23. Ibid., 12:14-20.

24. Merrill Jensen, ed., *The Documentary History of the Ratification of the Constitution*, 3 vols. (Madison: State Historical Society of Wisconsin, 1976), 1:79 ("Articles of Confederation and Perpetual Union").

25. Ibid. ("Articles of Conf.," Art. XIII, ¶ 1).

26. Ibid., 1:176-79.

27. Robert G. Ferris, ed., *Signers of the Constitution* (Washington, DC: National Park Service, 1976), 11-23.

28. Ibid., 23; H. H. B. Meyer, ed., *Formation of the United States: Documents Illustrative of the Formation of the Union of the American States* (Washington, DC: U.S. Government Printing Office, 1927), 39-43 ("Proceedings of Commissioners to Remedy Defects of the Federal Government, Annapolis in the State of Maryland, September 11, 1786").

29. Meyer, *Formation of the United States,* 43; Ferris, *Signers of the Constitution*, 23.

30. Meyer, *Formation of the United States*, 47 ("Report of Proceedings in Congress, Wednesday, February 21, 1787").

31. Jensen, *Documentary History of the Ratification of the Constitution,* 1:192-229. The General Assembly of Rhode Island and the Providence Plantations actually wrote to the Federal Convention on September 15, 1787, asserting that the State did not send delegates because of its "love of true constitutional liberty, and the fear we have of making innovations on the Rights and Liberties of the Citizens at Large."

32. Ferris, *Signers of the Constitution,* 31-34.

33. U.S. Constitution, Art. I.

34. Ibid., § 8.

35. Ibid., §§ 9, 10.

36. Ibid., Art. II.

37. Ibid., Art. III.

38. Ibid., Art. IV, §§ 1, 2, 4.

39. Ibid., Art. VI, cl. 2.

40. Ibid., Art. V.

41. Ibid., Art. VII.

42. Jonathan Elliot, *The Debates in the Several State Conventions on the Adoption of the Federal Constitution,* 5 vols. (Philadelphia: J. B. Lippincott, 1861), 1:230-31. The original preamble passed unanimously, as written, on August 7, 1787.

43. Catherine Drinker Bowen, *Miracle at Philadelphia: The Story of the Constitutional Convention, May to September, 1787* (Boston: Little, Brown, 1986), 240.

44. Elliot, *The Debates in the Several State Conventions on the Adoption of the Federal Constitution,* 1:317.

45. Ibid., 1:319, 322, 323.

46. Ibid., 1:322, 324-27.

47. Ibid., 1:327. It is important to note that when reference is made to "the people," the common understanding then was that it referred to the people of the States. Wrote James Madison in September 1829, "The real parties to the Constitutional compact of the United States are the States, that is, the people thereof respectively in their sovereign character." Ibid., 4:18.

48. Ibid., 1:327-31.

49. Ibid., 1:331-32, 334-36.

50. John Locke, *The Works of John Locke*, 10 vols. (London: W. Otridge & Son, 1812), 5:338-485. Locke wrote that governments are created by the consent of the governed who transfer to it only so much power as they possess in themselves, and are dissolved when the governments act contrary to the trust of the governed.

51. Gordon S. Wood, *The Creation of the American Republic, 1776-1787* (Chapel Hill: University of North Carolina Press, 1969), 283; Thad W. Tate, "The Social Contract in America, 1774-1787: Revolutionary Theory as a Conservative Instrument," *William and Mary Quarterly* 22, no. 3 (1965): 375-91.

52. Wood, *The Creation of the American Republic*, 284.

53. Massachusetts Constitution (1780).

54. Wood, *The Creation of the American Republic*, 290.

55. Max Farrand, ed., *Records of the Federal Conventions of 1787*, 3 vols. (New Haven: Yale University Press, 1911), 1:314-15.

56. Ibid., 1:315.

57. Ibid., 1:593.

58. Elliot, *The Debates in the Several State Conventions on the Adoption of the Federal Constitution*, 1:325-27, 334-37.

59. *Chisholm v. Georgia*, 2 Dallas 419, 471, 1 L.Ed. 440, 463 (1793).

60. The Virginia Comm'n. on Const. Government. *We The States: An Anthology of Historic Documents and Commentaries thereon, Expounding the State and Federal Relationship* (Richmond: The William Byrd Press, 1964), 143-44. Gordon S. Wood, *Empire of Liberty: A History of the Early Republic, 1789-1815* (New York: Oxford University Press, 2009), 267-71. For a narrative of Jefferson's role in the Virginia Resolution of 1798 and the drafting of the Kentucky Resolutions of 1798 and 1799, see: Dumas Malone, *Jefferson and the Ordeal of Liberty* (Boston: Little, Brown, 1962), 395-424. Jefferson actually wrote to James Madison on August 23, 1799, that if the people do not soon change the direction and tone of the federal government, Virginia and Kentucky ought "to sever ourselves from that union we so much value, rather than give up the rights of self-government which we have reserved, and in which alone we see

liberty." James Morton Smith, *The Republic of Letters: The Correspondence between Thomas Jefferson and James Madison, 1776-1826,* 3 vols. (New York: W. W. Norton, 1995), 2:1119.

61. *We the States,* 161.

62. Ibid., 159.

63. James Madison, *Letters and Other Writings of James Madison,* 4 vols. (Philadelphia: J. B. Lippincott, 1867), 3:223. (Letter from James Madison to Judge Roane, dated June 29, 1821.)

64. James M. Banner, Jr., *To the Hartford Convention: The Federalists and the Origins of Party Politics in Massachusetts, 1789-1815* (New York: Alfred A. Knopf, 1970), 301.

65. Ross M. Lence, ed., *Union and Liberty: The Political Philosophy of John C. Calhoun* (Indianapolis: Liberty Fund, 1992), 370-71. (Calhoun's "Fort Hill Address: On the Relations of the States and Federal Government," July 26, 1831.)

66. *We the States*, 161.

67. *Black's Law Dictionary, 4th Ed.* (St. Paul: West, 1968), 1298.

68. John Taylor of Caroline recorded an instance that occurred on May 8, 1794, five years after the ratification of the Constitution, where Sen. Rufus King of New York, a Federalist and former delegate to the Constitutional Convention from Massachusetts, called him into a Senate committee room. Taylor wrote about how King complained about the Southern interests that "clogged and counteracted every operation of government." King then said that "the eastern [States] would never submit to their [Southern] politics, and that under these circumstances, a dissolution of the Union by mutual consent, was preferable to a certainty of the same thing, in a less desirable mode." King was then joined by Sen. Oliver Ellsworth of Connecticut, also a Federalist and a former delegate to the Convention. Ellsworth concurred with King's suggestion. Both King and Ellsworth pressed Taylor "for fixing the outlines of a separation;" they claimed that they were "indifferent as to the line of division from the Potowmack to the Hudson." Taylor memorialized the extraordinary meeting in a letter to kinsman James Madison on May 11, 1794. It illustrates the sentiment among the framers and ratifiers

that States could withdraw from the Union and that the Union was not perpetual. Gaillard Hunt, ed., *Disunion Sentiment in Congress in 1794: A Confidential Memorandum Hitherto Unpublished Written by John Taylor of Caroline, Senator from Virginia, for James Madison* (Washington, DC: W. H. Lowdermilk, 1905), 21.

69. *McCulloch v. Maryland*, 4 Wheat. 316, 4 L.Ed. 579 (1819).

70. Ibid., 363-64, 4 L.Ed. 390-91.

71. Ibid., 402-6, 4 L.Ed. 600-601.

72. Robert Remini, *Daniel Webster: The Man and His Time* (New York: W. W. Norton, 1997), 27. It is interesting to note that, although he may not have actually attended the Hartford Convention in 1814, Daniel Webster publicly supported it using the same principles of the compact theory enunciated in the Virginia and Kentucky resolutions of 1798 and 1799. He was mocked as a hypocrite when he spoke against South Carolina's nullification of the Tariff of 1828 and 1832. Ibid., 129-31.

73. *Register of Debates in Congress*, Twenty-Second Congress, Second Session (Washington, DC: 1833), 174-92.

74. Charles M. Wiltse, ed., *The Papers of Daniel Webster, Speeches and Formal Writings*, 2 vols. (Hanover, NH: University Press of New England, 1886), 1:588.

75. South Carolina seceded from the Union on December 20, 1860; Mississippi on January 9, 1861; Alabama on January 11, 1861; Georgia on January 19, 1861; Louisiana on January 26, 1861; and Texas on February 1, 1861. After Lincoln called for 75,000 troops to "suppress the rebellion," Virginia, North Carolina, Tennessee, and Arkansas seceded from the Union. David M. Potter, *The Impending Crisis, 1848-1861* (New York: Harper & Row, 1976), 492-99. All of the States that seceded employed the use of popularly elected delegates to attend a convention for the purpose of rescinding their ratification of the Constitution, the very same method utilized by the first thirteen States to ratify the Constitution.

76. Roy P. Basler, ed., *The Collected Works of Abraham Lincoln*, 8 vols. (New Brunswick, NJ: Rutgers University Press, 1953), 4:252-53.

77. *Texas v. White*, 7 Wall. 724-25, 19 L.Ed. 237 (1869).

78. Ibid., 718-24, 19 L.Ed. 235-37.

79. Ibid., 725-26, 19 L.Ed. 237-38.

80. In an appeal seeking to overturn an injunction against an enactment by the Louisiana legislature asserting that federal decisions in school desegregation cases were a usurpation of State power, the Supreme Court agreed with a three-judge district court that "interposition is not a constitutional doctrine. If taken seriously, it is illegal defiance of constitutional authority." Interposition, to the Court, was an "objection without substance." *Bush v. Orleans Parish School Board*, 364 U.S. 500, 501, 81 S.Ct. 260, 5 L.Ed.2d 245 (1960). See also: *Cooper v. Aaron*, 358 U.S. 1, 78 S.Ct. 1401, 3 L.Ed.2d 5 (1958). Interposition may have been inappropriate as a means to resist court-ordered desegregation in 1960, but the Court was absolutely incorrect when it opined that it was not a constitutional doctrine. It was, and is, a very valid constitutional doctrine.

81. *U.S. Civil War Centennial Comm'n., The United States on the Eve of the Civil War, As Described in the 1860 Census* (Washington, DC: U.S. Government Printing Office, 1963), 61. There were 3,953,760 slaves in the United States according to the 1860 Census.

82. The Constitution, among other things, barred Congress from interfering in the slave trade prior to 1808, and a limit was set therein on terms that might be imposed on the slave trade (see Articles I and II). In Article I the existence of the slave institution was recognized in the "three-fifths" clause dealing with the counting of the population of slaves for purposes of apportionment, and Article IV provided for the extradition of an escaped "Person held to Service or Labor."

83. Steven A. Channing, *Crisis of Fear: Secession in South Carolina* (New York: Simon & Schuster, 1970), 18-20, 255-56.

84. Charles H. Lesser, *Relic of the Lost Cause: The Story of South Carolina's Ordinance of Secession* (Columbia: South Carolina Department of Archives and History, 1996), 6. On December 20, 1860, South Carolina rescinded its ratification of the Constitution of May 23, 1788, and declared the Union "dissolved."

85. Jon L. Wakelyn, ed., *Southern Pamphlets on Secession, November, 1860-April, 1861* (Chapel Hill: University of North Carolina Press,

1996), 108. For a detailed discussion of the right of secession, see: Alexander H. Stephens, *A Constitutional View of the War Between the States*, 2 vols. (Philadelphia: National, 1868).

86. *Missouri v. Holland*, 252 U.S. 416, 40 S.Ct. 382, 64 L.Ed. 641 (1920). Holmes served as a captain in the Twentieth Massachusetts Infantry and a major on the staff of Maj. Gen. Horatio G. Wright. He was badly wounded at the Battles of Ball's Bluff and Antietam and, in 1863, near Fredericksburg.

87. *Frothingham v. Mellon*, 262 U.S. 447, 43 Sup. Ct. 597, 67 L.Ed. 1078 (1923). In *Frothingham*, the Supreme Court considered a constitutional challenge by a taxpayer to an appropriations enactment of Congress, the Maternity Act of 1921. The Court concluded that because an ordinary taxpayer has such a miniscule interest in what Congress appropriates, he cannot illustrate harm sufficient to give him standing. The Court held that it did not have jurisdiction. In a companion case, *Commonwealth of Massachusetts v. Mellon, supra.*, the Court concluded that the State of Massachusetts presented no justiciable cause in its challenge to the Maternity Act that was predicated upon Congress having invaded the reserved powers of the States. That argument, the Court concluded, presented a "political" question over which it did not have jurisdiction. In *Flast v. Cohen*, 392 U.S. 83, 88 S.Ct. 1942, 20 L.Ed.2d 947 (1968), the Court allowed a taxpayer to proceed with an action against an act of Congress—the Elementary and Secondary Education Act of 1965—that arguably violated his First Amendment rights. That one exception to the *Frothingham* rule—a challenge under the First Amendment—is all the Court has ever allowed for taxpayer challenges to acts of Congress.

88. *Commonwealth of Massachusetts v. Mellon*, 262 U.S. 479-89, 43 S.Ct. 598-601.

The Founding Fathers of Constitutional Subversion

1. John C. Calhoun, *A Disquisition on Government*, http://www.constitution.org/jcc/disq_gov.htm, 26.

2. Ibid.

3. Ibid.

4. Ibid.

5. John Taylor, *New Views of the Constitution of the United States* (Union, NJ: Lawbook Exchange, 2002; originally published in 1823), 27-28.

6. Ibid., 29.

7. Ibid., 45.

8. Ibid., 46.

9. Ibid.

10. Clinton Rossiter, *Alexander Hamilton and the Constitution* (New York: Harcourt Brace, 1964), 196.

11. Ibid.

12. Jacob E. Cooke, ed., *The Reports of Alexander Hamilton* (New York: Harper & Row, 1964), 86.

13. Rossiter, *Alexander Hamilton and the Constitution,* 202.

14. W. B. Allen, ed., *George Washington: A Collection* (Indianapolis: Liberty Fund, 1980), 521.

15. Cooke, *The Reports of Alexander Hamilton,* 172.

16. Rossiter, *Alexander Hamilton and the Constitution,* 237.

17. Thomas Jefferson to Judge Spencer Roane, September 6, 1819, in Merrill D. Peterson, ed., *Thomas Jefferson: Writings* (New York: Library of America, 1984), 1426-27.

18. Taylor, *New Views of the Constitution of the United States,* 78.

19. Edward S. Corwin, *The Commerce Power Versus States Rights* (Gloucester, MA: Peter Smith, 1962), 131.

20. Rossiter, *Alexander Hamilton and the Constitution,* 244.

21. Ibid.

22. Joseph Story, *Commentaries on the Constitution*, http://www.constitution.org/js/js_303.htm, 4 (Book 3, Chapter 3).

23. Randolph Bourne, "War is the Health of the State," http://struggle.ws.histtextsw/warhealthstate1918.html.

24. Cecelia Kenyon, "Alexander Hamilton: The Rousseau of the Right," *Political Science Quarterly* 73 (1958): 161.

25. Felix Morley, *Freedom and Federalism* (Indianapolis: Liberty Fund, 1981), 36.

26. Claes Ryn, *America the Virtuous: The Crisis of Democracy and the Quest for Empire* (New Brunswick, NJ: Transaction, 2003), 72.

27.Story, *Commentaries on the Constitution,* 7.

28. Ibid., 13.

29. Daniel Webster, "Reply to Hayne," http://www.constitution.org/hwdebate/webstr2d.htm, 2.

30. John Taylor, *Tyranny Unmasked* (Indianapolis: Liberty Fund, 1992), 199.

31. Webster, "Reply to Hayne," 3.

32. Ibid., 11.

33. Ibid.

34. Ibid., 5.

35. Ibid., 7.

36. Ibid., 8.

37. http://en.wikipedia.org/wiki/Hartford_Convention; Banner, *To the Hartford Convention.*

38. William C. Wright, *The Secession Movement in the Middle Atlantic States* (Rutherford, NJ: Fairleigh Dickinson University Press, 1973).

39. Howard Cecil Perkins, *Northern Editorials on Secession* (Gloucester, MA: Peter Smith, 1964).

40. Adolf Hitler, *Mein Kampf* (New York: Houghton Mifflin, 1998), 565.

41. Ibid., 566.

42. Ibid., 575.

43. Ibid., 578.

44. Jeffrey Rogers Hummel, *Emancipating Slaves, Enslaving Free Men* (Chicago: Open Court, 1996), 279.

45. Ibid.

46. James McPherson, *Ordeal by Fire* (New York: Alfred A. Knopf, 1982), 476.

47. Hummel, *Emancipating Slaves, Enslaving Free Men,* 235.

48. Michael Lind, *Hamilton's Republic: Readings in the American Democratic Nationalist Tradition* (New York: The Free Press, 1997).

The Tenth Amendment Awakening,
the Supreme Court Be Damned

1. The Tenth Amendment Center is a valuable clearinghouse for Tenth Amendment initiatives and developments throughout the country. See http://www.tenthamendmentcenter.com/.

2. For example, on April 15, 2009, Gov. Rick Perry (Texas) remarked that "Texans might at some point get so fed up they would want to secede from the union." http://www.foxnews.com/politics/2009/04/15/governor-says-texans-want-secede-union-probably-wont/.

3. "A usually delusional idea that dominates the whole mental life during a prolonged period (as in certain mental disorders), called also fixed idea." http://dictionary.reference.com/browse/idee+fixe.

4. See Marshall DeRosa, *The Ninth Amendment and the Politics of Creative Jurisprudence* (New Brunswick, NJ: Transaction, 1996), 64.

5. See DeRosa, *The Ninth Amendment,* which adumbrates this development; and Yale Law professor Alexander Bickel's *The Least Dangerous Branch: The Supreme Court and the Idea of Progress* (New Haven: Yale University Press, 1962), which endorses this role for the courts.

6. *Missouri v. Holland,* 252 U.S. 416 (1920), 253.

7. http://myfloridalegal.com/webfiles.nsf/WF/MRAY-83TKWB/$file/HealthCareReformLawsuit.pdf.

8. http://www.politico.com/static/PPM152_101014_order.html.

9. See *Wickard v. Filburn,* 317 U.S. 111 (1942). http://supreme.justia.com/us/317/111/case.html.

10. Imperialism is defined as "the policy, practice, or advocacy of extending the power and dominion of a nation especially by direct territorial acquisitions or by gaining indirect control over the political or economic life of other areas; *broadly*: the extension or imposition of [cultural, economic, and military] power, authority, or influence." http://www.merriam-webster.com/dictionary/imperialism. See *McCulloch v. Maryland,* 17 U.S. 316

(1819) for an earlier case of the Court sanctioning national economic control over the States. http://www.law.cornell.edu/supct/html/historics/USSC_CR_0017_0316_ZS.html.

11. See Alexander Hamilton, *The Federalist Papers Nos. 13, 14,* and *22,* http://avalon.law.yale.edu/subject_menus/fed.asp.

12. Ibid., No. 8.

13. The Central Powers included the German Empire, the Austro-Hungarian Empire, the Ottoman Empire, and the Kingdom of Bulgaria; the U.S. was in alliance primarily with the British and French.

14. Donald Davidson, "That This Nation May Endure—The Need for Political Regionalism," in *Who Owns America? A New Declaration of Independence*, ed. Herbert Agar and Allen Tate (Wilmington, DE: ISI Books, 1999; originally published in 1936), 154.

15. Richard M. Weaver, *The Ethics of Rhetoric* (Chicago: Henry Regnery, 1965), 23.

16. Lincoln's rhetorical skills, especially as employed at Gettysburg, produced a "revolution in thought." See Garry Wills, *Lincoln at Gettysburg: The Words That Remade America* (New York: Simon & Schuster, 1992).

17. Michael Oakeshott, *Rationalism in Politics and Other Essays* (Indianapolis: Liberty Fund, 1991), 48.

18. William J. Watkins, Jr., *Reclaiming the American Revolution: The Kentucky and Virginia Resolutions and Their Legacy* (New York: Palgrave, 2004), 98-99.

19. http://www.nationalcenter.org/CalhounClayCompromise.html.

20. While the war was in progress, Lincoln and the Radical Republicans were at odds on how severely the Southern States should be treated in the postbellum. When contrasted with the severity of the Radicals, Lincoln appears to be moderate. But under no circumstances would Lincoln tolerate the reemergence of the consensual Union. In an 1863 proclamation on Reconstruction, in order to receive a presidential pardon "rebels" had to renounce secession as treasonous and swear their allegiance to the Union. See *The Proclamation of Amnesty and Reconstruction, By the*

President of the United States, December 8, 1863; U.S., *Statutes at Large, Treaties, and Proclamations of the United States of America,* vol. 13 (Boston, 1866), 737-39; http://www.history.umd.edu/ Freedmen/procamn.htm).

21. *Texas v. White,* 74 U.S. 700, 727.

22. Ibid., 741.

23. See the Insurrection Act of 1807: "§ 331. Federal aid for State governments: Whenever there is an insurrection in any State against its government, the President may, upon the request of its legislature or of its governor if the legislature cannot be convened, call into Federal service such of the militia of the other States, in the number requested by that State, and use such of the armed forces, as he considers necessary to suppress the insurrection." And "§ 332. Use of militia and armed forces to enforce Federal authority: Whenever the President considers that unlawful obstructions, combinations, or assemblages, or rebellion against the authority of the United States, make it impracticable to enforce the laws of the United States in any State or Territory by the ordinary course of judicial proceedings, he may call into Federal service such of the militia of any State, and use such of the armed forces, as he considers necessary to enforce those laws or to suppress the rebellion" (Title 10 of the United States Code).

24. See *Cummings v. Missouri,* 71 U.S. 4 Wall. 277 (1867) and *Ex parte Garland,* 4 Wall. 333 (1867).

25.   http://oll.libertyfund.org/?option=com_staticxt&staticfile= show.php%3Ftitle=2282&chapter=216239&layout=html&Itemid=27.

26. http://www.civilwarstlouis.com/history/oathofloyalty.htm.

27. Ibid.

28. *Ex parte Garland,* 71 U.S. 4 Wall. 333 (1866).

29. *Cummings v. Missouri,* 71 U.S. 4 Wall. 277 (1867).

30. For example, the House passed legislation requiring a two-thirds majority vote of the justices to declare an act of Congress to be unconstitutional. Fearful of the political backlash, the Senate took no action (40th Cong., 2d sess., 2127, March 26, 1868).

31. "The act of 27th March, 1868, repealing that provision of

the act of 5th of February, 1867, to amend the Judicial Act of 1789, which authorized appeals to this court from the decisions of the Circuit Courts in cases of habeas corpus, does not except from the appellate jurisdiction of this court any cases but appeals under the act of 1867." *Ex parte McCardle,* 74 U.S. 7 Wall. 506 (1868).

32. "Sec. 2. And be it further enacted, That whenever the laws of the United States shall be opposed or the execution thereof obstructed, in any state, by combinations too powerful to be suppressed by the ordinary course of judicial proceedings, or by the powers vested in the marshals by this act, . . . it shall be lawful for the President of the United States to call forth the militia of such state to suppress such combinations, and to cause the laws to be duly executed. And if the militia of a state, where such combinations may happen, shall refuse, or be insufficient to suppress the same, it shall be lawful for the President, if the legislature of the United States be not in session, to call forth and employ such numbers of the militia of any other state or states most convenient thereto, as may be necessary, and the use of militia, so to be called forth, may be continued, if necessary, until the expiration of thirty days after the commencement of the ensuing session."

33. http://teachingamericanhistory.org/library/index. asp?document=413.

34. Weaver, *The Ethics of Rhetoric,* 85-86. As a lawyer Lincoln used this ability to great effect in the courtroom, by largely ignoring legal precedent and instead relying on abstract first principles (ibid., 85).

35. Thomas J. DiLorenzo, *Lincoln Unmasked: What You're Not Supposed to Know About Honest Abe* (New York: Crown Forum, 2006), 92.

36. Ibid., 94-96.

37. See Marshall DeRosa, *Redeeming American Democracy: Lessons from the Confederate Constitution* (Gretna, LA: Pelican, 2007), 51-89.

38. "Suppose it is true that the Negro is inferior to the white in the gifts of nature; is it not the exact reverse of justice that the white should for that reason take from the Negro any of the little which he has had given to him?" Weaver, *The Ethics of Rhetoric,* 95.

39. Lincoln's 1838 Lyceum Address, http://showcase.netins.net/web/creative/lincoln/speeches/lyceum.htm.

40. http://teachingamericanhistory.org/library/index.asp?document=157.

41. Weaver, *The Ethics of Rhetoric,* 95.

42. Weaver misses this aspect of Lincoln. He praises Lincoln's honesty and refusal to "stay out of the excluded middle", i.e., political compromise. This is, indeed, a dangerous precedent to endorse. Pitting extremes against one another is a sure formula for heightened conflict and destabilization.

43. http://teachingamericanhistory.org/library/index.asp?documentprint=946.

44. http://avalon.law.yale.edu/19th_century/lincoln1.asp.

45. Ibid.

46. DeRosa, *The Ninth Amendment*, 55.

47. See Thomas E. Woods, *Nullification: How to Resist Federal Tyranny in the 21st Century* (Washington, DC: Regnery, 2010), 100, and DeRosa, *Redeeming American Democracy*, 25-26.

48. "The compact theory teaches that each state is a sovereign political society. The states created the central government as their agent, endowing it with only enumerated powers—mainly (national) defense, regulation of (interstate) commerce, and foreign treaties. The central government (including its supreme court) cannot have the final say as to what powers the states delegated and reserved because the central government is the agent and the states are the principals of the compact." Donald W. Livingston, "The Founding and the Enlightenment: Two Theories of Sovereignty," in *Vital Remnants: America's Founding and the Western Tradition*, ed. Gary L. Gregg II (Wilmington, DE: ISI Books, 1999), 255-56.

49. Chief Justice Chase winks and nods towards this conclusion

by remarking that if secession was constitutional, then such was the nature of the war against the C.S.A. See *Texas v. White,* 74 U.S. 700, 727.

50. Weaver, *The Ethics of Rhetoric,* 100.

51. See Wills, *Lincoln at Gettysburg.*

52. Senator McKinley sponsored the highest tariff in U.S. history, over 48 percent.

53. "The Paris Peace Treaty was signed on December 10, 1898. Under this treaty, the United States obtained Puerto Rico, Guam, and—for $20 million—the Philippine Islands. Spain also renounced its claim to Cuba, which remained under U.S. military occupation until 1902. Thereafter, Cuba would be a U.S. protectorate until 1934. Congress took nearly two months to ratify the treaty, but did so—securing the necessary two-thirds majority by a single vote— on February 6, 1899. Despite the heated debates and protests of congressional lawmakers, McKinley was able to secure the treaty's approval and to convince the House to appropriate funds for implementing and building the American empire. In demonstrating his political influence on the outcome of these matters, McKinley became the undisputed leader of the Republican Party. Furthermore, his actions represented a real expansion of presidential power at the turn of the century. Under McKinley's leadership, the United States had become one of the world's colonial powers." http://millercenter.org/academic/americanpresident/mckinley/essays/biography/5.

54. Kevin Phillips, *William McKinley* (New York: Times Books, 2003); Lewis L. Gould, *The Modern American Presidency* (Lawrence: University Press of Kansas, 2009).

55. Richard Gamble, "The United States as World Savior: Cost and Consequences," *The Political Science Reviewer* (2009): 106.

56. This metaphor is not meant to be cute hyperbole. By attacking the established monarchical political order of Germany and Austria and the constitutional rule of law in the U.S., the Progressives removed what Burke referred to as the "ballast in the vessel," making the ship of state vulnerable to Jacobin winds of

revolution. See Russell Kirk, *Edmund Burke: A Genius Reconsidered* (Wilmington, DE: ISI Books, 1997).

57. At one point in his academic career, Wilson considered himself to be disciple of Edmund Burke (see Kirk, *Edmund Burke*, 221). In a 1901 laudatory essay cited by Kirk titled "Edmund Burke and the French Revolution," Wilson makes manifest his profound understanding of Burke and the *modus operandi* of the French Jacobins. However, Wilson's praise of Burke is not based upon the latter's conservative policy preference but Burke's statesmanship, i.e., his political analytical skill set, and his passing the "test of fire," i.e., Burke was "undaunted, unstained, unchanged in purpose and principle." Wilson viewed Burke not as a conservative opposed to change but as a liberal favoring slow-paced inevitable change. *The Century Illustrated Monthly Magazine* 62, New Series 40 (May-October 1901): 784-92, http://babel.hathitrust.org/cgi/pt?view=ima ge;size=100;id=inu.32000000493355;page=root;seq=7;num=i.

58. See Hamilton, *The Federalist Papers No. 47.*

59. http://www.presidency.ucsb.edu/ws/index.php?pid=65394.

60. Address to Congress Requesting a Declaration of War Against Germany (April 2, 1917), http://millercenter.org/scripps/archive/speeches/detail/4722.

61. *The Century Illustrated Monthly Magazine,* 784. Wilson admired Burke not for condemning the French Revolution *per se* but for raising and correctly addressing the "radical question" whether developments in France posed a threat to Britain (ibid., 785). Wilson intimated that Burke's statesmanship should be credited for preventing the "French spirit of disorder" from crossing the Channel into Britain (ibid., 787). "If the French revolutionary doctrine *had* taken root in England, what then? They did not. Who shall say how much this vehement and eloquent Irishman did to keep them out?" (ibid., 788).

62. The term democracy as used by Lincoln and Wilson is not synonymous with Jeffersonian democracy, i.e., government based upon the consent of the governed. Lincoln did not advocate a consensual union of States or the enfranchisement of

African-Americans, and Wilson considered the Bolsheviks to be his democratic compatriots.

63. In his debate with Judge Douglas, Lincoln stated, "But this argument strikes me as not a little remarkable in another particular—in its strong resemblance to the old argument for the 'Divine right of Kings.' By the latter, the King is to do just as he pleases with his white subjects, being responsible to God alone. By the former the white man is to do just as he pleases with his black slaves, being responsible to God alone. The two things are precisely alike; and it is but natural that they should find similar arguments to sustain them." http://millercenter.org/scripps/archive/speeches/detail/3503. For Wilson, "making the world safe for democracy" required ridding it of monarchy. See Hans-Hermann Hoppe, *Democracy: The God That Failed* (New Brunswick, NJ: Transaction, 2001); Ralph Raico, "World War I: The Turning Point," in *The Costs of War: America's Pyrrhic Victories,* ed. John V. Denson (New Brunswick, NJ: Transaction, 1999); and Erik von Kuehnelt-Leddihn, *Leftism Revisited: From de Sade to Pol Pot* (Washington, DC: Regnery, 1990), 210. On Wilson and Wilsonianism, see further Murray N. Rothbard, "World War I as Fulfillment: Power and the Intellectuals," *Journal of Libertarian Studies* 9, no. 1 (1989); Paul Gottfried, "Wilsonianism: The Legacy that Won't Die," *Journal of Libertarian Studies,* 9, no. 2 (1990); idem, "On Liberal and Democratic Nationhood," *Journal of Libertarian Studies* 10, no. 1 (1991); Robert A. Nisbet, *The Present Age* (New York: Harper & Row, 1988), cited in Hoppe.

64. Richard M. Gamble, *The War for Righteousness: Progressive Christianity, the Great War, and the Rise of the Messianic Nation* (Wilmington, DE: ISI Books, 2003), 157.

65. The total death tally resulting from World War I is approximately 8.5 million, with 21 million being wounded.

66. My working definition of constitutional liberalism is the distribution of political power in such a manner that political power is both fragmented and competitively self-checking. It is essentially the Madisonian model, in which "ambition is made to counteract

ambition," and the interests of the officeholders (e.g., national and state legislators, executives, judges) are integrally connected to their offices and to identifiable constituencies. See *The Federalist Papers Nos. 10* and *51.*

67. Ibid., No. 1.

68. http://docs.fdrlibrary.marist.edu/011144.html.

69. See Bertrand De Jouvenel, *On Power: The Natural History of Its Growth* (Indianapolis: Liberty Fund, 1993), 120-24.

70. http://senate.legis.state.la.us/documents/constitution/.

71. Charles Alan Wright, *Law of Federal Courts* (St. Paul: West, 1983), 1-2.

72. In *Martin v. Hunter's Lessee,* 14 U.S. 304 (1816), the U.S. Supreme Court decided that it had appellate jurisdiction over State supreme courts. It based this claim on the supremacy clause in Article VI of the Constitution and section 25 of the Judiciary Act of 1789, which stipulate: "That a final judgment or decree in any suit, in the highest court of law or equity of a State in which a decision in the suit could be had, where is drawn in question the validity of a treaty or statute of, or an authority exercised under the United States, and the decision is against their validity; or where is drawn in question the validity of a statute of, or an authority exercised under any State, on the ground of their being repugnant to the constitution, treaties or laws of the United States, and the decision is in favour of such their validity, or where is drawn in question the construction of any clause of the constitution, or of a treaty, or statute of, or commission held under the United States, and the decision is against the title, right, privilege or exemption specially set up or claimed by either party, under such clause of the said Constitution, treaty, statute or commission, may be re-examined and reversed or affirmed in the Supreme Court of the United States upon a writ of error, the citation being signed by the chief justice, or judge or chancellor of the court rendering or passing the judgment or decree complained of, or by a justice of the Supreme Court of the United States, in the same manner and under the same regulations, and

the writ shall have the same effect, as if the judgment or decree complained of had been rendered or passed in a circuit court, and the proceeding upon the reversal shall also be the same, except that the Supreme Court, instead of remanding the cause for a final decision as before provided, may at their discretion, if the cause shall have been once remanded before, proceed to a final decision of the same, and award execution. But no other error shall be assigned or regarded as a ground of reversal in any such case as aforesaid, than such as appears on the face of the record, and immediately respects the before mentioned questions of validity or construction of the said constitution, treaties, statutes, commissions, or authorities in dispute." http://www.constitution.org/uslaw/judiciary_1789.htm.

73. Robert A. Carp, Ronald Stidham, and Kenneth L. Manning, *Judicial Process in America, 8th Ed.* (Washington, DC: CQ Press, 2011), 105.

74. Oakeshott, *Rationalism in Politics*, 49.

75. *The Federalist Papers No. 47.*

76. Thomas Jefferson to William C. Jarvis (1820), ME 15:277, http://etext.virginia.edu/jefferson/quotations/jeff1030.htm.

American Republicanism and the Forgotten Question of Size

1. Johannes Althusius, *Politica* (Indianapolis: Liberty Fund, 1995), 17-79.

2. Ibid., 17-19, 27, 39, 51.

3. Ibid., 197.

4. Ibid., 69.

5. Ibid.

6. See Bernard Bailyn, *The Ideological Origins of the American Revolution* (Cambridge: Harvard University Press, 1967).

7. J. Y. T. Greig, ed., *The Letters of David Hume*, 2 vols. (Oxford: Clarendon Press, 1969), 2:303.

8. "Hume's Early Memoranda, 1729-40: The Complete Text," *Journal of the History of Ideas* 9 (1948): 504.

9. *Letters of Thomas Jefferson, 1743-1826* (Charlottesville:

Electronic Text Center, University of Virginia, http://www.2.lib.virginia.edu/etext/index.html), 1492.

10. Ibid., 1381.

11. Ibid., 1227.

12. Ibid., 1493.

13. Banner, *To the Hartford Convention,* 100.

14. Quoted in Daniel Boorstin, *The Americans: The National Experience* (New York: Random House, 1966), 270. Boorstin discusses the nineteenth-century vision of the United States as the mother of new States and federations on the continent, similar to the way the Latin American continent developed into a number of nations.

15. Ibid., 271.

16. Ibid., 270.

17. Ibid.

18. Hamilton proposed at the Philadelphia Convention a constitution with a president for life, who would appoint State governors, have veto power over the States, and a senate with members for life. This was the dreaded monarchy that Jefferson and others feared. Hamilton's proposal did not even receive a second. Yet he was an icon for John Marshall, Joseph Story, Daniel Webster, Abraham Lincoln, and the entire nationalist tradition. He was the enemy of all things Jeffersonian. For a contemporary Jeffersonian view of Hamilton's baneful influence, see Thomas DiLorenzo, *Hamilton's Curse: How Jefferson's Archenemy Betrayed the American Revolution—and What It Means Today* (New York: Crown Forum, 2008).

19. Richard J. Ellis, *To the Flag: The Unlikely History of the Pledge of Allegiance* (Lawrence: University Press of Press, 2005), 116-17.

20. David Hume, "Idea of a Perfect Commonwealth," in *Essays Moral, Political and Literary*, ed. Eugene Miller (Indianapolis: Liberty Fund, 1985), 512-16, 525.

21. Ibid., 516-25.

22. Kennan, *Around the Cragged Hill,* 143. See the chapter "Dimensions."

23. For an unanswerable critique of how the Supreme Court has usurped power from the States and made the Court into a policymaking body rather than a judicial one, see Berger, *Government by Judiciary.*

24. Hume, "Idea of a Perfect Commonwealth," 529.

25. See Douglas Adair, "'That Politics May Be Reduced to a Science': David Hume, James Madison, and the *Tenth Federalist*," *Huntington Library Quarterly* 20 (1957): 343-60. Americans who prefer a centralized state of continental scale over a federative polity have made much of Madison's *Tenth Federalist*, which argues in favor of large-scale republicanism. Adair and others think the source of Madison's view is Hume's argument that the republic, if properly ordered, can and should be expanded. But Hume's expanded republic is about the size of Virginia. It is not continental in scale. At that scale, entirely new problems emerge, which Madison does not begin to consider in his much-overrated *Tenth Federalist.*

26. For the contemporary political relevance of State nullification as a lawful manner of resisting federal tyranny, see Woods' splendid study, *Nullification,* and Watkins, *Reclaiming the American Revolution.* For a systematic historical account of nullification, see Kirk Woods' magisterial study, *Nullification: A Constitutional History, 1776-1833,* 2 vols. (Lanham, MD: University Press of America, 2008). See also Forrest McDonald, *States' Rights and the Union: Imperium in Imperio* (Lawrence: University Press of Kansas, 2000).

27. See Donald Livingston, "The Secession Tradition in America," in *Secession, State, and Liberty,* ed. David Gordon (New Brunswick, NJ, 1998), 1-34. The other essays on secession in this volume are worthy of study.

28. Don E. Fehrenbacher, ed., *Abraham Lincoln, Speeches and Writings 1859-1865* (New York: Library Classics of the United States, 1989), 201-2 ("Speech at Indianapolis").

29. Alexis de Tocqueville, *The Old Regime and the French Revolution,* trans. Stuart Gilbert (New York: Anchor Books, 1955).

30. See Hoppe's comparative study of monarchy and mass

democracy in *Democracy*, especially chapters 1-3, and De Jouvenel's *On Power*. See Books III-V for a study of how twentieth-century mass democracies have been more destructive than eighteenth- and nineteenth-century monarchies.

31. Hoppe, *Democracy*, 54-57.

32. Marshall DeRosa *The Confederate Constitution of 1861* (Columbia: University of Missouri Press, 1991). DeRosa explains how the Confederate Constitution is an expression of Jeffersonian constitutionalism, which was the dominant strain in American thought and practice up to 1861.

33. DeRosa explains the reforms instituted by the Confederate Constitution to prevent centralization in the work just cited. In *Redeeming American Democracy*, he explores how failure to heed these reforms has led not only to the consolidation of the American States into a unitary state but has opened the door to supranational forms of centralization.

34. The Confederate Constitution did not write in a right of secession. The reason was that to do so would imply that if the right had not been written, it would not exist. But the States were sovereign political societies going into the Union. Consequently, what was not prohibited to them by the Constitution was reserved. Secession was not prohibited by the Constitution; therefore it was a reserved right. The Confederate Constitution made this clearer than the U.S. by declaring in the preamble that each State retained its freedom, sovereignty, and independence. Lincoln justified his invasion of the Southern States on the preposterous claim that the States were not and had never been sovereign political societies. In his first inaugural, he said the States did not create the Union; the Union created the States. Though contradicted by the historical record, this is, nonetheless, the foundational belief of American nationalists. The jurisprudence of John Marshall and Joseph Story rests upon it. An early and unanswerable refutation of it, as a theory of the Constitution, was given by Abel Upshur, in *A Brief Inquiry into the True Nature and Character of Our Federal Government, Being a Review of Judge Story's Commentaries* (Petersburg, VA, 1840). For

more on the right of an American State to secede, see Gordon, *Secession, State, and Liberty*, and John Remington Graham, *A Constitutional History of Secession* (Gretna, LA: Pelican, 2002).

35. Rufus J. Fears, ed., *Selected Writings of Lord Acton*, 3 vols. (Indianapolis: Liberty Fund, 1985), 278.

36. For the GDP of countries, see http://en.wikipedia.org/wiki/List_of_countries_by_GDP_(nominal). For the GDP of States, see http://www.census.gov/compendia/statab/2010/tables/10s0655.pdf.

37. Alexander Hamilton, "Federalist No. 13," in *The Federalist*, ed. George Carey and James McClellan (Dubuque: Kendall/Hunt, 1990), 60. See also John Jay, "Federalist No. 2 and 5," and Hamilton, "Federalist No. 1."

38. St. George Tucker, *A View of the Constitution of the United States, with Selected Writings* (Indianapolis: Liberty Fund, 1999), 84-87.

39. William Rawle, *A View of the Constitution of the United States* (Philadelphia: H. C. Carey & I. Lea, 1825).

40. *North American Review* 22 (1965): 450.

41. See William C. Wright, *The Secession Movement in the Middle Atlantic States*, 177-78.

42. Quoted in Albert Taylor Bledsoe, *Was Davis a Traitor, or Was Secession a Constitutional Right Previous to the War of 1861?* (North Charleston: Fletcher & Fletcher, 1995; originally published in 1866), 149.

43. Ibid., 146.

44. Gordon, *Secession, State, and Liberty*, 14.

45. See Berger for an analysis of how the Court has arbitrarily interpreted the Fourteenth Amendment to usurp the reserved powers of sovereign States.

46. State nullification in the area of civil rights is available to a Canadian province through what is called the "notwithstanding clause" of the constitution.

47. Aristotle, *The Politics*, trans. Jonathan Barnes, ed. Stephen Everson (Cambridge: Cambridge University Press, 1988), 162, 7:25, 1326a.

48. Ibid., 162-63, 7:35, 1326a.

To the Size of States There Is a Limit

1. Ibid., 4:6.

2. Ibid., 5.

3. Ibid., 7.

4. On the general question of the optimum size of political units there is a considerable literature, besides Aristotle's. Besides my own work in *Human Scale* (Gabriola Island, BC: New Society, 2007; originally published in 1980), there is the treasure of Leopold Kohr's *The Breakdown of Nations* (White River Junction, VT: Chelsea Green, 2001; originally published in 1978), the classic *Small Is Beautiful,* by E. F. Schumacher (Vancouver: Hartley & Marks, 1999; originally published in 1985), and Lewis Mumford's magisterial *The City in History* (New York: Harcourt, 1961). Each of those authors has an additional corpus of works on scale and size (Kohr also has Leopold Kohr Online), and to them should be added several more important figures, such as G. K. Chesterton, Paul Goodman, Ivan Illich, Arthur Morgan, Wendell Berry, Murray Bookchin, Thomas Berry, John Papworth, and Jane Jacobs. Needless to say, their voices, though elegant and forceful, have been scarcely heeded—until now, perhaps.

5. Wikipedia, List of Countries by Population; http://CIA.gov/ World Factbook.

6. Ibid.

7. Wikipedia, World Index of Economic Freedom.

8. Freedom House, *Freedom in the World 2010,* Table of Independent Countries.

9. Wikipedia, List of Countries by Literacy Rate.

10. WHO ranking of world health systems, http://photius.com/ rankings/healthranks.

11. Steven D. Hales, *Good Society* 15, no. 2 (2006): 35-50.

12. http://sustainablesocietyindex.com.

13. Wikipedia, List of Countries by Total Area.

14. Sale, *Human Scale*, 129-42.

15. Wikipedia, List of States by Population.

16. Wikipedia, List of States by Area.

17. http://CNN.com, February 21, 2010.

Too Big to Fail? Lessons from the Demise of the Soviet Union

1. The lucky ones escaped and continued the development of the Russian intellectual tradition elsewhere. Among notable Russian émigrés were Vladimir Nabokov, Ayn Rand, Pitirim Sorokin, Mark Aldanov, André Andrejew, Yul Brynner, Ivan Bunin, Alexandra Danilova, Serge Diaghilev, Oleg Cassini, Dmitri Nabokov, Sergei Rachmaninoff, Nikolai Berdyaev, Anna Pavlova, Igor Stravinsky, Alexander Procofieff de Seversky George Ignatieff, Igor Sikorsky, Otto Struve, economists Peter Struve, Wassily Leontief, and Alexander Gerschenkron, and tens of thousands of others. See: M.V. Nazarov, *The Mission of the Russian Emigration* (Moscow: Rodnik, 1994).

2. Ludwig Von Mises, *Human Action,* 3rd Rev. Ed. (Chicago: Henry Regnery, 1949), 684.

3. Richard Pipes, *Property and Freedom* (New York: Alfred A. Knopf, 1999), 217.

4. "The first pattern (we may call it the Lenin or the Russian pattern) is purely bureaucratic. All plants, shops and farms are formally nationalized (verstaatlicht); they are departments of the government operated by civil servants. Every unit of the apparatus of production stands in the same relation to the superior central organization, as does a local post office to the office of the postmaster general. The second pattern (we may call it the Hindenburg or German pattern) nominally and seemingly preserves private ownership of markets, prices, wages, and interest rates. There are, however, no longer entrepreneurs, but only shop managers (Betriebsfuhrer in the terminology of the Nazi legislation)." Von Mises, *Human Action,* 651.

5. Ibid.

Most Likely to Secede: U.S. Empire and the Emerging Vermont Independence Effort

1. See Donald Livingston, "The New England Secession Tradition," *Vermont Commons: Voices of Independence* news journal (May 2007), now featured at the homepage at www.vtcommons.org.

2. Bill Kauffman, *Bye Bye Miss American Empire: Neighborhood Patriots, Backyard Rebels, and Their Underdog Crusades to Redraw America's Political Map* (White River Junction, VT: Chelsea Green, 2010), xv.

3. For a state-by-state list of secession organizations, visit the Middlebury Institute at www.middleburyinstitute.net.

4. Ibid., "Chattanooga Declaration."

5. Christopher Ketcham, "The American Secessionist Streak," *Los Angeles Times* (September 10, 2008). Read the online article through www.latimes.com.

6. Kauffman, *Bye Bye Miss American Empire,* xx.

7. Christopher Ketcham, "Most Likely to Secede," *Good,* no. 008 (January 2008).

8. Visit www.vtcommons.org/essentialreadings for the books and resources most useful for understanding the U.S. as Empire.

9. Thomas Naylor, *Secession: How Vermont and All the Other States Can Save Themselves from the Empire* (Port Townshend, WA: Feral House, 2008), 43-44.

10. Quoted in Naylor, *Secession,* 47.

11. John Saltmarsh, *Scott Nearing: An Intellectual Biography* (1991), quoted in http://en.wikipedia.org/wiki/Scott_Nearing.

12. Hale is quoted in *Current Concerns* news journal, Zurich, Switzerland, http://www.currentconcerns.ch/archive/2004/04/20040408.php.

13. Quoted in http://www.vtcommons.org/blog/2006/04/29/poll-8-vermonters-favor-secession-vermont-independence-movement-leads-nation (April 29, 2006).

14. Author's correspondence with Naylor (November 21, 2010).

15. This information is recounted in "A History of the Second Vermont Republic," http://vermontrepublic.org/history-of-the-second-vermont-republic-2. The final quotation comes from author's correspondence with Naylor.

16. Author's correspondence with Naylor.

17. Ibid.

18. Bill Kauffman, "Green Mountain Boys Ponder Secession,"

American Conservative, http://www.amconmag.com/article/2005/dec/19/00016/.

19. Ibid.

20. Author's correspondence with Naylor.

21. Quoted in "A History of the Second Vermont Republic."

22. Author's correspondence with Naylor.

23. See "2010 Electoral Wrap Up," http://www.vtcommons.org/blog/2010/11/04/thanking-you-reloading-2012.

24. This section based on author's correspondence with Naylor.

25. Naylor, *Secession*, 47.

26. Ibid., 97.

27. This section authored with major input from Naylor and the Second Vermont Republic.

28. H. Newcomb Morse, "The Foundations and Meaning of Secession," *Stetson Law Review* 15 (1986).

29. Ibid.

30. Frank Bryan, "The Case for Vermont Secession," http://www.vtcommons.org/journal/2005/04/frank-bryan-case-vermonts-secession.

31. See Christopher Ketcham, "Vermont Revolutionaries and the Rise of a Green Tea Party," *Huffington Post* (August 30, 2010). http://www.huffingtonpost.com/christopher-ketcham/vermont-revolutionaries-a_b_699954.html.

32. This section authored with major input from Naylor and the Second Vermont Republic.

33. Kauffman, *Bye Bye Miss American Empire*, xxix.

34. Author's correspondence with Naylor.

35. Paul Starobin, "Divided We Stand," *Wall Street Journal* (June 13, 2009). www.wsj.com.

Index